THE ASIAN MICROWAVE COOKBOOK

Carol Selvarajah

Times Books International
Singapore • Kuala Lumpur

To Sarah & Selva.
One taught me to cook,
the other gave me a taste for life.
Thank you, both.

Photography:
Lee Jen of First Photo Suppliers
Yim Chee Peng (cover & pages 9-12)
Andrew Merewether (pages 81, 119, 193 & 249)

Crockery and other tableware by courtesy of Tangs

Illustrations by Michelle Teo & Andros Wong

Cover and pages 9-12 were prepared with
information and assistance from
Hagemeyer Electronics (S) Pte Ltd and
the National Microwave Kitchen Studio.

© **1987 Times Books International**
Times Centre, 1 New Industrial Road
Singapore 1953
2nd Floor, Wisma Hong Leong Yamaha
50 Jalan Penchala
46050 Petaling Jaya
Selangor Darul Ehsan
Malaysia

Second edition 1987
1st reprint February 1988
2nd reprint May 1988
3rd reprint December 1988

Printed by Kim Hup Lee Printing Co. Pte Ltd.

ISBN 9971 65 420 2

Contents

Chicken

Eggs

Introduction

We are in an age of transition; our lifestyle is changing, especially in Asia where the older maidservants are becoming a vanishing breed, and younger girls have gone on to better lives as factory hands.

To manage on one's own seems to be a way of life and those fortunate enough to have help pay dearly for the services of maids and are at great pains to keep them happy. One is amused to hear of the lengths the lady of the house would go to, to make 'Ah Mooi' happy.

The fact is, as help is being phased out slowly, the family has to cope with more household chores. One way to overcome this is with a microwave oven.

My family solved this problem with a microwave oven seven years ago. There were the usual protests and dark mutterings of doom from family and friends: 'Microwaves are dangerous, you could be exposed to diseases after eating food cooked by microwaves.'

This and other microwave myths were dispelled soon after microwave ovens came into domestic use some 25 years ago. There seems to be a great deal of mystery surrounding the concept of microwaves and how it affects cooking, but microwaves are really quite similar to existing energy forms we are familiar with, such as police radar, household energy, or even sunlight. In the microwave oven, they are merely emitted from the magnetron and converted to heat energy once they make contact with the food.

Once you have decided to purchase a microwave oven, you will have made a commitment that will change your ideas about food and the time spent in preparing meals.

Microwave cookery is a totally new and different concept in cooking and some of the preconceived ideas we have about food will have to be readjusted. Food behaves differently when microwaved; microwaves pass through the food, cooking it so fast that it does not brown. So why does microwaved Asian food always look attractively browned? It is because an Asian meal rarely leaves the kitchen without spices or sauces, and our sauces and oils react favourably with microwaves. And today, 'combination' ovens are available so the user has the advantages of speedy microwave cooking with grilling and convection oven facilities.

Changes in Lifestyle

The introduction of a microwave oven into our home has resulted in the whole family becoming involved in cooking. Although for the first two years it was only a novelty — a gadget merely for defrosting and heating up frozen food — gradually we began to rely on it more for actual cooking. Today it has virtually replaced conventional cooking in our home, except in a couple of areas.

We pre-plan our meals and now always have a freezer stocked full of food. I spend less time in the kitchen as a result of this microwave oven. Some of the recipes included in this book have in fact been created by the family who have become enterprising cooks since our move to Australia left them bereft of househelp. If Mother was out and one was hungry, one simply had to learn to cook, and what easier way than to 'microwave it'!

Buying our microwave oven not only meant a change of lifestyle, it gave us the advantage of cutting housework time and expenses, among other things.

Cutting Housework Time and Energy

The microwave oven is a wonderful cooking

device which speeds up thawing, cooking and reheating and provides other shortcuts to cooking with ease and safety. Most meals can be cooked and served in the same dish, thus virtually eliminating the washing up of pots and pans, saving effort for those on tight work-schedules.

It is also simple and quick to clean as baked-on grease does not accumulate on the smooth plastic or stainless steel surfaces. There are no difficult corners or grooves where dust may accumulate. A quick wipe with detergent and hot water is all that is necessary to keep it clean. It is possible to save between two-thirds and half the cooking time on microwave cooking depending on the starting temperature of the food, the density and the amount of food cooked each time.

Cutting Expenses

The microwave oven is economical as it uses about 50% less cooking time than a conventional oven and the short bursts of microwave energy cost half as much as conventional electrical cooking. It is light, compact, portable and does not need any special installation as it works off a normal 13 amp power point anywhere in the house. There is also no expensive preheating time involved (as in conventional oven usage) and no installation costs.

Nutritional Advantage

Microwaves are odourless and tasteless so they cannot affect the flavour of the foods you cook. Since the cooking is rapid, the cooked foods taste better, and vitamins and flavours are preserved. This is a definite nutritional advantage, as 90% of the value of all food cooked in the microwave oven is retained.

Since very much less water is used in microwave cooking, any mineral salts and flavours 'sweat' and make for tastier meals. The microwave oven contains most of the cooking odours as the metal cabinet is equipped with efficient seals. Food colours remain naturally bright and vegetables crisp. Also, as microwave frying is unique and there is little need for fat, food can also be cooked with minimal oil, additives or butter. Microwave cooking is therefore excellent for those on diet.

Some Limitations of the Microwave Oven

The microwave oven will not make you a better cook, merely a more efficient one, in terms of time. It helps, however, to realise that certain foods do not cook well and certain cooking techniques are inadvisable in a microwave oven:

- Pastry does not crisp as well as in a conventional oven.
- Oil catches fire when overheated. However, stir-frying can be done in a browning dish.
- Eggs should never be cooked in shells as steam builds up inside and the egg bursts.
- Meat should be cooked on a 'Roast' setting or it could toughen. Tougher cuts of meat should be cooked on 'Low' or 'Medium' setting.
- Large amounts of food are better cooked in the traditional way as the time taken in a microwave oven would not be economical.
- Moist foods cook well in the microwave oven but foods which require crisping are not as successful as food does not brown normally. This can be overcome by using Asian browning sauces, spices, or by browning food in a browning dish.

The longer you use your microwave oven, the more you will appreciate its versatility and usefulness. The microwave oven will not completely replace your conventional stove or oven, but it is an invaluable complement to the other cooking appliances in your kitchen. You will find you need to spend less time in the kitchen and you will have a life-style that allows for tastier, more efficiently prepared and nutritious meals with an overall saving of time, energy and effort.

The Asian Microwave Cookbook has been designed to help overcome the problems experienced by new microwave oven users. An understanding of the principles involved will increase confidence and encourage adaptation and experimentation with the oven. Used in conjunction with conventional cooking methods, it could save time, effort and money. The thought of cooking on paper plates, in plastic bags and in ice cream containers may be daunting at first, but shorter hours spent in the kitchen, reduced electricity bills and a complete change of lifestyle may spur one on to using the microwave oven to its full potential.

Microwave Oven Controls

Microwave oven controls are designed to help you. In fact, in this age of computer language, they are, by comparison, so simple a child could cook a meal. Let us run through the function of each 'touch pad'* on the control panel, to see if you have gained a thorough understanding of the potential of a microwave oven.

Illustrated below is the comprehensive control panel of a 'combination' oven. Other than cooking solely on microwave energy or convection heat alone, you can also use the grill by itself. You may even cook food on a combina-tion of microwave and convection methods simultaneously. (See page 11.)

Some of the controls, such as the Auto Weight and Auto Sensor pads, are designed for failsafe cooking. These user-friendly controls are just what you need on days you don't feel up to making those tough time and temperature decisions!

Of course, there are available microwave ovens with less comprehensive features. The user alone can make his/her choice, based on personal needs and microwave cooking experience.

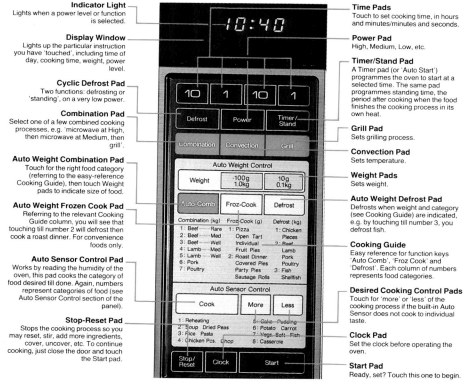

Indicator Light
Lights when a power level or function is selected.

Display Window
Lights up the particular instruction you have 'touched', including time of day, cooking time, weight, power level.

Cyclic Defrost Pad
Two functions: defrosting or 'standing', on a very low power.

Combination Pad
Select one of a few combined cooking processes, e.g. 'microwave at High, then microwave at Medium, then grill'.

Auto Weight Combination Pad
Touch for the right food category (referring to the easy-reference Cooking Guide), then touch Weight pads to indicate size of food.

Auto Weight Frozen Cook Pad
Referring to the relevant Cooking Guide column, you will see that touching till number 2 will defrost then cook a roast dinner. For convenience foods only.

Auto Sensor Control Pad
Works by reading the humidity of the oven, this pad cooks the category of food desired till done. Again, numbers represent categories of food (see Auto Sensor Control section of the panel).

Stop-Reset Pad
Stops the cooking process so you may reset, stir, add more ingredients, cover, uncover, etc. To continue cooking, just close the door and touch the Start pad.

Time Pads
Touch to set cooking time, in hours and minutes/minutes and seconds.

Power Pad
High, Medium, Low, etc.

Timer/Stand Pad
A Timer pad (or 'Auto Start') programmes the oven to start at a selected time. The same pad programmes standing time, the period after cooking when the food finishes the cooking process in its own heat.

Grill Pad
Sets grilling process.

Convection Pad
Sets temperature.

Weight Pads
Sets weight.

Auto Weight Defrost Pad
Defrosts when weight and category (see Cooking Guide) are indicated, e.g. by touching till number 3, you defrost fish.

Cooking Guide
Easy reference for function keys 'Auto Comb', 'Froz Cook' and 'Defrost'. Each column of numbers represents food categories.

Desired Cooking Control Pads
Touch for 'more' or 'less' of the cooking process if the built-in Auto Sensor does not cook to individual taste.

Clock Pad
Set the clock before operating the oven.

Start Pad
Ready, set? Touch this one to begin.

* A control pad has an automatic 'count-up' feature. Touch repeatedly, or leave a finger on any function pad, and you see, lighted on the display window, a changing function or a particular measure — weight, time, power, etc.

Even Cooking

The even cooking of food in a microwave oven depends on two things:

1 Even distribution of energy throughout the oven. But, however advanced the oven, hot and cold spots will remain. So the second factor is

2 Rotation of food so that every part of it passes through the hot and cold spots.

Rotating Wave Guide

Energy waves reach the oven cavity from the bottom in some new microwave oven models. The rotating wave guide then distributes microwave energy in an even pattern throughout the oven cavity. A uniform pattern of waves effectively surrounds the food for even cooking.

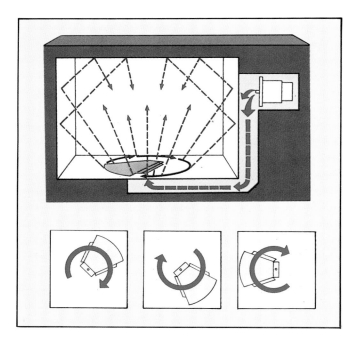

Food Rotation

An automatic turntable is important because it eliminates the need to frequently rotate food for even cooking when longer cooking times are required.

Experienced microwave users are aware, though, that even with an automatic turntable, food tends to cook faster at one particular spot in the oven. For long cooking times, take the trouble to manually rotate your dish 180°.

Limitations? What are Those?

Microwave cooking brought freedom to many slaves of the stove. With the advantages of easy operation, healthier food, cleaner living – what could possibly deter one from complete conversion to microwave cooking? Tradition, some may answer.

Now, the microwave oven has been expanded to include the features of convection cooking, giving the user greater versatility and choice of cooking methods. You can choose to cook using microwave or convection energy, or combine the cooking processes.

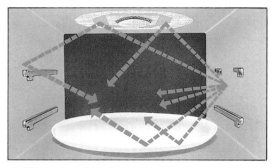

1 Microwave Cooking
Microwave cooking is fast, clean and cool, saving time and energy. Foods such as rice, Chinese pastries, casseroles, vegetables, fruits and convenience foods are ideal for cooking by microwaves. Cooking for one or two, a chore for some, becomes fun when you cook whole meals on the serving plate. And microwave-heated leftovers retain their original fresh-cooked flavour.

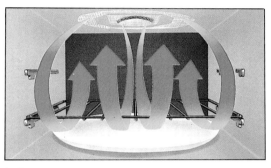

2 Convection Cooking
Traditionalists argue that cooking by convection heat is ideal for baking cakes, pies, pastries, breads, etc. In convection cooking, a heating element produces hot air that is circulated around the food by a quiet-operating fan. The gentle action of the constantly circulating heat allows you to bake even the most delicate pastries to perfection. You can do all this today, in the microwave oven.

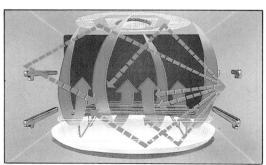

3 Combination Cooking
The microwave oven is capable of 'combination cooking', combining the advantages of two cooking methods. This is especially convenient when cooking roasts. Convection heat browns and seals the food's natural juices while the microwave energy speeds up the cooking process. Preprogrammed settings alternately release microwave energy and convection heat in on/off cycles during the cooking process.

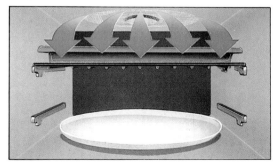

4 Grilling
The most up-to-date microwave oven allows you to grill steaks, hamburgers, fish, poultry or chops. Two settings are provided so that adjustment may be made for specific foods.

Combination Cooking, using a Simple Programme

Steamed Red Snapper

1 piece red snapper (approx. 150 g/5 oz)
1 tablespoon preserved soybean paste
2 cloves garlic, chopped
1 stalk spring onion, chopped
1 knob ginger, shredded
1 red chilli, shredded
30 g (1 oz) salted vegetable (*kiamchye*), shredded
½ teaspoon vegetable oil
1 teaspoon sesame oil

Preparation:
Put fish section in a casserole.
Top with all the other ingredients and
2 tablespoons water.

Combination Cooking Method:
Cover the casserole. Programme the oven and
cook.

1 Power, High: 3 minutes

Touch power pad till you see 'High' displayed.

Touch time (minute) pad 3 times for 3 minutes.

2 Power, Medium: 3 minutes, 30 seconds

Touch power pad till you see
'Medium' displayed.

Touch time (minute) pad 3 times.

Touch time (second) pad 3 times.

3 Timer/Stand: 2 minutes

Touch Timer/Stand pad once.

Touch Time (minute) pad twice.

Know Your Microwave Oven

What is a Microwave?

It is a type of high frequency radio wave. The electromagnetic wave within a particular frequency band (or radar) which the police use to detect speeding traffic is a form of microwave. When you use the microwave oven, electricity is converted by the magnetron tube and, in the form of invisible microwaves, enters the cooking area of the microwave oven where it cooks the food.

There is no direct heating applied to the food but when food which contains moisture comes into contact with microwaves, they cause the water molecules within the food to vibrate at high speed. This friction (as when you rub your palms together to get warmth) produces the intense heat that cooks the food.

Microwaves heat food quickly because they penetrate the food immediately. In conventional oven cooking the oven must be heated before food begins to cook. In microwave ovens this is not necessary as the waves are totally absorbed by the food. The walls of the oven merely reflect this energy into the food and no energy is required to heat the air or the interior walls of the oven.

The advantage of microwaves is that they penetrate the food immediately and heat the centre as quickly as the outer layers. Heating is therefore more uniform and food is cooked quickly.

How Safe is the Microwave Oven?

The term 'radiation' has always been a cause for alarm in the past. However, if one approaches the concept of radiation in a rational and sensible way, such fears can be dispelled. A simple definition of radiation is the sending out of energy and heat in rays; for example, a stove radiates its warmth.

What about wavelengths? And what about the different effects of varying wavelengths and frequencies with which they are emitted? Don't let these terms get you down, as they did with me initially. It is a well-known and established fact that when there is close body contact between two human beings, as in hugging, radiation occurs at a frequency of 3200 megahertz. (This figure is determined by calculating the radiation frequency emitted by the body at the normal body temperature.)

Now, this figure is in fact much higher than the frequency emitted in a microwave oven! It is only when frequencies reach the 'ionising' stage that wavelengths become dangerously short enough to cause (if coupled with a high enough frequency) disruption of cell structure, as in the case of X-rays. The laws of Physics have determined that lower frequencies will not cause such damage. What is important to note is that the energy in microwave cooking is non-ionising energy. It cannot change cell structure and it cannot be stored in the body.

In any case, each microwave oven is fitted with safety features that prevent radiation leaks. Microwaves are reflected by metal containers but are transmitted by non-metallic ones like glass, paper or plastics.

The National Health and Research Council of Australia gives the following information and advice on safe practices in the use of microwave ovens.

All-metal Construction Seals in Microwaves. Microwave radiation will not readily penetrate a metallic object but will be reflected by it. A microwave oven is basically a microwave generator enclosed in a metal box which has a large metal door on one side. The purpose of the all-metal construction is to contain the microwaves. All microwave ovens have glass doors to permit viewing of its contents while the metal grille inside the glass is designed to prevent the escape of microwave radiation.

No Leakage of Microwaves. The door of a microwave oven is interlocked to the microwave generator to prevent the production of microwave radiation. When the door is moved from its fully closed position, a switch is activated and the microwaves are turned off. Two switches are usually used, one acting as a back-up should the first fail. The leakage of radiation between the door and the oven is usually prevented by the provision of a special seal. This may be a metal seal or a separate cavity filled with absorber.

Cool Walls. The main advantage of a microwave oven is that it is simple to operate and it remains cool to the touch throughout all its cooking functions. This is an important factor as the old, the young and even the disabled can use it safely.

Checklist when Buying a Microwave Oven. Your inspection of the oven should confirm all the following items:
1   The grille is not damaged or broken.
2   The door fits squarely and securely and opens and closes smoothly.
3   The door hinges are in good condition.
4   The door does not open more than a small fraction of an inch (a few millimetres) without the user hearing the safety switches operate.
5   The metal plates of a metal seal on the door are not buckled or deformed.

Microwave Rules to Remember. Observe the following rules when using a microwave oven:
1   Never tamper with or inactivate the interlocking devices on the door.
2   Never poke an object, particularly a metal object, between the door and the oven while the oven is operating.
3   Never place metal objects inside the oven. These include saucepans, trays or any other metal utensils, metal-rimmed or metal decorated utensils.
4   Clean the oven cavity, the door and the seals with water and a mild detergent at regular intervals. Never use any form of abrasive cleaner that may scratch or scour surfaces, especially around the door.
5   Never use the oven without the trays provided by the manufacturer.
6   Never operate the oven without a load – an absorbing material such as food or water – in the oven cavity unless specifically allowed in the manufacturer's manual.
7   Never rest heavy objects such as food containers on the door while it is open, as damaged or bent doors will prevent tight or secure sealing.
8   Use the correct dials to stop and start the microwave oven. Opening the door will automatically turn off the microwave oven, thus activating the safety switches.

Features of a Microwave Oven

Your microwave oven is able to replace the functions of an ordinary oven in all aspects, even (in the case of 'combination' ovens) grilling and stir-frying.

The latest microwave ovens are computerised masterpieces containing two functional ovens – the microwave oven and the conventional oven. One could begin by cooking a meal using microwaves and then complete the cooking using conventional methods. This means that a dish could be cooked quicker, using both traditional and modern cooking methods in one oven.

As no special wiring is required the microwave oven can be plugged into an existing power point and located on any bench or shelf that provides sufficient air ventilation.

To get to 'know' your microwave oven, you must first understand how it operates. All microwave ovens have the following components.
1   **Magnetron:** converts electrical energy (240 volts) to high frequency waves of energy called microwaves. These waves are absorbed by the food and create friction that heats and cooks the food.
2   **Wave Guide:** directs microwaves from the magnetron to the oven cavity.
3   **Stirrer Fan:** distributes microwaves into the oven cavity to give even cooking.
4   **Power Control:** determines the speed at which the oven cooks. Power settings such as Defrost, Simmer or Roast vary the effective microwave energy in the oven cavity.

5 **Timer:** cooking time is calculated and set by the operator – a bell indicates when time has expired and power is automatically cut off.

6 **Cook Button:** is depressed to put the microwave oven into operation. Each time the door is opened, the oven is switched off and the Cook button must be pressed to recommence operation.

7 **Memory Controls:** are dials and buttons available on certain models. The cook can pre-set the electronic brain which stores instructions on power levels and times and will operate without the cook's supervision once the instructions are fed into the oven.

8 **Auto Combination:** a special setting now available in many models, this provides the speed and convenience of microwave cooking and the convection heat that browns food.

9 **Automatic Weight Defrost:** a function that determines the correct defrost times and power levels for a variety of meat, poultry and seafood items. The user merely enters the weight and category of food, and the oven does the rest.

10 **Automatic Weight Cook:** this is similar to the auto weight defrost, except that, this time, the controls are meant to cook the food.

11 **Automatic Defrost-Cook:** by 'programming' the oven (entering category and weight), it is possible to leave food to defrost, then continue cooking – an obvious advantage for those with busy schedules.

12 **Automatic Turntable:** helps cook all sides of food at the same time.

Cleaning a Microwave Oven

Cleaning is relatively simple because no heat is generated to the interior surfaces to cause burn or bake splatter. A quick wipe with a wet sponge soaked in detergent is sufficient to remove spills. To freshen the oven and dispel cooking odours that accumulate, a steaming bowl of lime or lemon juice and water cooked in the oven for 6 to 8 minutes on a High setting will produce condensation which can be wiped off easily.

Some foods produce more condensation than others. When cooking foods such as rice that normally produce moisture, a small dry towel placed next to the dish will absorb the excess moisture. The oven vents should always be clean and clear of all obstruction.

Microwave ovens should not be cleaned with scouring agents. Check the manufacturer's instruction manual.

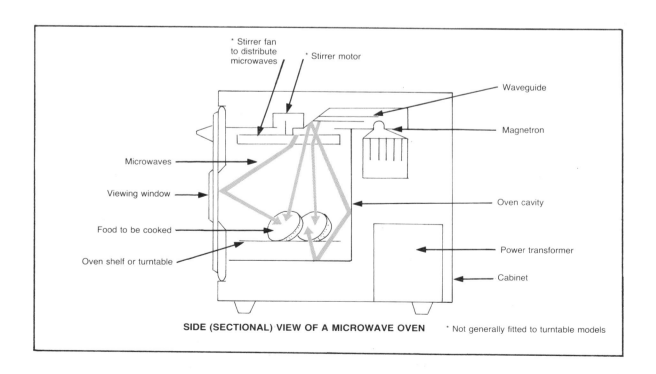

SIDE (SECTIONAL) VIEW OF A MICROWAVE OVEN   * Not generally fitted to turntable models

Comparisons: Conventional vs Microwave Cooking

CONVENTIONAL COOKING	MICROWAVE COOKING
HEAT transfers through the pan to the bottom of the food.	STIRRING is necessary for heated food to circulate. Often, the surface of the dish is the last area to be heated.
STIRRING food occasionally prevents food-burn and circulates heat by conduction.	COVERING the dish with plastic wrap speeds cooking time as steam builds up. Note: After cooking, plastic wrap should be lifted off *away* from the cook to prevent scalding from steam.
COVERING the pan with a tight lid speeds cooking as steam produced is retained in the pan and creates moist heat.	UNCOVERING the pan reduces moisture content a little, but not as much as in conventional cooking. It produces a better end result – as in rice.
UNCOVERING the pan reduces moisture content and thickens gravies.	A GLASS of water boiled in a microwave oven remains cool to the touch until the water that is heated inside it transmits heat to the glass.
A PAN which contains water has to heat up first in order to convey heat to the water inside.	BAKING – Microwaves transmitted through glass, paper or plastic penetrate evenly from all sides. If a roast or piece of meat were raised above an inverted saucer, waves would penetrate better. Energy is converted to heat the food surface before cooking begins.
BAKING in an oven is a process when heating elements heat up the cake or casserole from the outside and since the dish is suspended on a tray, the hot air circulates around the dish and heat gradually penetrates, from the outside areas to the centre of the dish.	LARGER AMOUNTS of food need longer microwave cooking times. For double the quantity, double the cooking time. For each additional proportionate amount, add original time divided by half. For example:

LARGER AMOUNTS of food take a little longer to cook in conventional pans, in ovens, etc.	1 unit = 4 minutes
	    2 units = 8 minutes
	    3 units = 8 + (half of 4) = 10 minutes
	    4 units = 10 + (half of 4) = 12 minutes

FOOD COOKS externally and gradually transmits heat to the inside.	FOOD COOKS faster as waves penetrate meat up to 4 cm.
The waves penetrate up to 4 cm through all sides of the food surface.	

HOW MICROWAVES PENETRATE FOOD

Conventional Oven

sweet potato after 10 mins

same sweet potato after 15 mins: centre is cool

Microwave Oven

sweet potato after 1½ mins on High

same sweet potato after 5 mins on High

cool   semi-cooked   cooked

Conventional Temperature Terms and Equivalent Microwave Setting

CONVENTIONAL SETTINGS	MICROWAVE SETTINGS				APPROXIMATE % MICROWAVE POWER
	Sharp	National	G E	Amana	
Heat on Low	DEFROST	DEFROST WARM	1 2	1 2	30%
Simmer	SIMMER	LOW MED LOW	3 4	3 4	50%
Heat on Medium or Roast)	ROAST	MEDIUM MED HIGH	5 7	5 6	70%
Heat on High	FULL POWER	HIGH	10	7 8	100%

Levels worked on a 600-650 watt oven.

Converting Temperatures to Microwave Cooking

Converting temperatures from conventional cooking to microwave cooking is part of microwave mastery. Each microwave oven has its own variable temperature description that can be equated to conventional cooking terms.

Converting conventional recipes is easy, using the guidelines that follow. A safe method for conversion would be to compare the conventional recipe with a similar microwave recipe, noting the quantity and ingredients used and time settings. Thus, a general guideline for conversion is to use a conventional recipe, but

- lower cooking time for meats to a quarter of the conventional time;
- lower liquid content by half the conventional amount used.

It is always best to underestimate cooking times.

Oven Wattage

The recipes in this book are written for a 600-650 watt microwave oven, but cooking times for ovens of other wattage are given. Adjust your cooking to either a higher or a lower time setting according to this test, adding a few more minutes or a shorter time for cooking. It is always safer to undercook food as this can be remedied in a few seconds to get food to the correct temperature.

Hot and Cold Spots

Hot and cold spots are present in every microwave oven regardless of type or model. Microwaves tend to travel in circles and as they hit the oven and bounce off in angular lines, they create hot and cold spots. Once these spots are identified, the oven can be put to its maximum use.

To identify hot and cold spots, choose a large, circular shallow dish, fill it with water and cook on High. The spot where the first bubbles appear will be the hot areas. Even with a rotating turntable, the bubbles always appear initially in the same areas. For maximum efficiency, place food to be cooked on the hot areas and avoid the cold spots in your microwave oven.

Density and Size of Food

Cook food of the same size and density together to achieve best results. When using a large platter, arrange larger pieces of food on the outside and smaller pieces around the inside to cook evenly. As in conventional cooking, thinner areas cook faster than denser areas.

As in conventional cooking, too, food should be cut into even-sized pieces so that they cook evenly. As bubbles appear on the edges of the plate, the hotter food should be moved to the centre of the dish.

Defrosting

The forte of the microwave is in defrosting or thawing cooked foods that have been frozen. Less moisture is lost when thawing in this manner and there is less risk of food being contaminated by bacteria than if it were left sitting in a kitchen sink all day.

Efficient defrosting depends on the quantity of food. Check the manufacturer's instructions for best use of your microwave oven for these functions and for the variable control settings. Large amounts of food defrost unevenly: some areas begin to defrost while others remain rock hard. Since microwaves travel in circles, the outside of the frozen mass will always thaw first, as microwaves pass through ice crystals. To speed up thawing, cut through the mass if possible and use a larger container that will receive the food as it thaws.

Alternating defrosting with standing time prevents the surfaces from cooking before the central portions are properly defrosted.

Food that can be stirred could be thawed on full power, but food like custards which cannot be stirred should be microwaved on low, to thaw evenly. If the oven does not have a defrost cycle, short periods of heating followed by standing times will also serve to thaw out a dish. To prevent uneven defrosting, corners or thinner areas should be shielded with pieces of foil. (Small amounts of foil are allowed.) Do not allow the foil to touch the tops or sides of the oven. Shielding protects corners or less dense areas that may cook while part of the food is being thawed.

Heating and Reheating Foods

An advantage of microwaving is that foods can be heated and reheated with no loss of quality, taste or texture. Dishes such as noodles do not need to be stirred unduly while being microwaved and so retain the fresh texture of the original dish. Reheated food does not dry up as in conventional reheating.

However, successful reheating depends on two factors: the starting temperature of food and the quantity to be reheated. Frozen food would naturally take longer to reheat as it has to go through a defrost cycle before heating.

Food that requires crisping on the outside — for example, chips or Goreng Pisang (banana fritters) — needs only a kitchen paper towel over it, as plastic wrap would serve merely to soften the product. Liquids and gravies should be covered with plastic wrap and dry food should be covered with a paper towel.

Single plates of food should have food arranged so that larger, denser parts are outside and smaller areas face inward as microwaves travel in circles.

Chips, breakfast cereals or soft biscuits can easily be recrisped in a microwave oven.

For a more comprehensive guide to reheating foods, check the tables in 'Microwave Cooking at a Glance'.

Microwave Cooking Terms

Browning

Browning does not occur during normal microwaving so to compensate for this, a browning or colouring agent should be used to give the desired colour. Examples of colouring agents are soy sauce, brown malt sugar, red paprika or saffron coloured turmeric. It may be necessary to brush lighter coloured meats with these browning agents to give a desirable colour to cooked meats. This is a choice left entirely to the cook. Although the food is cooked, tastes normal and is similar in every way to food cooked in the traditional manner, it may look underdone or unpalatable because it is aesthetically desirable to have a golden 'cooked' look for food.

Pastry may be browned by brushing with a glaze of egg yolk and brown colouring or molasses. Alternatively, wholewheat flour gives a pleasing texture and colour to pastry.

Browning dishes, which are coated with tin oxide, are used to brown foods (see 'Microwave Ovensafe Utensils'). A browning element in some microwave ovens is similar to a conventional grill. It is not part of the microwave oven, but browns food by convection simultaneously (when using the combination method).

Density and Time

Density and time are relevant in microwave cooking. In a conventional oven, 1 potato would take 1 hour to cook. In a microwave oven, 1 potato takes 4 minutes. All the available microwave energy is used in cooking the single potato. It therefore takes double the time to cook 2 potatoes (6 to 8 minutes).

When a whole chicken is being cooked, the legs and wings will cook first, the denser areas later.

Liquid Content

Liquid content of food should be reduced when microwaving. Because of the speed of microwave cooking, less evaporation of liquid takes place. Liquid content of food should be reduced because of the speed and evenness of microwave cooking. Hence, halve the liquid normally added in conventional recipes, or add thickening agents to reduce liquid content. An effective thickening agent is a packet of instant soup mix of your choice.

Piercing

Piercing or slitting the membrane of certain foods prevents splatters and bursting of the food in the oven, e.g. egg yolks, tomatoes, potatoes, apples and fish eyes.

Rotating/Stirring

Rotating food is an important part of microwave cooking. This term should not be confused with stirring or stir-frying as in conventional cooking. Food needs to be rotated so that the micro-

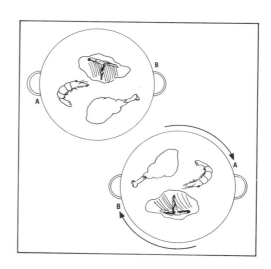

waves reach all sections of it. Even if your microwave oven has an automatically rotating turntable, food needs to be rotated at 90° turns, as the turntable only rotates on its own axis and food placed on it rotates in a set pattern. To rotate one half turn, place dish so that the side which faced the back of the oven now faces the front.

Stirring should not be confused with rotating, as it is the process of actually moving food around in the dish for even cooking. Food needs to be turned over within the dish so that heat waves can reach all areas of food and fewer hot and cold spots are created.

Shielding/Covering

Foil covering is sometimes used in microwave cooking
- as a heat deflector, to shield certain areas of food which may cook faster than others.
- to cover partially cooked food. By covering or 'tenting' the food with foil, the heat is retained and food is cooked further. This is called 'standing time'.

Plastic wraps or lids hold in moisture and speed up the heating process. When plastic wrap is used as a cover, a slit can be made in it through which steam can escape, or through which a spoon may be inserted to enable stirring. Plastic film should always be placed loosely over dishes so steam can escape. Always remove wrap away from the body to avoid scalding.

Plastic wrap with polythylene is non-toxic and safe.

Waxed paper placed loosely over dishes is effective especially in preventing splatters in bacon or rice cooking. Some meats 'pop' when cooked on high temperatures in the microwave oven. The meat is not harmed in any way and should only be covered to prevent splatters in the microwave oven.

Standing Time

Standing time is equivalent to the term 'resting time' in conventional roasting. Because of the intense heat generated during cooking, it is advisable to undercook the food and to 'stand' it while it completes the cooking in the heat thus dispersed. Foil may be used to cover the food while it cooks in its own heat. Standing time is particularly important while cooking meats, eggs, milk, and varieties of bread and cake.

Temperature Variables

The power of microwave ovens varies from 500 to 700 watts. The less the power, the slower the cooking process.

A 'variable control' on a microwave oven means the microwave oven has different settings that can be adjusted higher or lower. Some ovens use numbers (3-5) while others use names, i.e., Defrost, Low, Medium, Roast, etc.

Microwave cooking times vary with the size and shape of foods and cooking utensils. Round-shaped pans cook food more evenly – squared corners receive no energy as microwaves travel in circles.

To test microwave compatibility. Heat an ovenproof cup of water together with an empty dish in the oven. If the dish remains cool, it is microwave-safe. If it turns warm, it may be used with caution. If the dish is hot, it may not be used in the oven.

Aids to browning. Food cooks quickly in the microwave oven and appears pale in comparison to food cooked conventionally. A browning dish coated with tin oxide which prevents microwaves from passing through, sauces, syrup and turmeric are some of the agents used to brown food cooked in the microwave oven.

Microwave Compatible Cookware

(top right, clockwise)

browning dish
rattan/basketware
earthenware
plastic roasting
rack
stoneware
glasses with
plastic lids
toughened
tupperware
(not clear)
wooden bowls/trays
ceramic ware
paper plates,
styrofoam (not
to be re-used)
ovenproof ware
(such as
'Pyrex')
cork
rubber bands
raffia twine
wooden skewers
plastic/wooden
stirrers
plastic microwave
ware
banana leaf and
other leaves
used to
wrap food

**Unsafe
in the
Microwave
Oven**

*(top left,
clockwise)*

enamel ware
metallic dishes,
   trays and
   spoons
metal ties
foil containers
metal colanders
pewter
silver/metallic
   cutlery
foil (except
   in small
   amounts to
   shield meat)
crystal
glasses with
   metal rims
   (the same
   applies to
   dishes with
   metal rims)
jars with
   metal rims
marble
plastics that
   are not
   heatproof

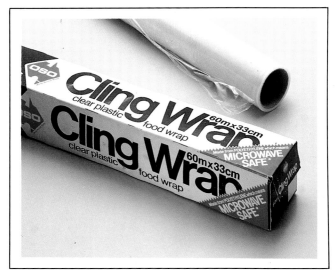

Plastic wraps. Use those made of polyethylene. Avoid other kinds which may give off noxious gases when heated to high temperatures.

Tenting. Use plastic wrap to cover or 'tent' a dish so that some air is allowed to escape while the food is cooked.

Rotating food. Food should be rotated if the microwave oven does not have a turntable. It should also be turned *over* so that microwaves can cook every part evenly. A metal turning fork should be removed from the oven before a cooking cycle is resumed.

Foil in the microwave oven. For even cooking, some areas of meat such as chicken can be covered with foil so that extremities do not cook before the rest of the meat. As long as the use of foil is restricted and it does not touch the top, bottom and sides of the microwave oven, it can be used to shield parts of food.

Shielding fish. The same applies to fish. Tail and other fins should be covered with foil. Remember to remove the eyes before the fish is placed in the microwave oven.

Sterilising. Bottles and jars may be sterilised by filling them to the brim with water and bringing to a boil in the microwave oven. Plastic lids can also be brought to a boil in an ovenproof jar or glass of water. Shake off excess water while glass is still hot. Do not sterilise metal lids in the microwave oven.

Piercing. Food which has a membrane or skin should be pierced to prevent the skin from bursting as microwave-cooked foods heat up from the inside.

Shellfish should be spaced out on the outer edges of a plate to cook evenly as microwaves travel in circles. Shellfish will open when cooked.

Correct positioning. Food should be placed so that thicker portions lie on the outer edge of the dish to cook faster.

Bacon. To cook bacon easily, place between sheets of paper towel and cook as recommended. Fat will be absorbed by the paper.

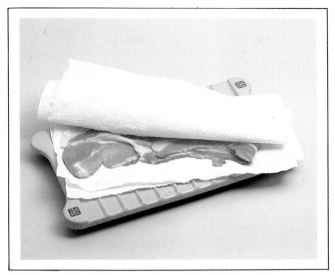

Standing time. This is necessary if food is not to be overcooked in the microwave oven. To retain heat of just undercooked food, it may be covered with foil (shiny side facing in) and allowed to stand outside the microwave oven while it completes cooking. Foil should be used only after the food leaves the microwave oven.

Defrosting. To defrost food effectively, it should be spread out or flattened so that microwaves can penetrate the frozen food effectively. Food should not be thawed in a large mass.

Vegetables. To retain nutrients, vegetables can be cooked in plastic or freezer bags without water. Metal ties should not be used.

Cooking without containers. Some foods may be cooked in their own skin or shell, thus eliminating the need for dishes. The flesh may then be scooped out and mixed with other foods or seasoning.

Microwave Ovensafe Utensils

It is not necessary to purchase a new set of dishes or ovenware to use in a microwave oven – most kitchens are stocked with glass dishes, earthenware crocks, firm plastic bowls, paper and cardboard or basket ware that can be used in the microwave oven.

Glass dishes with metallic gold or silver trims are unsuitable as they may spark when placed in the oven. Metal dishes, pans, thermometers, metal skewers or foil trays may not be used in any oven. Plastic that is labelled 'dishwasher safe' is often also microwave safe. Canned food should never be heated in the can and when foil is used, it should not touch the bottom, top or sides of a microwave oven.

Microwaves should be able to pass through a dish to enable food to cook in it. Some dishes and shapes are more suitable than others. Usually, round dishes are best, as microwaves travel in circles. Most modern plastics can withstand heat transmitted by cooked food. Lead crystal is unsuitable, so is delicate glass.

What's Safe?

Clear, heatproof glass and ceramic bowls are ovensafe and ideal microwave cooking containers. So is heavy pottery or chinaware, subject to the restrictions mentioned earlier. Corningware or Pyrex and similar brands are commonly used as microwave cookware.

Plastic and dishwasher-proof plastic containers are suitable for use in microwave ovens. They should not be used for longer heating periods or contain sweetened or salted liquids as the temperatures these liquids reach are too high for plastic dishes.

Heavy-duty plastic 'speciality' microwave cookware are excellent for microwave cooking and roasting. Check outlets for other brands. Heavy-duty tupperware is suitable, but not the softer plastics. Melamine contains metal and should not be used.

Plastic freezer bags are ideal containers for vegetable cooking, e.g. spinach (ready-cut) or peas in their freezer bag containers. Metal ties should not be used in a microwave oven.

Paper towels may be used in a variety of ways. Use the towel to prevent rice or meat splatters, and in between bacon slices to absorb liquid or fat. Pastry is wrapped in towelling to crisp it and steamed food can be resteamed using a damp dishcloth wrapped over the food to provide the required moisture.

Styrofoam cups may be used once but not re-used. The high temperatures of liquids may melt these cups.

Browning dishes are trays or casserole dishes specially coated with tin oxide bases. These bases do not allow microwaves to pass through the dish, but absorb the waves and act as a heat surface, thereby enabling food to be browned in a little oil or sautéed, as in onion and garlic sautéeing in Asian cookery.

For a browning dish to work effectively, it has to be preheated (without a lid on) on High (100%) for 7 minutes. Some oil may be added after or during preheating. Browning dishes have been known to crack at high temperatures. Check individual recipes using browning dishes and heat only for the prescribed heating times.

A browning dish should not be heated for longer than 8 minutes or it may get too hot and crack the oven shelf which is made of glass.

Test for Microwave Suitability

Place the empty dish and a glass of water in the microwave oven. Cook on High for 1 minute.

- If the water becomes hot and the dish is cool to the touch, it is safe for microwaving.

- If the dish is warm, it may be used for microwaving or reheating foods. In this case, however, continued use could damage the dish eventually.
- If the dish is hot, it is unsafe for microwaving.

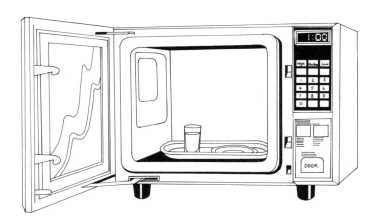

Freezers in Microwave Cooking

The freezer is an excellent complement to the microwave oven as the Defrost cycle in the microwave oven allows the freezer to be used to its full potential. One should make maximum use of both these appliances.

While cooking a meal, plan to cook double the amount so that half of it can be frozen. Freezing is a simple way to cut down on cooking time and it is the safest method of preserving food. When you have frozen meals stacked away in the freezer and a microwave oven to defrost these meals, you are super-organised. Meals can be planned in advance and entertaining on a large scale becomes a relatively simple exercise.

To make your freezer and your microwave oven work for you, be sure to understand the principles involved with both these appliances. Freezers work best when they are filled and the microwave enables you to cook food quickly and economically. When proper cooling and freezing methods are used, the food will retain its nutritional value, quality and texture. Following are some tips:

1   The main advantage of freezing is that cooking double the quantity of food does not take double the time and food bought in bulk is often cheaper.

2   The freezer should be used not only to store cooked frozen food, but major fresh protein foods such as meat, fish and poultry. This provides a reliable and handy food source and reduces the time spent shopping. 'Blast freezing' at the supermarket is the best way to freeze meats so that they can be stored all at once in your freezer. Usually only 10% of the total capacity should be put in your freezer at a time, as a large quantity all at once will strain the freezer motor.

3   Apart from freezing complete meals, there are many short cuts and aids to cooking where the freezer can be put to optimum use:
   - An onion, garlic and ginger blended mixture that is stored in its frozen state can be defrosted at little notice for use in all Asian meals.
   - Liquified blended 'wet' chilli may also be stored in its frozen form and defrosted as the need arises.
   - Root ginger preserves its flavours in its frozen state and yet with 30 seconds on a Defrost cycle, it softens sufficiently to be peeled and cut up or pounded for a recipe.
   - Belacan (dried shrimp paste) can be pre-roasted and stored frozen then defrosted and crumbled into a sambal as needed.
   - Cooked rice, noodles and grated coconut freeze, defrost and heat up with absolutely no change in texture or flavour. So do most daily needs.
   - I make up lime juice when limes are in season. A few seconds of microwaving softens the lime and gives up more juice. The extracted juice can then be frozen into ice blocks and stored until needed, for curries or for refreshing drinks.

If these foods are frozen in small quantities, defrosting for daily use will be simplified.

Some cooked foods freeze and reheat well in the microwave oven: curries, curry puffs (brought to room temperature then crisped, covered with kitchen paper), Nasi Bungkus or Ceylonese Lampries wrapped in banana leaves, casseroles, blanched vegetables and soups.

Freezer Facts

A proper understanding of how freezers work is an important step in competent kitchen management. There are two basic freezer designs in the market today: the 'chest' or elongated box freezer and the upright freezer designed to look like a refrigerator. There is also the smaller freezer compartment of the refrigerator that can always be put to maximum use. (However, if you plan to cook and freeze and use your microwave to defrost meals each evening, a larger capacity of freezer space would be most practical.)

Chest and upright freezers work on the same principle but chest freezers are more economical to run as they are cheaper, have greater capacity and require less electricity. The disadvantage is that food stored in a chest freezer is difficult to reach. In an upright freezer, cold air is lost each time the door is opened, causing a bigger build-up of frost and heavier running costs. However, food is more accessible and one can see at a glance what is available in the freezer.

On a rough estimate, each cubic foot of space in a freezer will hold at least 8 to 9 kg (17-20 lb) of food.

Make sure that floors are even when siting a freezer and that switches and plugs are securely attached. Masking tape may be used to tape over the switch to prevent any accidental shut-off.

Freezer Containers and Storage Notes

To preserve food well, it has to be frozen well. There are a variety of containers that can be used successfully. Rigid plastic containers with lids, special microwave plastic ware, tupperware or even ice cream containers can be used but the food should be filled right up to within 1 cm (½ in) of the top of the container. Trapped air in a container will also trap bacteria. Always remove air from containers by 'burping'.

Heavy-duty plastic freezer bags make excellent freezer containers as they can be moulded around the food and will take up less space in the freezer. Metal ties may be used to seal the bags but should be removed before defrosting or reheating in a microwave oven.

Foil-ware or 'take-away' foil-lined cardboard containers freeze well but cannot be used to defrost food in the microwave oven.

The glass ovenproof dish makes the perfect freezer-to-microwave-to-table container but glass lids are seldom airtight. This can be remedied by wrapping plastic cling film over the lid and dish before freezing. Beware of metal or cast-iron dishes that have been enamelled over. These cannot be used in a microwave oven.

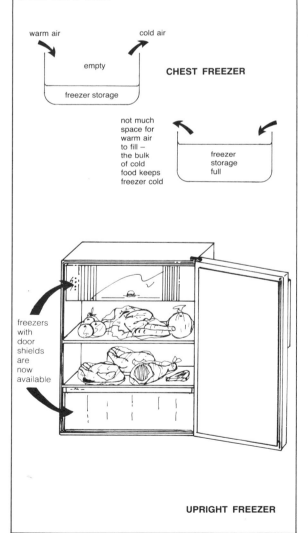

**Freezers – a Basic Principle:
heated air rises and cold air sinks.**

A chest freezer retains cold air because of its depth but if it is not filled to capacity, warm air enters and activates the thermostat each time the freezer door is opened.

In an upright freezer, cold air rushes out and warm air moves in each time the door is opened, unless each shelf has its own plastic door or shield.

warm air   cold air

empty   **CHEST FREEZER**

freezer storage

not much space for warm air to fill – the bulk of cold food keeps freezer cold

freezer storage full

freezers with door shields are now available

UPRIGHT FREEZER

Seals and Labels

Proper sealing and labelling is an important part of freezer organisation. Label each dish with the date it was cooked and its approximate shelf-life. Wax pencils or indelible marker pens should be used to label all items with self-stick labels.

Organise the freezer so that fresher foods are stocked behind older food. Use old stocks first to prevent needless waste. Pack the refrigerator in the same order each time so that each item can be identified at a glance, i.e., meats on the left, ice cream touching one of the cold surfaces, etc.

Cleaning the Freezer

The freezer needs thorough cleaning every two months but any excess ice build-up should be scraped away regularly if the freezer is expected to perform efficiently. Short blasts from a hot hair dryer works well as a quick defroster. Do not use sharp instruments to prise thick ice from freezer walls.

A weak soda bicarbonate solution or vanilla drops will eliminate the stubborn odours of onions or of fish.

Some Precautions To Take

1 Always allow food to cool sufficiently before it is frozen.
2 Cover all food, cooked or otherwise, to prevent freezer burn.
3 Never refreeze defrosted food – this invites bacteria.
4 Always use clean, smooth containers. Dented or peeling plastic containers may contain bacteria that will affect the quality of food.
5 Follow reheating instructions, especially when microwaving, defrosting or reheating.
6 Use your freezer to the maximum but do not expect to freeze a large supply of food at once as this puts a strain on the freezer motor.

Finally, re-educate your family on the merits of preparing and eating pre-cooked, frozen and microwaved food. Then sit back and enjoy your newly acquired freedom.

A Brief Outline of the Freezer Shelf Life of Raw Foods

FOOD	PREPARATION	STORAGE	SHELF LIFE (months)
Beef	Remove gristle. Store in small amounts sufficient for each meal.	Wrap in freezer bags, or foil interleaved with greaseproof paper.	12
Lamb, Pork, etc.	Remove fat, gristle. Store in family servings.	Pack as in beef. Thaw according to instructions in 'Microwave cooking at a glance'.	9
Poultry	Wash inside and out. Remove offal.	Plastic, foil, tupperware	4
Fish	Gut, clean. Freeze fresh fish only.	Tupperware, plastic freezer bags	1-2
Other Seafood	Devein prawns, skin squid.	Tupperware, plastic freezer bags	1-2
Vegetables (generally)	Choose fresh vegetables. Wash, blanch in hot water. Remove and pack in bags, removing all air.	Tupperware, plastic freezer bags	3
Fruit (generally, not bananas)	Cook in syrup of sugar and water. Bottle in sterilised jars.	Bottles	8-12

Microwave Cooking at a Glance

As you refer to the defrosting and cooking chart that follows, remember that:
- Frozen foods in plastic or paper containers (but not foil) may be cooked in these containers.
- Frozen foods should be completely defrosted before beginning the cooking process.
- Cooking time is increased with quantity, though not necessarily in the same ratio as weight.

FOOD	DEFROSTING	REHEATING	COOKING
BISCUITS Frozen slices, brownies	Thaw uncovered for 1 minute on Low (30-40%).		20 cm (8 in) toughened glass square dish of brownies. Cook on High (100%) for 6-8 minutes. Turn dish twice. Cool.
BREADS Crust will be soft, outside colour same as inside. Brown bread is more successful.	Loaves: Defrost on High (100%). Wrap in newspaper – 2 minutes on High.		Bread-making: Dough can be proved by heating on Low (30%/Simmer) for 15 seconds every 9-10 minutes. Best cooked in conventional oven. In microwave, use Roast (70%) setting.
Chapati, Roti Chanai, etc.		Heat 2 minutes on High (100%), covered with damp kitchen paper.	Heat 2-3 minutes on High, covered with damp kitchen paper.
Rolls	Microwave unwrapped in kitchen paper or newspaper for 7-9 seconds each on Low (30%).	Microwave unwrapped for 1 minute on High (100%). Leave for 2 minutes to cool as inside of roll could be too hot.	
BUTTER, GHEE MARGARINE	Microwave on Low (30%) to return 250 g (½ lb) to spreading consistency.		To melt 2 tablespoons butter, heat 30 seconds on Medium (50%). To clarify 250 g (½ lb) ghee, heat 6 minutes on High (100%).
CAKES	Cakes freeze well. Wrap in plastic wrap. Defrost on Low, 10 minutes per 500 g (1 lb).		20 cm (8 in) greased round or square dish. Cook for 8-10 minutes on Medium (70%/Roast). Ignore wet patch on top: Cake is cooked inside. Let it stand 5 minutes before inverting.

FOOD	DEFROSTING	REHEATING	COOKING
Basic Cakes, Sponge	Frozen icing will defrost to spreading consistency on Low (30%) in 10 seconds.		Cook 1 cup sugar, pinch of cream of tartar, 4 tablespoons water for 2 minutes on High (100%). Beat 3 egg whites till stiff. Pour syrup onto egg whites in gradual stream while still beating. Whip mixture until frothy (about 5 minutes).
Bean cakes	8 minutes per 500 g (1 lb). Do not freeze well.		Cook 8-10 minutes per 250 g (½ lb). Cover with plastic wrap.
Caramel (¼ cup water with 4 level tablespoons sugar)		2 minutes on Medium (70%/Roast) to soften once it caramelises.	Blend sugar and water. Stir. Cook till boiling (1 minute). Stir for 2 minutes after boiling. Sugar will caramelise. Watch carefully as sugar turns golden brown. It burns quickly.
Cheesecake	Defrost on Low (30%) uncovered for 2-3 minutes. Let stand.		Microwave to dissolve gelatin in water. Cook on High (100%) 3-4 minutes then on Medium (70%) for 6 minutes. Refrigerate when set.
Chocolate (50 g/1⅔ oz)			Microwave on Medium (70%/Roast) for 1½ to 2 minutes. It retains shape even when soft and could burn easily. Stir. Use as desired to coat nuts, raisins, etc. Cook 1 minute on High (100%) to soften.
Malay and Nonya Kuih (Local cakes)	Rice cakes do not freeze well unless covered with plastic wrap. Defrost on Low (30%), 8 minutes per 500 g (1 lb).		Cakes that need steaming cook well in the microwave oven. A general rule: steam 6 minutes per 250 g (½ lb) on High (100%).
CEREALS			Mix cereal and hot water. Stir well. Add salt, sugar, etc. 2 tablespoons with ½ cup water: 2½ minutes on High (100%). Stir well after ½ minute.
CHEESE		Melting must be done on Low (30%) as high temperatures make cheese stringy.	Microwave Low (30%) for Fondue, etc., then add heated wine and some flour. Heat till it bubbles on Low for 3-4 minutes. Stir.
COCONUT	Flakes freeze and defrost well. 150 g (5 oz): 8 minutes on Low (30%). Milk expressed after adding water does not freeze well.	150 g (5 oz): 6-8 minutes on Low (30%).	Cook as for any other liquid: 1 cup, 3 minutes on High (100%).

FOOD	DEFROSTING	REHEATING	COOKING
CRACKERS (Kropok, Papadam)			1 minute on a kitchen paper on High (100%).
CUSTARD			1½ cups: 5 minutes on High (100%). Stir or whisk every ½ minute. Add 2 egg yolks to 1¼ cups milk. Beat and microwave for 30 seconds on High (100%). Stir and whisk. Continue on Low (30%) for 4 minutes. Stir and cook till set.
Packet Custard			Blend recipe quantities of custard with cold milk. Whisk well, add all the required milk and microwave. 1½ cups: 2½ minutes on High (100%). Whisk every ½ minute.
DOFU	Freezes well. Defrost 200 g (7 oz) 8 minutes on Low (30%).	200 g (7 oz): 6 minutes on Medium (70%).	As for Stir-fried Vegetables.
EGGS			See separate recipes. Do not cook in shell — they will explode. Pierce membrane of yolk. Poached egg: 6 minutes in boiling water in a dish. Pierce membrane. Basic cooking: (no oil required) 1½ minutes on High (100%). Use plastic wrap.
Omelette			Whip egg, add salt, pepper and onion. About 40 seconds an egg.
Kaya (egg custard) (See also Custards)	10 minutes on Defrost per 250 g (½ lb).	7 minutes on High for 250 g (½ lb).	
LEGUMES (DHAL, MUNG/BLACK/ GREEN/RED/LIMA BEANS)	They freeze well but could turn mushy after defrosting. Defrost 250 g (8 oz) on Low (30%) for 10-12 minutes.	Slow reheating needed to avoid overcooking. Use short bursts of heat. stir in between till heat desired is reached. 250 g (8 oz): 4 minutes on High (100%) or 8 minutes on Medium (70%).	No need to soak overnight. Add water to just cover beans. 200 g (7 oz): 15 minutes on High (100%), covered with plastic wrap. Add more water if needed. Reduce cooking time by 2 minutes if a less mushy dish is desired.
LIQUIDS: DRINKS, SAUCES, ETC.			
Coffee		1 cup 1 minute on Medium (70%).	Boil 1 cup water for 1½ minutes on High (100%). Add coffee, milk and stir. Cook 1½ minutes on High (100%) to bring to a boil.
Gravies, Sauces, Curries	1 cup: 4 minutes on Low (30%). Stir to distribute heat.	1 cup: 2 minutes on Medium (70%).	1 cup: 5 minutes on High (100%). Use a larger container.

FOOD	DEFROSTING	REHEATING	COOKING
Gravies, Sauces, Curries			To make sauce: Microwave equal amounts of butter and flour (seasoned) together and whisk as butter melts. Cook, stop and stir often. (See notes on custard.)
		For thick curry and spaghetti sauce: 3 minutes at room temperature. Keep stirring to distribute heat.	Spaghetti/Curry Sauce: 1 cup (covered): 6 minutes. Keep stirring to distribute heat.
Milk		To warm 1 cup: 1 minute on Medium (70%).	To boil 1 cup: 2¼ minutes on High (100%).
Soups	1 cup: 40 seconds on Low (30%).	1 cup: 2 minutes on High (100%).	Cook each cup 3½ minutes on High (100%).
Spirits, wine, brandy (to flambé fruit or dessert, ignite and pour over)			7 minutes on High (100%).
Tea		To warm 1 cup tea with milk: 1 minute on Medium (70%).	Boil 1 cup water for 2½ minutes on High (100%). Add 1½ teaspoons tea. Cover for ½ minute. Strain the tea.
Water		To warm 1 cup: 1 minute on Medium (70%).	To boil 1 cup: 2¼-3 minutes on High (100%).
MEAT			
Beef			
Curry	500 g (1 lb): Cover and microwave 20 minutes on Medium (70%). If you want curry to come to room temperature, and not overcook, stir to move thawed pieces. Begin cooking only when pieces are thawed.	500 g (1 lb): 10 minutes on Medium (70%). Stir twice as in conventional cooking to distribute heat to warm dish.	As in normal cooking, slow cooking produces better results. Brown meat in a preheated and oiled browning dish. Use tenderiser for 500 g (1 lb), cook ½ hour on High (100%) or 1½ hours on Medium (70%).
Minced	Smaller pieces defrost quicker than large chunks. Remove wrap, place in dish, keep moving so defrosted areas around edges can be moved inward. Do not refreeze once defrosted. Defrost 500 g (1 lb) 8-10 minutes on Low or Defrost (30%).	Mince casserole 500 g (1 lb) 4 minutes on High (100%). Mince curries, etc. 500 g (1 lb) 4 minutes on High (100%). Meatloaf 500 g (1 lb) on Medium (70%).	500 g (1 lb) for 7 minutes on High (100%). 500 g (1 lb) 8½ minutes on High (100%). 500 g (1 lb) 10 minutes on High (100%). Use a browning dish to brown: preheat, add oil, sauté onions and garlic. Add mince and cook, stirring once or twice according to time and settings. Add other ingredients and cook on High (100%) for a third the conventional cooking time.
Rendang	Freezes well. Defrost as for curry.	As above.	Cook using Low and Medium cycles as this dish needs slow cooking.

FOOD	DEFROSTING	REHEATING	COOKING
Beef			
Roast	500 g (1 lb): 10 minutes on Low (30%). Defrost on Low or meat will begin to brown at edges. Best to defrost part of the way, then leave to defrost naturally at room temperature; or shield thinner or exposed areas with foil.	500 g (1 lb): 8 minutes on Medium (70%). Let roast stand for a while before serving.	Best cooked on Medium (70%/Roast). Every 500 g (1 lb): 18-20 minutes on Medium (Roast/ 70%), in a shallow dish, uncovered after basting. Rotate dish 4 times during cooking to cook sides evenly. Cover in foil and let stand to cook further in its own heat. Brown under grill if desired.
Stir-fried	Freezes well. Defrost as for curry. Do not add thickening until serving.	As for Curry.	Cut into thin slices, season and cook on High (100%) for 2 minutes per 200 g (7 oz).
Lamb, Mutton			
Casserole	500 g (1 lb): 15 minutes on Low (30%).	500 g (1 lb): 6 minutes on Medium (70%).	500 g (1 lb): 25 minutes on Medium (70%/Roast). Use sauces to colour meat. Preheat browning dish 3 minutes on High (100%). Turn over. Cook a further 3 minutes on High (100%). Transfer to casserole. Casserole cooking time: for every 500 g (1 lb), 20 minutes on Medium (70%). Stir, then cook for 5 minutes on High (100%).
Chops	Cover with paper and defrost on a plate. 500 g (1 lb): 5 minutes on Low (30%). Turn frequently and move chops around.	500 g (1 lb): 3 minutes on High (100%).	Arrange meat to touch rim of plate. Solid pieces cook slower. Use sauces to colour meat. Preheat browning dish 7 minutes on High (100%). Dot with oil. Cook chops 8 minutes on Medium (70%). Allow 5 minutes standing time.
Curry, Kurmah	These freeze well. Defrost 500 g (1 lb) for 10 minutes on Low (30%). Bring to room temperature. Stir to distribute heat so dish defrosts evenly.	500 g (1 lb): 10 minutes on Medium (70%). Stir twice to distribute heat as in conventional cooking.	As for beef, use browning dish to sauté onions, garlic, etc. Cook curry on Medium (70%) as for casserole cooking. To tenderise meat, slow cooking is needed. Add flour to thicken curry as natural evaporation is not possible in microwave cooking.
Roast	500 g (1 lb): 10 minutes on Low (30%). Shield thin areas and bone with foil to prevent cooking before defrosting.	500 g (1 lb): 10 minutes on Medium (70%). Allow standing time.	Brush roast with oil and seasonings. Cover with plastic wrap. Preheat browning dish 6 minutes on High (100%). Cook 500 g (1 lb) 20 minutes on Medium (70%/Roast). Turn roast once. Let it stand for 10 minutes before carving.

FOOD	DEFROSTING	REHEATING	COOKING
Pork			
Bacon	To separate frozen slices, place on kitchen paper. 200 g (7 oz): 2 minutes on Low (30%). Let stand for 1 minute.		Place bacon on 2 pieces of kitchen paper. 2 rashers: 60 seconds on High (100%). Overcooking toughens bacon.
Pieces	As with lamb.	As with lamb.	As with lamb. Cover with plastic.
Roast	500 g (1 lb): 10 minutes on Low (30%). Give short bursts of power, allow standing time between.		Slit skin and sprinkle with salt. Make slits in meat and insert slivers of garlic. Cook on a trivet. Every 500 g (1 lb): 10 minutes on High (100%). Remove skin on top, place between 2 sheets of kitchen paper and let it crisp – 3 minutes on High (100%). More time for larger crust.
Spare ribs	500 g (1 lb): 10 minutes on Low (30%).		Season spare ribs. Preheat browning dish for 6 minutes on High (100%). Oil dish and heat for 1 minute on High (100%). Cook 500 g (1 lb) ribs 5 minutes on High (100%), then turn over and cook 15 minutes on Medium (70%). Cover with plastic.
Sausages	Open and separate or microwave on High (100%) for 30 seconds to allow sausages to separate. To defrost 500 g (1 lb): 5 minutes on Low (30%). Allow 5 minutes standing time.	500 g (1 lb): 3 minutes on High (100%). Keep turning sausages.	Do not cook frozen sausages. Heat browning dish for 7 minutes on High (100%). Dot with oil. Cook sausages, turning in dish. Sausages will sizzle. For every 2 sausages: 2 minutes on High (100%). Brown under grill if desired.
Chinese sausages			For every 2 Chinese sausages (sliced), 1½ minutes on High (100%).
NUTS/SEEDS Almonds, Cashewnuts, Chestnuts, Peanuts, Sesame Seeds	Nuts do not freeze well.		Roast 100-150 g (3-5 oz) on High (100%) for 3 minutes, stirring once to avoid burning. Dredge in butter.
POULTRY			
Chicken			
Casserole	500 g (1 lb): 7 minutes on Low (30%). Arrange pieces so thicker parts point outward where microwaves hit more often. Keep moving pieces.	500 g (1 lb): 10 minutes on Medium (70%). Stir once or twice to distribute heat.	Preheat browning dish for 6 minutes on High (100%). Add oil. Brown pieces. Add seasoning and liquid (not too much).

FOOD	DEFROSTING	REHEATING	COOKING
Chicken casserole			500 g (1 lb): 20 minutes on Medium (70%). Keep larger pieces at outer edge of dish. Stir often to cook evenly. 1 kg (just over 2 lb): 28 minutes on Medium (70%).
Curry	Freezes well. Tastes penetrate meat. 500 g (1 lb): 10 minutes on Low (30%).	As above.	Start curry as for casserole, sauté onion, etc. first. Total cooking time for curry is 20 minutes. Add flour to thicken as evaporation is not present as in conventional cooking.
Whole	500 g (1 lb): 10 minutes on Low (30%). Turn to make sure all of chicken is exposed to microwaves. Let stand and wash under tap to complete defrost.	500 g (1 lb): 10 minutes on Medium (70%).	Rub with seasoning and browning agent (e.g. soy sauce). Cover with plastic wrap. 500 g (1 lb): 10 minutes on High (100%). 1 kg (just over 2 lb): 10 minutes for each on High (100%). Wings should be shielded with foil to prevent burning. Do not let foil touch sides of microwave oven.
Turkey	It is not practical to defrost a turkey in a microwave oven. It is best left to defrost slowly in the refrigerator.	500 g (1 lb): 12 minutes on Low (30%). Larger amounts impractical.	Season and rub with salt. Cook in large dish loosely covered with plastic. Shield wings with foil. 500 g (1 lb): 13 minutes on Medium (70%/Roast). Large turkeys (more than 2 kg/ 4½ lb) are best cooked in a conventional oven.

RICE AND PASTA

FOOD	DEFROSTING	REHEATING	COOKING
Macaroni			500 g (1 lb): 12 minutes on High (100%), in boiling salted water.
Noodles		500 g (1 lb): 10 minutes on High (100%).	
Rice	Loosen rice grains, sprinkle with water and cover with plastic wrap. 1 cup rice: 6 minutes on Medium (70%).	Sprinkle with water, cover with plastic wrap. 1 cup: 4 minutes on Medium (70%).	1 cup: 12 minutes on High (100%). Rinse rice 3 times. Place in casserole, add 1½ cups water. Cover with kitchen paper and cook. When water is absorbed, let rice stand for 3 minutes. Fluff out with a fork.
	Cooked rice as in Fried Rice, Chicken Rice and Pilaf freezes well. To defrost each cup: 6 minutes on Low (30%).	As for rice, above.	Refer to individual recipes.

FOOD	DEFROSTING	REHEATING	COOKING
Spaghetti		500 g (1 lb): 10 minutes on Medium (70%). Cover with plastic wrap.	500 g (1 lb): 15 minutes on High (100%), in salted boiling water.

SEAFOOD

Fish

FOOD	DEFROSTING	REHEATING	COOKING
Curry	500 g (1 lb): 6 minutes on Low (30%). Fish curry freezes well.	500 g (1 lb): 6-8 minutes on Medium (70%). Do not reheat too long. Reposition fish.	500 g (1 lb): 6 minutes on High (100%).
Fillets	500 g (1 lb): 6 minutes on Low (30%). Rinse under tap to wash off ice crystals.	500 g (1 lb): 8 minutes on Medium (70%).	Arrange fillets with large ends on outer edge of plate. Turn dish around and turn fillets over half way through cooking. 500 g (1 lb): 6 minutes on High (100%).
Whole	Remove eyes. 500 g (1 lb): 8-10 minutes on Low (30%). Rinse under tap to defrost fully. Let stand before cooking. Cover tail with foil to prevent overcooking.	300 g (10 oz): 6 minutes on Medium (70%).	The ideal way to cook fish is to cover with greaseproof paper. Before covering, season, make slits on the sides to allow seasoning to penetrate. 500 g (1 lb): 8 minutes on Medium (70%) or 5 minutes on High (100%). Steaming: 4 minutes on High (100%), covered with a plastic wrap.
Lobster	Defrost in shallow dish, soft side up. 500 g (1 lb): 12 minutes on Low (30%). Turn over halfway through defrosting. Remove before lobster turns warm.	Reheat 500 g (1 lb) lobster mornay or curry 10 minutes on Medium (70%). Do not overheat cooked lobster as meat will toughen.	Cook lobster in shallow dish. Sprinkle with water, cover loosely with plastic wrap. Turn dish around and turn lobster over halfway through cooking. 500 g (1 lb): 8 minutes on High (100%). Let lobster stand 5 minutes, covered in foil to keep the heat in, before serving. Cooked lobster meat is translucent.
Prawns	(Clean and devein before freezing.) 500 g (1 lb): 5 minutes on Low (30%).	For sambals, curries, etc., 500 g (1 lb): 4 minutes on High (100%). Stir twice to distribute heat.	Arrange larger pieces on outer edge. Preheat browning dish 6 minutes on High (100%). Add oil. Heat 30 seconds on High (100%). Fry prawns and garlic. 500 g (1 lb): 5 minutes on High (100%), stirring once. Add *sambal* sauces. Cook further 8 minutes on Medium (70%).
Prawn Paste (*Belacan*)			To roast, heat a 1½ cm (¾ in) cube for 2 minutes on High (100%).

FOOD	DEFROSTING	REHEATING	COOKING
Shellfish (Clams, etc.)			Clean and wash off grime. Place in a dish and cook 3 minutes on Medium (70%). Shellfish will open and meat can be removed from shell. Discard unopened shellfish.
VEGETABLES			
Cabbage		3 minutes on Medium (70%). Stir once.	For 4 cups cabbage use 2 tablespoons margarine. Cook covered for 10 minutes on High (100%).
Canned Vegetables (Remove from can)			
Root: carrot, potato, etc.		4 minutes on High (100%) per can. (Remove from can first.)	250 g (8 oz): 8 minutes on High (100%).
Soft vegetables		4 minutes on High (100%) per can.	250 g (8 oz): 5 minutes on High (100%).
Frozen Vegetables	3-5 minutes on Low (30%).	3 servings: 3 minutes on High (100%).	500 g (1 lb): 4 minutes on High (100%).
Hard Vegetables			
(Most)		5 minutes on Medium (70%) if at room temperature.	Cook covered. 500 g (1 lb): 12 minutes on High (100%) for tender consistency; 10 minutes on High (100%) for crisp consistency.
Beetroot			2 large: 10 minutes on High (100%). Stand for 8 minutes.
Brinjal			2 large: 8 minutes on High (100%).
Broccoli (cut in pieces)	500 g (1 lb): 10 minutes on Low (30%).	500 g (1 lb): 5 minutes on Medium (70%).	500 g (1 lb): 10 minutes on High. Stir and add sauces.
Carrot (cut in pieces)	Freezes well. 500 g (1 lb): 10 minutes on Low (30%).	500 g (1 lb): 6 minutes on Medium (70%).	500 g (1 lb): 12 minutes on High (100%), thicker parts facing outward.
Cauliflower (Whole)	500 g (1 lb): 10 minutes on Low (30%).	500 g (1 lb): 5 minutes on High (100%).	500 g (1 lb): 12 minutes on High (100%).
(Pieces)			500 g (1 lb): 10 minutes on High (100%).
Potato			1 potato: 4 minutes on High (100%). 2 potatoes: 7 minutes on High (100%). Impractical to cook too many in a microwave oven.
(Boiled Potato)		2 minutes on Medium (70%) if at room temperature.	500 g (1 lb): add water to half-cover. Cook for 10 minutes on High (100%).

FOOD	DEFROSTING	REHEATING	COOKING
Pumpkin, Taro, Chinese Yam (wu tow)	500 g (1 lb): 10 minutes on Low (30%).	500 g (1 lb): 6 minutes on High (100%).	Cook with some water, or just 'in the shell'. 500 g (1 lb): 15 minutes on High (100%) to soften.
Leafy Vegetables	Kai Lan, Chye Sim, and Kangkung – in fact most greens – do not freeze well and change in texture. Spinach, however, freezes well.		Greens cook very quickly. Sprinkle with water. Cook on High (100%) a minute, stop and test-taste, then continue. Do not add too much oil or water. Greens 'sweat' in the heat and taste better with natural salts.
Mushroom (Dried)			100 g (3½ oz): 5-6 minutes on High with water to soak mushrooms.
Soft Vegetables (Zucchini, Tomato, Tender Mushroom)		2-3 minutes on Medium (70%). Stir once.	For tender consistency, 500 g (1 lb) in covered dish: 6 minutes on High (100%). For crisp, 5 minutes (covered) on High (100%).
Stir-fried Vegetables	6-8 minutes per 100 g (3½ oz).	4 minutes per 100 g (3½ oz).	Pieces (green pepper, corn, mushroom, carrot, leafy vegetable, etc.) cut even-sized. 500 g (1 lb): 9 minutes on High (100%). Stir twice. Add sauces. Precook carrot for 4 minutes before adding other vegetable.

Time Savers

Here are ways to make the most of your microwave oven. Times and temperature settings will vary according to quantity and starting temperatures of food. Settings are based on a 650 watt microwave oven, but as ovens and ingredients do vary, time and temperature adjustments may be required for some items.

	TEMPERATURE SETTING	TIME
To soften butter 250 grams	Low	3 minutes. Check consistency, give more time if needed.
To soften cream cheese 100 grams	Low	30-50 seconds
To freshen stale bread 2 slices (wrap bread in damp towel).	Med/Low	30 seconds
To crisp softened biscuits.	High	10 seconds
To crisp softened cereals (cornflakes) 1 cup.	High	20 seconds
To refresh bread rolls/ *yu char kuay*/croissants (wrap in paper towel).	Med	30 seconds per roll
To heat limes, lemons, oranges to yield more fruit juice.	High	30 seconds
To soften hard ice cream 1 litre.	Low	3-4 minutes
To dry grated rind of lemon or lime ¼ cup.	High	1½ minutes
To dry fresh herbs (curry leaves, lemon grass, etc.) ½ cup between paper towels. Dried herbs will crumble between fingers.	High	2 minutes
To toast desiccated coconut ½ cup. Spread evenly on heatproof plate. Stir coconut after ½ minute.	High	3 minutes

Dom Yam Gung (56) and Hua Hom Sod Sai (97)

Ikan Pepes (65)

	TEMPERATURE SETTING	TIME
To heat baby food in jar (remove metal lid).	Med	1½ minutes — warm 2½ minutes — hot
To heat baby's milk in bottle 1 medium sized 8 oz bottle.	High	55 seconds
To defrost butter icing for spreading or icing 100 g (3½ oz).	Low	20-30 seconds
To flambé liqueurs/brandy ¼ wine glass (pour over Christmas pudding or dessert and light).	High	30 seconds
To make bread crumbs from dry bread. Break up 1 slice. Add ½ tablespoon butter. Mix and stir well during cooking.	High	3 minutes
To soften lumpy sugar. Add a wedge of apple to 1 cup sugar. Apple helps to separate sugar crystals.	High	1-2 minutes
To plump dried fruit 1 cup. Add some liqueur or water. Cover with plastic wrap.	High	1½ minutes
To roast nuts and sesame seeds, spread ½ cup evenly on a flat dish. Stir after 1½ minutes.	High	3 minutes
To melt chocolate ½ small bar. Do not overcook. Chocolate burns.	High	1½ minutes depending on size of bar. Chocolate retains its shape although soft.
To crisp pork fat and to make crackle. Remove from meat and place between kitchen towelling paper. Rub with salt.	High	4 minutes or till skin crackles. Will depend on size of piece or amount of crackling required.
To reheat cold tea or coffee without a stewed flavour 1 cup.	High	1½ to 2 minutes
To soften 1 tablespoon honey, liquid glucose or golden syrup.	High	30 or 50 seconds
To liquify crystallised honey 1 cup.	Med	3 minutes
To dissolve 1 tablespoon gelatin. Sprinkle on top of liquid stated in recipe.	High	Heat about 1 minute till dissolved. Give mixture a stir.
To open mussels or cockles easily. Place 6-8 on a plate.	High	30 seconds each. As each shell opens, remove from the microwave oven.
To heat cold dinner plates (without metallic rims). Interleave with moistened tea towels.	High	1 minute per plate.

	TEMPERATURE SETTING	TIME
To reheat an individual pie or banana fritter. Wrap in damp kitchen paper or banana leaf.	High	1 minute
To resteam cakes, especially Puttu Piring (2-3). Wrap in moistened kitchen paper or banana leaf.	High	2-3 minutes
To heat individual serves of soup in a cup.	High	2 minutes
To soften dried chillies before grinding. Add some water to ½ cup dried chillies	Med	2 minutes. Drain water then grind softened chillies.
To quick-steam fish to make fish patties 250 g (½ lb). Rub turmeric and salt over fish. Add water. Cover with plastic wrap.	High	4-5 minutes or until fish flesh is white and flakes off bone.
To quick-cook brinjals in the skin for sambals 1 medium-sized brinjal.	High	Halve and cook 5 minutes. Scoop out cooked flesh.
To quick-cook pumpkin in shell 200 grams.	High	6-8 minutes. Scoop out flesh and use as desired.
To soften large cabbage leaves as in Cabbage Rolls. Wrap in moistened towels. Cook singly.	High	1-2 minutes depending on size of cabbage leaf.
To dry out wet papers or newpapers. Fold to fit oven.	High	1-2 minutes. *Do not let it overdry or paper will ignite.*
To pre-roast *belacan* before using in sambals 1 cm (½ in) cube.	High	20 seconds. Pre-roasted *belacan* will crumble easily when crushed with the fingers.
To cook Papadams singly without oil. Place on a plate or kitchen paper. All crackers may be treated similarly.	High	About 1 minute each, depending on size.
To warm a sandwich. Cover with a paper towel to prevent drying out.	Med	1 minute. Eat at once.
To warm stall-cooked noodles, etc. Remove metal ties. Heat in wrapping of plastic, paper or banana leaf. Open up packet.	High	3-5 minutes, depending on amount.
To heat towels for hot water fomentation, a face-steam (facial) or after a Chinese dinner. Moisten towel.	High	2 minutes per towel.

	TEMPERATURE SETTING	TIME
To peel tomatoes. Place 1 tomato in a cup of boiling water. Slit skin a little to prevent 'membrane-burst'.	High	30 seconds. Remove from hot water and run cold water over. Skin peels easily.
Dry sweet-smelling flowers or shredded *pandan* leaves for homemade potpourri. The result will be dry but not crumbly. For ½ cup.	High	2-3 minutes
To quick-roast chicken. The weight of a chicken determines the number of minutes cooked on each side:		
1 kg (2¼ lb) chicken	High	10 minutes on each side.
1¼ kg (2¾ lb) chicken	High	12 minutes on each side.

Curry Cooking in a Microwave Oven

Curries are best cooked on top of a stove as the flavours need to penetrate meat. However, when cooked on a Roast or Simmer setting (Medium/Medium High/50-70%), the meat is cooked slowly and the same effect is achieved.

The advantage of microwaving a curry is that it is clean and efficient and the curry may be served in the dish in which it was cooked.

Flour may be used to thicken a curry, as liquids are not reduced in the microwave oven — it cooks too quickly for natural evaporation to take place as would happen in conventional cooking. Alternatively, add ground uncooked rice to the curry powder as an effective gravy-thickener. Curries should be covered loosely if meat is cooking slowly, but uncovered at some stage in the cooking cycle so that gravy may thicken.

Basic Curry Starter

500 g (1 lb) shallots
100 g (3½ oz) garlic
200 g (6⅔ oz) ginger
a little vinegar to facilitate
    grinding

Use this as a base for all your cooking needs as it cuts preparation time by half.

Preparation

Peel and wash all ingredients, then blend till fine, using a little vinegar (rather than water) to facilitate grinding. If you prefer to grind on a grinding stone, remember to use vinegar, not water.

Place blended ingredients in a clean sterilised bottle and freeze for use as needed, for cooking Malaysian curries. The starter may be used in its frozen state, or defrosted.

Note: A piece may be chipped off as required. In its frozen state, the mix turns a light green but this does not affect its quality or taste.

Nam Prik Pao (Thai Roasted Curry Paste)

7 dried red chillies
6 shallots
4 cloves garlic
2 tablespoons dried shrimp paste
    (*kapee*)
1 teaspoon brown sugar
1 tablespoon fish sauce (*nam pla*)
some oil

Use this for Thai curries.

Preparation

Preroast chillies, shallots and garlic over an open flame till smoky black, holding them with tongs.

Cool and pound the ingredients, adding *kapee*, brown sugar and *nam pla*.

Microwave Cooking Method

Preheat a browning dish. Add 1 tablespoon oil and heat for 30 seconds on High (100%), uncovered.

Cook the curry paste for 2 minutes on High (100%), uncovered, stirring once. Cook for another minute on High (100%).

Cool and bottle for use with curries.

Note: This amount is sufficient for 3 Thai curries.

Measures & Equivalents

In this book, conversions are approximate and rounded off where the extra few grammes or ounces do not affect cooking time. It is important to remember that all equivalents given below are also approximate and rounded off to the nearest useful figure.

Liquids

Imperial liquid measures	Imperial/Metric Cup and tablespoon measures	Metric liquid measures
1 fl. oz	1½ tablespoons	30 ml
2 fl. oz	¼ cup	60 ml
3 fl. oz	5 tablespoons	100 ml
4 fl. oz	½ cup	125 ml
5 fl. oz/¼ pint	7½ tablespoons	150 ml
6 fl. oz	¾ cup	185 ml
8 fl. oz	1 cup	250 ml

Imperial liquid measures	Imperial/Metric Cup and tablespoon measures	Metric liquid measures
10 fl. oz/½ pint	1¼ cups	310 ml
12 fl. oz	1½ cups	375 ml
14 fl. oz	1¾ cups	430 ml
15 fl. oz/¾ pint	1⅘ cups	475 ml
16 fl. oz	2 cups	500 ml
20 fl. oz/1 pint	2½ cups	625 ml

Equivalents

	Equivalent/Substitute
Achuete seeds	Annatto seeds
Brinjal	Aubergine, Eggplant
Candlenut	Macadamia
Capsicums	Peppers
Champignons	Button mushrooms
Citrus leaf	Double lime leaf Kaffir lime leaf Lime zest
Coconut cream	Thick coconut milk
Egg noodles	Yellow noodles
Garam masala	Curry powder
Kitchen paper	Paper towels
Lemon zest	Lemon rind
Lentils	Dhal

	Equivalent/Substitute
Palm sugar	Jaggery, Molasses, Treacle
Plastic wrap	Cling wrap
Rice wine	Sherry
Sago	Tapioca pearls
Sake	Sherry
Semolina	Wheatola, 'Breakfast Delight'
Snow peas	Mange tout
Sweet cummin	Fennel
Tamarind paste	Lime juice, Vinegar
Tomato sauce	Tomato ketchup
Wholewheat bread	Wholemeal
Zucchini	Courgette

Matching Spoonfuls

1 tablespoon	3 teaspoons
1 tablespoon	2 dessertspoons
1½ teaspoons	1 dessertspoon

Cup Measures

	Metric	Imperial	Metric cup/spoon
Almonds	120 g	4 oz	¾ cup
Breadcrumbs, dried	120 g	4 oz	2 cups
fresh	120 g	4 oz	1 cup
Butter	5 g	⅙ oz	1 teaspoon
	15 g	½ oz	1 tablespoon
	120 g	4 oz	1 cup
Cheese, grated	120 g	4 oz	1 cup
Coconut, grated	120 g	4 oz	1 cup
Flour, unsifted	7 g	¼ oz	1 tablespoon
	120 g	4 oz	1 cup
	450 g	1 lb	3⅔ cups
Herbs, chopped	15 g	½ oz	1 tablespoon
Meats, cooked and chopped	250 g	8 oz	1 cup
Nuts, chopped	7 g	¼ oz	1 tablespoon
	120 g	4 oz	1 cup
Onions, chopped or sliced	120 g	4 oz	1 cup
Rice, uncooked	9 g	⅓ oz	1 tablespoon
	200 g	6⅔ oz	1 cup
Sugar, granulated or castor	15 g	½ oz	1 tablespoon
	250 g	8 oz	1 cup
Vegetables, hard (e.g. carrot)	240 g	8 oz	1 cup

SOUPS

Microtips on Cooking Soups

Soups are ideally cooked in the microwave oven. They heat evenly and thick soups will cook without sticking to the container. Some rules are:

- Water-based soups should be heated on High (100%).
- Cream- or milk-based soups should be heated on Medium (70%).
- Liquids do not evaporate as much as in conventional cooking, so flavours – such as garlic or fish – remain strong.
- Plastic wrap should be used only to cover container loosely, allowing a vent to stir the soup.
- Vegetables break down easily in a microwave oven, and can then be pureed or blended with cream.

Canton Chicken and Sweetcorn Soup

CHINESE

PREPARATION: 10 mins
COOKING: 700 watt – 21-22 mins
650 watt – 28-29 mins
500 watt – 37-39 mins
Times given here are for a
650 watt oven. Decrease time
by 15 seconds per minute for
a 700 watt oven. Increase time
by 20 seconds per minute for a
500 watt oven.
KCAL 884
SERVES 6

300 g (10 oz) chicken thighs
2 × 2 cm (¾ × ¾ in) ginger
8 stalks spring onion
4 peppercorns, crushed
1 tablespoon sweet sherry
3-4 cooked corncobs (use kernels
  only)
1 egg
1 tablespoon flour
salt
pepper

Preparation

Cut chicken into pieces. Discard skin and fat. Peel ginger, clean spring onion and slice both thinly.

Place chicken, ginger, spring onion and crushed peppercorns in a casserole with 3 cups water. Cook, covered with plastic wrap, 5 minutes on High (100%), then 10 minutes on Medium (70%). Remove chicken and shred meat.

Microwave Cooking Method

Put chicken stock, shredded meat, sherry and corn kernels in a casserole and cook on High (100%) for 10 minutes, covered.

Trail beaten egg in boiling soup. Stir, then add flour mixed with a little water. Cook 3-4 minutes on High (100%).

Serve hot with a spring onion garnish.

Nethali Rassam

PREPARATION: 8 mins
COOKING: 700 watt – 12 mins
650 watt – 16 mins
500 watt – 21 mins
Times given here are for a
650 watt oven. Decrease time
by 15 seconds per minute for
a 700 watt oven. Increase time
by 20 seconds per minute for a
500 watt oven.
KCAL 284
SERVES 6

50 g (1⅔ oz) dried anchovies
2 cloves garlic
½ teaspoon peppercorns
2 teaspoons coriander seeds
2 shallots
4 cm (1½ in) cube of tamarind
     paste
1 teaspoon cummin
salt
1 teaspoon oil
2 dried chillies, each torn into 2-3
     pieces
3-4 stalks curry leaves torn from
     stalks
½ teaspoon mustard seed

Rassam or 'pepper water' and its pidgined equivalent, the famous Mulligatawny, have always been known to aid digestion. It is an integral part of South Indian cooking. 'Nethali' or Anchovy Rassam is typically Sri Lankan and especially nutritious when microwaved as the flavours mature favourably.

Rassam can also be cooked with tomato or chicken pieces. Add at the beginning of cooking time and cook for 4 minutes longer on High (100%).

Preparation

Remove heads and black offal from anchovies. Rinse in a colander and drain.

Bruise garlic, leaving skin intact. Crush peppercorns and coriander seeds roughly. Peel and slice shallots.

Work tamarind and ½ cup water with fingers and strain off dregs.

Microwave Cooking Method

Place tamarind juice, shallots, garlic, pepper, coriander, cummin, salt, anchovies and 2 cups water in a casserole.

Cover loosely with plastic wrap, leaving a vent for steam to escape and to insert a spoon. Cook for 7 minutes on High (100%), stirring once during the cycle.

Continue cooking on Medium (70%) for 6 minutes and allow to stand, covered with foil.

In another heatproof bowl, heat 1 teaspoon oil on High (100%) for 1 minute. Add dried chillies, curry leaves and mustard seed. Cook on High (100%) for 2 minutes, stirring at the end of the cycle. Add immediately to Rassam and serve hot.

Dom Yam Gung (Hot Sour Prawn Soup)

PREPARATION: 15 mins
COOKING: 700 watt – 20 mins
            650 watt – 27 mins
            500 watt – 36 mins
Times given here are for a
650 watt oven. Decrease time
by 15 seconds per minute for
a 700 watt oven. Increase time
by 20 seconds per minute for a
500 watt oven.
KCAL 752
SERVES 6

500 g (1 lb) prawns
6 stalks lemon grass
6 red bird's eye chillies
1 lemon or large lime
3-4 stalks coriander leaves
4 stalks spring onion
salt to taste
1 tablespoon fish sauce
1 tablespoon chilli oil
6 citrus leaves

Be prepared to work up a sweat over this delicious soup from Thailand.

Preparation

Clean and devein prawns, reserving heads for broth after rinsing them twice in clean water. Strip leaves off lemon grass and bruise stalks. Chop chillies, seeding them if you wish.

Grate rind of lemon or lime. Extract juice, strain and keep aside.

Wash and chop coriander leaves and spring onion.

Microwave Cooking Method

Cook prawn heads in 1½ cups water (covered with plastic wrap) on High (100%) for 7 minutes.

Strain, discard heads and add lemon grass, chopped chillies, grated rind, salt and 3 cups water to stock.

Cook, covered with plastic wrap, for 12 minutes on Medium (70%). Stir.

Add cleaned prawns. Cook for 8 minutes on High (100%), covered loosely. Add fish sauce, lemon/lime juice, chilli oil and citrus leaves 4 minutes before end of cycle.

Correct for salt.

Serve garnished with chopped coriander and spring onion – and gallons of iced water.

Buddhist Monk's Soup (Canh Kiem)

VIETNAMESE

PREPARATION: 20 mins
COOKING: 700 watt – 35 mins
               650 watt – 47 mins
               500 watt – 63 mins
Times given here are for a
650 watt oven. Decrease time
by 15 seconds per minute for
a 700 watt oven. Increase time
by 20 seconds per minute for a
500 watt oven.
KCAL 938
SERVES 6

100 g (3½ oz) raw peanuts
60 g (2 oz) green mung beans
20 g (⅔ oz) cellophane noodles
1 firm soybean square
½ coconut, grated or
   ½ packet coconut cream
100 g (3½ oz) pumpkin
150 g (5 oz) or one medium-sized
   sweet potato
salt
pepper

Sauce
1 tablespoon chilli sauce
2 tablespoons *tuong*
1 tablespoon fish sauce
1 teaspoon sugar
1 teaspoon peanut butter

This nutritious soup recipe was painstakingly translated by one of my Vietnamese students. His only source of food came from kind Buddhist monks who helped his family as they made their long trek through sharp bamboo and barbed wire to the Thai border. Canh Kiem represents life to one who very nearly lost it.

Preparation

Shell peanuts and soak for 30 minutes, then pound roughly.

Wash and soak green mung beans for 1 hour. Soak cellophane noodles for 20 minutes, then drain and cut into 2-3 cm (1 in) lengths.

On a conventional stove, brown soybean square in some oil on both sides. Drain from oil and cut into strips.

Work grated coconut with ½ cup water to express 1 cup thick coconut milk, or add water to packet coconut cream to make up 1 cup milk.

Microwave Cooking Method

Cook pumpkin and sweet potato in shell/skin for 8 minutes on High (100%). Remove and scoop out flesh from both. (Always use a plate under food in a microwave oven.)

Into a casserole, pour 2 cups water, adding pumpkin, sweet potato, green mung beans and peanuts. Cook, covered loosely with plastic wrap, for 30 minutes on High (100%).

Stir and check if beans are cooked. If not, give soup another 5 minutes on High (100%). Then add 1 cup water and mash vegetables with the back of a fork.

Add coconut milk, salt and pepper to taste. Heat for 4 minutes on High (100%), then add cellophane noodles and fried soybean square strips.

Mix sauce ingredients. The soup, served hot with the sauce, is a meal in itself.

Hanoi Beef Soup (Pho Bo Ha Noi)

PREPARATION: 15 mins
COOKING: 700 watt – 26 mins
                650 watt – 35 mins
                500 watt – 47 mins
Times given here are for a
650 watt oven. Decrease time
by 15 seconds per minute for
a 700 watt oven. Increase time
by 20 seconds per minute for a
500 watt oven.
KCAL 1280
SERVES 6

2 × 2 cm (¾ × ¾ in) young ginger
2 shallots
4 stalks coriander
3 stalks spring onion
100 g (3½ oz) beansprouts
100 g (3½ oz) beef fillet (to serve
** raw)**
500 g (1 lb) beef bones
100 g (3½ oz) beef
2 star anise
3 tablespoons fish sauce
pepper
salt
200 g (7 oz) rice sticks (*banh pho*)
** or rice noodles**
½ lime in wedges
2 red chilles, sliced
3 tablespoons light soy sauce

This dish, typical of North Vietnam, is traditionally eaten for breakfast, at the many stalls that serve early risers both a hearty bowl of noodles and a chat. A bowl of Beef Hanoi Soup is a meal in itself.

This broth can be made days ahead and frozen. The meat can be removed and wrapped separately in foil and the broth stored in a bottle or other suitable container. The meal can be assembled when needed.

Preparation

Peel ginger and shallots and hold over a flame to 'roast' until blackened.

Clean and chop coriander and spring onions. Tail beansprouts.

Slice fillet into wafer-thin slices and set aside till needed.

Microwave Cooking Method

Put beef bones and beef in 4 cups boiling water, adding shallots, star anise and ginger. Cook, covered with plastic wrap, for 25 minutes on High (100%).

Remove scum on top. Continue to boil for 10 minutes on High (100%).

Remove beef and slice. It should be tender. Set aside.

Add fish sauce, pepper and salt to soup.

Serving

Arrange noodles at the bottom of individual bowls. Add raw beansprouts, cooked beef slices, then distribute raw wafer-thin fillet on top. Sprinkle on chopped spring onion and coriander.

Pour boiling soup over. The hot soup will cook the wafer-thin fillet.

Garnish with lime wedges and sliced chillies. Serve with light soy sauce.

Bedok Crab and Corn Soup

PREPARATION: 10 mins
COOKING: 700 watt – 21 mins
650 watt – 28 mins
500 watt – 37 mins
Times given here are for a
650 watt oven. Decrease time
by 15 seconds per minute for
a 700 watt oven. Increase time
by 20 seconds per minute for a
500 watt oven.
KCAL 713
SERVES 6

1 slice ginger
2 shallots
3-4 stalks spring onion
1 tablespoon cornflour
1 tablespoon Chinese wine or
   sherry (optional)
4 cups stock
2 eggs
1 anchovy (*ikan bilis*) stock cube
1 cup crabmeat
1 cup creamed corn or young corn
1 teaspoon sesame oil
pepper
salt
onion crisps

Bedok's beach stalls in the 1950s provided many an inexpensive romantic meal under the stars. This was also where most starving students ended a Saturday night revelry.

Preparation

Peel and slice ginger and shallots thinly. Slice spring onion into 2-3 cm (1 in) lengths.

Mix cornflour and sherry/wine with a little stock till smooth.

Beat eggs till frothy.

Microwave Cooking Method

In a deep casserole, boil the stock with the stock cube. Cook for 10 minutes on High (100%), covered loosely with plastic wrap. Break cooking cycle to stir stock once.

Add sliced ginger and shallots, crabmeat and corn. Stir and cook, covered, for 10 minutes on High (100%). Stir well.

Add cornflour and sherry/wine mixture, sesame oil and seasoning. Cook another 8 minutes on Medium (70%). Break cycle to stir as mixture thickens. Remove when steaming, drizzle in beaten egg, stirring as egg streaks the soup.

Serve garnished with spring onion and onion crisps.

Note: Boiling water may be added for a thinner soup. Remember to correct for seasoning.

Shan Soup

PREPARATION: 5 mins
COOKING: 700 watt – 29-30 mins
                   650 watt – 38-40 mins
                   500 watt – 51-53 mins
Times given here are for a
650 watt oven. Decrease time
by 15 seconds per minute for
a 700 watt oven. Increase time
by 20 seconds per minute for a
500 watt oven.
KCAL 260
SERVES 6

2 tomatoes
2 cups tender shoots of mustard
**   greens**
100 g (3½ oz) garlic shoots or
**   spring onion bulbs**
4 cups stock (beef, chicken or
**   pork)**
2 green chillies
1 teaspoon black bean paste
½ teaspoon oil
salt
pepper

The Shans are a hardy people of Burma, preferring pork or beef soups thickened with fresh seasonal vegetables growing as green as the jade mined in their hills. This soup takes on varied forms, depending on the vegetables in season.

Preparation

Slice tomatoes. Clean and break off tender shoots of mustard greens and garlic or the bulbs of spring onion.

Microwave Cooking Method

In a deep casserole, heat stock on High (100%) for 10-12 minutes, or until it starts boiling. The casserole should be covered loosely with plastic wrap.

Add tomatoes and whole chillies, mustard leaves and black bean paste. Continue cooking soup on High (100%) for 15 minutes, then remove from heat.

Heat browning dish for 5 minutes on High (100%), add oil and garlic shoots or onion bulbs. Stir and fry in hot oil till vegetables change colour – 3 minutes on High (100%).

Pour this into hot soup and continue cooking soup for 5 more minutes on High (100%). Season with salt and pepper.

Serve hot as a starter in a meal of rice and vegetables.

SEAFOOD

Microtips on Cooking Seafood

Fish cooks quickly and efficiently in the microwave oven and the finished product is delicious, moist and flavourful. It can be cooked whole, provided it is small enough to be placed flat on a dish, or on a piece of plastic wrap, or even on a banana leaf.

To bake a fish whole (for example, pomfret or snapper), first scale and gut it, removing entrails, gills and stomach. The eyes must be removed as they are covered by membrane and will splatter when cooked in a microwave oven. The eye socket can later be decorated with a green pea, a slice of carrot cut decoratively, or a sprig of parsley.

Preparation of Fish Brush with seasoning according to the recipe. Add some dark, thick soy sauce and turmeric for colour as microwaves will not brown food. The head and tail should be covered with a little foil (harmless if used in small areas) to protect the thinner areas from overcooking.

Cooking Fish Cook fish on High (100%) for 6 minutes every 500 g (1 ib). Turn after 3 minutes to cook the other side. Fish is cooked when flesh turns white and flakes easily with a fork.

Crumbed Fish can be cooked successfully in a microwave oven. After seasoning with sauces, coat the fish with toasted breadcrumbs (shake fish in a plastic bag of crumbs). Either (1) place in a heated microwave browning dish with 1 tablespoon hot oil to cook for 6 minutes on High (100%) or (2) place on a roasting rack to cook on High (100%) for 7 minutes. The times refer to a fish of about 400 g (13 oz).

Freezing and Defrosting Fish and Seafood To keep fish fresh, it should be gutted, cleaned and frozen in a plastic freezer bag with some water. Fillets may be separated with plastic sheets for easy removal.

When defrosting fish, take into account the following:
- The shape and weight of fish may affect defrosting times.
- Fish should not be over-defrosted. This toughens the flesh.
- Fish should be cold and pliable, not warm and soft.
- Thinner sections should be covered with foil, shiny side in, to prevent overcooking. (Small amounts of foil may be used, provided it does not touch the oven sides.)

To defrost fish, use this guide:
Fish fillets (500 g or 1 lb):
8 minutes, turning over after 4 minutes
Whole fish (500 g or 1 lb):
6-8 minutes, turning over after 4 minutes
Remember that once fish has thawed, micro-organic activity will begin and it spoils unless cooked immediately. Thawed fish should not be left unrefrigerated for any length of time.

Cooking Other Seafood

Prawns: Allow 6 minutes per 500 g (1 lb) on High (100%), on a plate loosely covered with plastic wrap. Check colour which should be opaque or pink.

Clams: Instead of plunging into boiling water, wash and pat dry. Allow about 6 minutes per 250 g (½ lb) on High (100%). Stop cooking as soon as clams open partially. Clams that do not open should be discarded.

Crabs: Wash and drain. Break claws before cooking. Allow 7 minutes per 250 g (½ lb) on High (100%) in a casserole covered with plastic wrap. Leave a vent in the cover for steam to escape. If shells are hard, you may need to cook another 2-3 minutes till flesh turns opaque and pink.

Defrosting Other Seafood

Shellfish: Allow 6-7 minutes per 500 g (1 lb) on a Defrost cycle. For crabs, allow 10 minutes per 300 g (10 oz) on a Defrost cycle. Defrosted shellfish should feel cool to the touch. Allow standing time for it to thoroughly defrost. Over-microwaving may cause meat to cook through.

Prawn/Crab Blocks: Allow 10-22 minutes per 500 g (1 lb) on a Defrost cycle. Place block in a shallow casserole so as it thaws liquid melts into the container. Turn over and break ice block with a fork to defrost efficiently. Defrosted pieces should feel cool and be given standing time to come to room temperature.

Unpeeled Prawns: Allow 7 minutes per 500 g (1 lb) on High (100%).

Vietnamese Stuffed Fish (66)

Pinais (91)

Ikan Pepes (Fish in Sour Sauce)

PREPARATION: 15 mins
COOKING: 700 watt – 10 mins
           650 watt – 13 mins
           500 watt – 17 mins
Times given here are for a
650 watt oven. Decrease time
by 15 seconds per minute for
a 700 watt oven. Increase time
by 20 seconds per minute for a
500 watt oven.
KCAL 940
SERVES 4

Marinade A
2 cm (¾ in) cube tamarind
1 teaspoon sugar

500 g (1 lb) medium-sized whole
   red snapper/mackerel
   (***ikan merah/tenggiri***)

Marinade B
6 shallots
4 cloves garlic
6 red chillies
2 × 2 cm (¾ × ¾ in) ginger
2 cm (¾ in) turmeric

2 stalks lemon grass
3-4 kaffir lime leaves
   (***daun limau purut***)
½ coconut, grated
salt

Garnish
cut chillies
shredded lettuce

Traditionally, banana leaves are used to wrap the Ikan Pepes. In this case, plastic wrap would be as effective as long as it is loosely wrapped around the fish. I tested this recipe with canned coconut milk which proved very satisfactory.

Preparation

Prepare Marinade A: Work tamarind with 2 tablespoons water into a paste. Mix with sugar till completely dissolved.

Clean, gut and scale fish. Remove fish eyes. Cut slits on both sides and rub in Marinade A. Spread marinade on both sides of fish.

Prepare Marinade B: Blend or pound together shallots, garlic, chillies, ginger and turmeric.

Bruise lemon grass and shred kaffir leaves.

Work grated coconut with fingers. Squeeze out 4 tablespoons thick coconut milk.

Mix Marinade B with coconut milk, lemon grass, shredded kaffir leaves and salt.

Shield fish tail with foil (do not allow foil to touch sides of oven). Spread marinade mixture well over and under fish.

Microwave Cooking Method

Wrap fish in plastic wrap, leaving a tent-like vent for steam to escape. Place parcel on a heatproof plate and cook for 9 minutes on High (100%). Turn parcel over (rearranging wrap to prevent leaking of marinade) and cook for another 4 minutes on High (100%).

Serving

Serve fish on a flat platter, with marinade poured around it. Garnish with cut chillies and shredded lettuce. Decorate eye socket with cut chilli or a carrot slice.

Stuffed Fish (Ca' Rut Xuong Dut Lo)

PREPARATION: 12 mins
COOKING: 700 watt – 9 mins
                650 watt – 12 mins
                500 watt – 16 mins
Times given here are for a
650 watt oven. Decrease time
by 15 seconds per minute for
a 700 watt oven. Increase time
by 20 seconds per minute for a
500 watt oven.
KCAL 1309
SERVES 4-5

**700 g (1½ lb) whole grouper/
   bream (*ikan kerapu/kerisi*)**
**3 red chillies, seeded if a less
   spicy flavour is preferred**
2 stalks lemon grass
1 clove garlic
2 shallots
salt
pepper
100 g (3½ oz) minced pork
**1 tablespoon fish sauce (*nuoc
   mam*)**
1 teaspoon sugar
1 teaspoon sherry
½ teaspoon groundnut oil

Garnish
2 hardboiled eggs
2 limes
1 carrot
coriander sprigs

This tasty and impressive dish makes an ideal centrepiece. The Vietnamese do not use much chilli but this recipe, which is much hotter and spicier, may be influenced by Thai food.

Preparation

Clean and gut fish. Cut a slit from head to tail and carefully remove main bone without cutting off head or tail. Remove eyes. Make cuts on both sides of the fish.

Blend or pound chillies, lemon grass, garlic and shallots, adding salt and pepper to taste. Mix with minced pork, fish sauce and sugar.

Rub a little salt and pepper into cut slits on fish. Cover tail with foil (do not allow foil to touch sides of oven). Stuff fish with pounded mixture and pork. Sprinkle fish with sherry to moisten it.

Microwave Cooking Method

Grease a baking dish with ½ teaspoon groundnut oil. Place fish carefully on the dish and steam, covered with plastic wrap for 8 minutes on High (100%). Turn fish carefully and cook for another 4 minutes on High (100%).

Serving

Serve garnished with hardboiled eggs, lime slices and a carrot. Peel carrot and slice a piece to cover eye socket. Cut thin strips from the rest. Halve eggs and limes. Use carrot strips as basket handles for the egg baskets, and fill them with coriander sprigs.

Captain's Table Sweet 'n' Sour

PREPARATION: 10 mins
COOKING: 700 watt – 12 mins
            650 watt – 16 mins
            500 watt – 21 mins
Times given here are for a
650 watt oven. Decrease time
by 15 seconds per minute for
a 700 watt oven. Increase time
by 20 seconds per minute for a
500 watt oven.
KCAL 1110
SERVES 4

500 g (1 lb) red snapper
  (*ikan merah*)
pepper
salt
2 carrots
2 green peppers
1 onion
1 cucumber
½ cup vinegar
1 tablespoon sugar
2 × 2 cm (¾ × ¾ in) ginger
4 cloves garlic
2 tablespoons cornflour
3 tablespoons tomato sauce
oil
1 teaspoon chilli sauce

Simple and economical to prepare, use the freshest ingredients to raise this dish to gourmet level. Fresh fish always imparts a special flavour which is enhanced by the subtle use of spices. An advantage of this recipe is that it can be cooked and served in the same dish, saving the fish from breaking up through too much handling.

Preparation

Clean and wash fish, removing eyes. Make diagonal cuts across fish for sauces to penetrate. Season with pepper and salt and cover tail with foil. (Make sure foil does not touch sides of oven.)

Scrape carrots. Cut carrots and green peppers into thin slices. Peel and quarter onion and loosen onion sections.

Peel and slice cucumber. Soak in a vinegar and sugar mixture for 1 hour.

Peel and slice ginger and garlic. Blend or pound to a paste.

Mix cornflour and tomato sauce with ¼ cup water.

Microwave Cooking Method

Preheat a browning dish for 6 minutes on High (100%). Add 2 tablespoons oil and heat 1 minute on High (100%). Brown ginger and garlic paste for 2 minutes on High (100%).

Add seasoned fish and cook for 3 minutes on High (100%). Add more oil if needed. Turn fish and cook for another 2 minutes on High (100%).

Add cornflour and tomato sauce mixture, chilli sauce, sugar-vinegar pickled cucumber, carrots, green peppers and onion. Cook for 2 minutes on High (100%), stirring once during cooking.

Serve in the same dish, after wiping sauce splatter from edges. Arrange vegetables decoratively, using a slice of carrot to cover the eye socket.

Note: If you do not like raw carrot or green pepper, cook them with 2 tablespoons water for 3 minutes on High (100%). Drain water then add to fish with pickled cucumber.

Nonya Otak Otak (Spicy Steamed Fish)

PREPARATION: 15 mins
COOKING: 700 watt – 21 mins
                  650 watt – 28 mins
                  500 watt – 37 mins
Times given here are for a
650 watt oven. Decrease time
by 15 seconds per minute for
a 700 watt oven. Increase time
by 20 seconds per minute for a
500 watt oven.
KCAL 1010
SERVES 6-8

500 g (1 lb) white fish fillet
1 coconut, grated
2 stalks lemon grass (*serai*)
2 × 2 cm (¾ × ¾ in) galangal
  (*lengkuas*)
6 cloves garlic
10 shallots
10 dried chillies, seeded
2 cm (¾ in) square dried shrimp
  paste (*belacan*)
salt
6 banana leaves
wooden skewers

This is not 'brain' food in spite of its name, which probably originated from the texture of this cooked fish. However, in our home it is the equivalent of soul food. The Malays call this food, which is often grilled over charcoal, Pais (pronounced pah-is) when it is wrapped in banana leaf and Otak Otak when it is wrapped in coconut leaf. It is better known by the latter name.

Preparation

Cut fish fillet into small thin slices.

Roast 1 tablespoon of the grated coconut in the oven for 2 minutes on High (100%), stirring once. Mix the rest with ¼ cup water and extract ½ cup thick coconut milk.

Peel and cut lemon grass, galangal, garlic, shallots and dried chillies into small pieces. Roast *belacan* for 2 minutes on High (100%), turning it once during the cycle. Blend these ingredients and the roasted coconut in a blender, or grind till fine.

Cut banana leaves into 20 cm (8 in) squares and steam in the oven for 1½ minutes on High (100%) to soften leaves.

Microwave Cooking Method

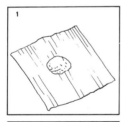

Mix ground ingredients in a dish with ½ cup thick coconut milk. Cook for 3 minutes on High (100%), stirring well twice during the cycle. Add salt to taste. Remove from the microwave oven and let it cool.

Mix cooked ingredients with fish. This mixture can also be blended to a smooth paste in a blender.

Place 1 tablespoon of the mixture on each banana leaf. Wrap as illustrated and secure with skewers or toothpicks. There should be 14 small bundles.

Microwave each bundle for 1½ minutes on High (100%). If you wish to cook a few bundles together, multiply the number of bundles by 1½ minutes.

Grill bundles under a conventional grill for a few minutes before serving as an entrée to a main meal.

Note: If banana leaf is not available, grease a large flat platter, pour in mixture and smoothen the top with the back of a spoon. Cover loosely with plastic wrap and steam on High (100%) for 8 minutes. The Otak Otak can be cut into squares and served hot or cold.

A-Nee's Taucheo Fish

PREPARATION: 10 mins
COOKING: 700 watt – 15 mins
          650 watt – 21 mins
          500 watt – 27 mins
Times given here are for a
650 watt oven. Decrease time
by 15 seconds per minute for
a 700 watt oven. Increase time
by 20 seconds per minute for a
500 watt oven.
KCAL 838
SERVES 4-6

**500-600 g (1-1⅓ lb) white
  firm-fleshed fish, preferably
  *ikan senangin***
1 clove garlic
1 × 1 cm (½ × ½ in) ginger
**2 tablespoons preserved
  soybeans**
oil
1 teaspoon sugar
1 tablespoon dark soy sauce
1 tablespoon light soy sauce
1 teaspoon oyster sauce
1 tablespoon cornflour
salt
pepper

Garnish
lemon wedges
parsley

The Babas and Nonyas were the early Chinese settlers in Pulau Pinang, Melaka and Singapore who adopted Malay customs, culture and language. Nonya cooking is distinctive in that it blends the delicacy of Chinese sauces with the fiery chilli taste of Malay foods. This dish is dedicated to Annie, who taught me to cook Nonya food.

Preparation

Scale, gut and clean fish, removing eyes and trimming fins. Cover tail with foil. (Make sure foil does not touch the sides of the microwave oven.)

Pound garlic and ginger to a paste. Pound preserved soybeans to a paste and rub half onto the inside of the fish.

Microwave Cooking Method

Cook fish in a shallow, greased casserole, covered with plastic wrap, for 8 minutes on High (100%). Turn fish over halfway through the cycle. Remove fish from the microwave.

Preheat browning dish for 7 minutes on High (100%). Add 1 tablespoon oil and cook for ½ minute on High (100%).

Add ginger, garlic and remaining preserved soybean paste. Cook 1 minute on High (100%). Add sugar, soy sauces, oyster sauce and ½ cup water. Cook 1 minute on High (100%).

Blend cornflour with a little sauce from the dish and add to the rest of the sauce with salt and pepper to taste. Cook for 1 minute on High (100%). Stir evenly. Add fish and spoon sauce over. Cook for 2 minutes on Medium (70%).

Garnish with cut lemon wedges and some parsley over the eye socket.

Sour Fish Curry

PREPARATION: 10 mins
COOKING: 700 watt – 14 mins
              650 watt – 20 mins
              500 watt – 27 mins
Times given here are for a
650 watt oven. Decrease time
by 15 seconds per minute for
a 700 watt oven. Increase time
by 20 seconds per minute for a
500 watt oven.
KCAL 810
SERVES 4-6

**500 g (1 lb) fillet of Spanish
  mackerel (*ikan tenggiri*)**
½ teaspoon turmeric
pepper
salt
2 cloves garlic
4 shallots
1 lemon or large lime
½ cup tamarind paste
¼ cup water
1 teaspoon cummin powder
1 teaspoon fennel powder
1 tablespoon coriander powder
**1 teaspoon chilli powder
  (optional)**
1 tablespoon oil
sugar to taste

This recipe, made for us by a charming Sinhalese cook at a guesthouse, evokes memories of the holidays spent in Sri Lanka: emerald waters of the Paradise Island, the gently swaying palms and the log catamarans that slip easily into the sea – and fish always fresh, plentiful and beautifully cooked. The dish keeps well, for the tamarind acts as a preservative.

Preparation

Season fish with turmeric, pepper and salt.

Peel and chop garlic and shallots into tiny pieces.

Extract juice from lemon or lime. Work tamarind with water to make a thick paste. Strain and discard seeds.

Roast cummin, fennel and coriander powder for 2 minutes on High (100%).

Microwave Cooking Method

Mix chopped shallots and garlic, curry powder and chilli powder to a paste.

Preheat browning dish for 6 minutes on High (100%). Heat oil for 1 minute on High (100%), then add spiced shallot-garlic mixture. Cook for 1 minute on High (100%), covered. Add lemon/lime juice and sugar to make a thick sauce.

Poach fish in this sauce, cooking (covered with a plastic wrap) for 3 minutes on High (100%). Add tamarind paste and turn once during cooking cycle, making sure fish does not burn. Keep basting sauce over fish during a further 6-minute cooking cycle on High (100%).

Taste and correct for salt and cook for 1 minute on High (100%), covered.

Garnish with crisp fried onion and serve as a main course.

Morobe 'Tin Fish' Cakes

PREPARATION: 15 mins
COOKING: 700 watt – 12 mins
               650 watt – 16 mins
               500 watt – 21 mins
Times given here are for a
650 watt oven. Decrease time
by 15 seconds per minute for
a 700 watt oven. Increase time
by 20 seconds per minute for a
500 watt oven.
KCAL 1330
SERVES 6-8

**500 g (1 lb) canned pilchards/
  mackerel in oil or brine**
**1 cup soft breadcrumbs (from 3½
  slices fresh crustless bread)**
2 egg yolks
1 teaspoon chilli powder
1 teaspoon fennel powder
4 small onions, chopped very fine
1 clove garlic, chopped very fine
1 tablespoon lemon juice
¼ cup milk
salt
pepper
2 egg whites, beaten
**½ cup flour, mixed with
  ½ teaspoon turmeric**
1 tablespoon oil
sprigs of mint

Two years spent in Papua New Guinea were a time of culinary surprises; one of the most bizarre was that although the islands are surrounded by crystal clear teeming waters, the people prefer fish canned in oil or tomato sauce. This recipe grew out of a desperate attempt to create a new meal from the limited ingredients available.

Preparation

Drain fish well. In a bowl, mix fish with breadcrumbs, yolks, chilli and fennel powder, chopped onions and garlic, and lemon juice. Add milk gradually. The mixture should be firm yet moist. Season with salt and pepper.

Divide mixture into 20 small balls. Flatten into cakes, dip into egg white and then into flour-turmeric mixture.

Microwave Cooking Method

Heat a browning dish on High (100%) for 7 minutes.

Add oil and heat on High (100%) for 1 minute. Place 10 fish cakes in oil. Cook on High (100%) for 2 minutes. Turn fish cakes and cook for another 2 minutes on High (100%). They should be removed carefully from the dish. Cook the second batch in the same way.

Garnish with sprigs of mint leaves.

Note: Dried breadcrumbs may be purchased commercially. It can also be made quite easily in the microwave oven by breaking up day-old bread and microwaving this on High (100%) for 3-6 minutes, depending on the quantity of bread. Keep stirring to prevent burning.

Ikan Gulai Rempah (Fish in Spicy Sauce)

INDONESIAN

PREPARATION: 15 mins
COOKING: 700 watt – 22 mins
　　　　　 650 watt – 29 mins
　　　　　 500 watt – 38 mins
Times given here are for a
650 watt oven. Decrease time
by 15 seconds per minute for
a 700 watt oven. Increase time
by 20 seconds per minute for a
500 watt oven.
KCAL 1067
SERVES 4-6

500 g (1 lb) threadfin/red snapper
　　(*ikan kurau/merah*)
½ cup flour mixed with
　　1 teaspoon turmeric
1 cm (½ in) square dried
　　shrimp paste (*terasi*)
6 shallots
2 cloves garlic
1 × 1 cm (½ × ½ in) ginger
6 dried chillies or
　　2 teaspoons *sambal olek*
2 × 2 cm (¾ × ¾ in) tamarind
　　paste
1 tablespoon oil
2 tablespoons dark soy sauce
2 tablespoons vinegar
salt
sugar
pepper
2 tablespoons tomato sauce
lime peel, grated or cut into thin
　　strips

This Gulai originates from the Lake Toba district of Sumatra where the Bataks serve a cuisine unique to their part of Indonesia. The Spanish influence is evident in their music which we enjoyed for a week in their spectacular crater-lake resort. I could easily believe paradise began and ended there, where little babies crawled out onto the plank walkways connecting stilted houses and plonked into the deep lake, paddling joyously as mothers went about their chores, apparently unconcerned.

Preparation

Cut fish into bite-sized pieces, about 4 cm (1½ in) square. Coat by rolling in flour and turmeric mixture.

Toast *terasi* in an ovenproof dish for 3 minutes on High (100%).

Peel and slice onions, garlic and ginger. Plump dried chillies with 1 tablespoon water for 2 minutes on High (100%) or use *sambal olek*.

Combine chilli, onion, garlic, ginger and *terasi*, and blend with 2 tablespoons water till quite fine.

Work tamarind with ½ cup water till a thick brown liquid is obtained. Strain and set aside.

Microwave Cooking Method

Preheat browning dish for 6 minutes on High (100%). Add 1 tablespoon oil and heat for 1 minute on High (100%).

Cook blended mixture in hot oil for 2 minutes on High (100%), stir, then cook a further 2 minutes on High, stirring twice.

Add other ingredients: dark soy sauce, vinegar, salt, sugar, pepper and tamarind juice. Correct for salt. Cook for 4 minutes on Medium (70%), then add tomato sauce and ½ cup water.

Place fish pieces in the sauce carefully, so that liquid surrounds all of them. Cover loosely with plastic wrap.

Cook on Medium (70%) for 7 minutes or till sauce is simmering. Uncover and stir, then cook for another 3 minutes on High (100%).

Serve garnished with lemon peel.

Fish Moolee

PREPARATION: 8 mins
COOKING: 700 watt — 13.5 mins
650 watt — 18 mins
500 watt — 24 mins
Times given here are for a
650 watt oven. Decrease time
by 15 seconds per minute for
a 700 watt oven. Increase time
by 20 seconds per minute for a
500 watt oven.
KCAL 1486
SERVES 4-6

500 g (1 lb) fish fillet
¼ cup flour mixed with
  1 teaspoon cummin powder and
  salt
6 shallots
2 cloves garlic
2 × 2 cm (¾ × ¾ in) ginger
1 lime
2 tablespoons oil
½ teaspoon fenugreek
1 cup thick coconut milk
3-4 chillies, slit lengthwise
3 tablespoons fish curry powder
  or
  1 tablespoon coriander powder,
  ½ tablespoon cummin powder,
  ½ teaspoon turmeric powder,
  1 teaspoon chilli powder and
  pinch of pepper
salt
mint leaves
nuts or almonds, chopped

This spicy fish curry originates from South India where the use of fenugreek and lime juice replaces tamarind. This is eaten with mountains of rice, cool yogurt and a pepper-soup called Rassam. Throw in a few Papadams (Indian crackers) and a lime pickle for an authentic flavour.

Preparation

Cut fish into 4 cm (2½ in) squares and dip in flour-cummin-salt mixture.

Peel and slice shallots, garlic and ginger. Extract lime juice.

Microwave Cooking Method

Preheat a browning dish for 6 minutes on High (100%).

Add 2 tablespoons oil and heat for 30 seconds on High (100%). Add garlic at once. It will brown in hot oil.

Add shallots and fenugreek. Brown in garlic oil on High (100%) for 2 minutes, stirring once.

Add coconut milk, chillies, curry powder, salt and fish, placing fish around the outer edge of the dish. Cover loosely with plastic wrap.

Microwave the fish curry for 6 minutes on Medium (70%), stirring well to coat fish with sauce.

Uncover, sprinkle with lime juice and cook another 4 minutes, this time uncovered, on High (100%).

Serve in the same dish or platter, garnished with mint leaves and chopped nuts.

Haw Mok (Steamed Fish Curry)

PREPARATION: 25 mins
COOKING: 700 watt – 21-23 mins
          650 watt – 28-30 mins
          500 watt – 37-40 mins
Times given here are for a
650 watt oven. Decrease time
by 15 seconds per minute for
a 700 watt oven. Increase time
by 20 seconds per minute for a
500 watt oven.
KCAL 1695
SERVES 6

800 g (1¾ lb) fish fillets
1 coconut, grated
1 tablespoon rice flour
1 egg, beaten
3-4 stalks spring onion
2 citrus leaves
½ teaspoon oil
6-8 curry leaves
2 tablespoons green curry paste
   (krung gaeng keo wan)
1½ tablespoons fish sauce (nam
   pla)
3 red chillies, chopped

A Thai fish dish traditionally steamed in banana leaf bundles, so ideally suited to the microwave oven. Prepare to work up a sweat over this tasty but extremely spicy curry.

Preparation

Slice fish into thin strips.

Blend grated coconut with ½ cup water and extract 1 cup thick coconut milk. Mix rice flour evenly with beaten egg and coconut milk.

Shred spring onions and citrus leaves.

Microwave Cooking Method

Preheat browning dish for 6 minutes on High (100%). Add oil and cook for 30 seconds on High (100%).

Add curry paste and cover. Cook on High (100%) for 1 minute, stirring at the end of the cycle. Cook uncovered for another 30 seconds.

Add *nam pla*, flour-egg-coconut milk mixture, chillies and citrus leaf and spring onion shreds. Cook on High (100%) for 5 minutes, stirring twice during the cycle so that mixture thickens evenly. Remove from the oven and stir mixture well.

Place fish fillet in a greased shallow container and pour Haw Mok mixture over. Cover with plastic wrap and cook on High (100%) for 10-12 minutes, or until firm. You may have to stir from the centre to the edges of the dish so that cooking is even. Cook for 5 minutes uncovered on High (100%).

Serve as a hot accompaniment to a meal, or as a cold savoury.

Note: I have, for testing purposes, also used a packet of coconut cream powder instead of fresh. This reconstitutes easily into a cup of coconut milk.

Haw Mok may also be made in a casserole with fillets lining the dish and sauce poured all over. The casserole should be covered loosely with plastic wrap and steamed on High (100%) for 10 minutes.

Sakaido Salt-Grilled Fish

PREPARATION: 5 mins
COOKING: 700 watt – 8 mins
            650 watt – 10 mins
            500 watt – 13 mins
Times given here are for a
650 watt oven. Decrease time
by 15 seconds per minute for
a 700 watt oven. Increase time
by 20 seconds per minute for a
500 watt oven.
KCAL 715
SERVES 6

**700 g (1½ lb) grouper/flounder
(*ikan kerapu/sebelah*)**
1 tablespoon salt
2 × 2 cm (¾ × ¾ in) ginger
1 medium *daikon* (white radish)
2 leeks
2 tablespoons *tamari shoyu*
2 tablespoons vinegar
2 tablespoons lemon juice

Japanese grilled foods are known as sugata-yaki *or 'form-grilled'. Fish especially lends itself to this method of cooking. The salt tenderises the fish and acts to bring delicious fats and oils to the surface.*

Preparation

Scale and clean fish, and remove eyes. Dry with kitchen paper or a towel, and rub in salt thoroughly. Cover tail with foil. (Make sure foil does not touch sides of the microwave oven.)

Peel and bruise ginger, extracting as much juice as possible, and sprinkle this on fish. Grate *daikon* and mix with leeks, sliced thinly.

Microwave Cooking Method

Place fish on a platter, uncovered, and cook for 6 minutes on High (100%). Turn fish carefully. Cook uncovered, 2 minutes for each side, on High (100%). The salt will crackle as fish cooks.

Pour off liquid that collects with the fish as it will be very salty. Cover eye socket with a piece of parsley or carrot.

Combine *tamari shoyu*, vinegar, lemon juice, leeks and *daikon* in a small bowl. Serve with grilled fish.

Note: When fish cooks uncovered, the splatter of salt may mess up the walls of the microwave oven. Powerful scourers or brushes should not be used, but a wet sponge rinsed once or twice in water will be sufficient to clean the surfaces.

Harbourside Fish in Almond Sauce

PREPARATION: 20 mins
COOKING: 700 watt – 14 mins
          650 watt – 18 mins
          500 watt – 24 mins
Times given here are for a
650 watt oven. Decrease time
by 15 seconds per minute for
a 700 watt oven. Increase time
by 20 seconds per minute for a
500 watt oven.
KCAL 1490
SERVES 6

2 small *ikan senangin*
   (250 g/8 oz each)
1½ lemons or large limes
1 large onion
1 clove garlic
3 stalks spring onion
2 stalks lemon grass (*serai*)
1 firm soybean square
3-4 tablespoons butter
½ cup almond slivers
½ cup fresh breadcrumbs, from 2
   slices bread
salt
pepper
wooden skewers
½ cup chopped parsley
lemon zest

A special creation that has become a family favourite. Fish needs spice to lift it from the bland to the exotic. Here, this is achieved by using slivered almonds and parsley with lemon grass and dofu (soybean cake). This dish makes a stunning centrepiece for a luncheon.

Preparation

Scale and gut fish and remove gills and eyes.

Extract juice from lemons or limes.

Peel and chop onion and garlic and slice spring onion.

Strip outer leaves from lemon grass and slice into fine circles. Use only about 4 cm (1½ in) from the fragrant root end.

Break soybean cake into little pieces.

Microwave Cooking Method

In a shallow casserole, melt 1 tablespoon butter for 1 minute on High (100%). Add almond slivers and stir. Cook for 2 minutes on High (100%). Stop, stir and cook a further 2 minutes on High (100%).

Remove almonds. Add remaining butter.

Add chopped onion and garlic and cook for 1 minute on High (100%). Add soybean cake bits and cook another minute on High (100%). Remove with a slotted spoon.

Mix onion, garlic and soybean cake with spring onion, lemon grass, breadcrumbs, a third of the lemon/lime juice, salt and pepper. Stuff fish with this mixture and use wooden skewers to keep stuffing in place.

Place fish in butter in the casserole, making sure fish is coated with it. Cover with sheets of kitchen paper to prevent splatters and cook on High (100%) for 6 minutes. Turn and cook for another 5 minutes on High (100%).

Remove casserole from the oven. Pour remaining lemon juice over fish and arrange almond slivers on top. Cover with foil and let it stand to finish cooking in its own heat.

Serve fish in the casserole, garnished with chopped parsley and some lemon zest to decorate the eye socket.

Ikan Merah Belanda

PREPARATION: 10 mins
COOKING: 700 watt – 14 mins
650 watt – 18 mins
500 watt – 24 mins
Times given here are for a
650 watt oven. Decrease time
by 15 seconds per minute for
a 700 watt oven. Increase time
by 20 seconds per minute for a
500 watt oven.
KCAL 1715
SERVES 8

1 kg (2⅓ lb) red snapper (*ikan merah*)
salt
pepper
1 lemon or large lime
1 tablespoon butter
1 clove garlic
1 large onion

Stuffing
1 cup cooked rice
¼ cup peas
½ cup chopped parsley
1 red chilli, seeded and chopped fine
1 teaspoon light soy sauce
1 teaspoon butter

raffia twine
1 teaspoon oregano
1 teaspoon breadcrumbs
1 tomato, sliced

The Dutch influence in Indonesia produced many European-style dishes cooked with the spices of the East. The name of this recipe betrays its origin, for 'Belanda' is the Indonesian term for Holland. The Indonesians are a nation of fish and seafood eaters and produce some of the tastiest fish dishes in the world.

Preparation

Scale and gut fish by cutting it open to the stomach. Remove eyes. Clean and pat dry with kitchen paper.

Season inside of fish with salt, pepper and juice from half the lime. Dot surface of fish with a little butter. Cover tail with foil. (Make sure foil does not touch sides of the microwave oven.)

Peel and chop garlic, and slice onion into rings.

Microwave Cooking Method

Mix stuffing ingredients together and cook on Medium (70%) for 2 minutes to melt butter and cook peas.

Stuff fish with these ingredients and tie it up carefully with raffia twine (or skewer shut).

Brush fish with remaining butter and lime juice, oregano and breadcrumbs. Place it on a greased dish. Place garlic and onions on top and cook on High (100%) for 8 minutes. Turn fish and cook another 8 minutes on High (100%).

Remove from oven and cover with foil for a few minutes' standing time for fish to continue cooking in its own heat.

Uncover fish and garnish with tomato slices and a slice of tomato or some peas over the eye socket.

Fish Head Cantonese

PREPARATION: 15 mins
COOKING: 700 watt – 26 mins
           650 watt – 34 mins
           500 watt – 45 mins
Times given here are for a
650 watt oven. Decrease time
by 15 seconds per minute for
a 700 watt oven. Increase time
by 20 seconds per minute for a
500 watt oven.
KCAL 1290
SERVES 6

1 red snapper (*ikan merah*)
   head, approx. 1 kg (2¼ lb)
½ teaspoon salt

Marinade
1 tablespoon Chinese wine
1 teaspoon light soy sauce
1 tablespoon ginger juice
½ teaspoon sugar

100 g (3½ oz) pork
50 g (1⅔ oz) canned bamboo
   shoot
1 clove garlic
1 red chilli
2 slices ginger
5 dried Chinese mushrooms
3 stalks spring onion
2 tablespoons cornflour
2 tablespoons oil

Sauce
½ teaspoon sesame oil
1 teaspoon dark soy sauce
pepper
salt
½ cup water

½ tablespoon preserved soy
   beans (mashed)
2 soft soybean squares

A Cantonese speciality popular because of the fine texture of meat from the fish head. Snapper is the favourite fish.

Preparation

Remove eyes and rub fish head with salt, then with marinade ingredients for 1 hour.

Slice pork into thin slices across the grain. Shred bamboo shoot. Peel and chop garlic finely. Seed the chilli and slit lengthwise. Shred the slices of ginger.

Wash and soak mushrooms in 1 cup water. Microwave on High (100%) for 3 minutes. Drain, cut off stalks and shred mushrooms.

Wash and chop spring onions for garnish.

Microwave Cooking Method

Heat a browning dish for 6 minutes on High (100%). While dish is heating, drain marinade from fish head and coat it with cornflour, turning it so head is coated on all sides. Discard excess cornflour.

Add 2 tablespoons oil to the browning dish and cook on High (100%) for 1 minute.

Fry fish head on High (100%) for 3 minutes on each side, pressing it down so that fish sizzles in hot oil. Remove fish head and drain on a paper towel.

To remaining oil in the dish, add garlic, ginger, pork, bamboo shoot, mushrooms and chilli. Cook for 4 minutes on High (100%).

Add sauce ingredients, preserved soybean paste and soft soybean squares. Stir well, and cook for 4 minutes on High (100%). Spoon sauce over fish head and cook for another 10 minutes on Medium (70%), covered with plastic wrap.

Remove from heat, spoon sauce over and sprinkle with chopped spring onions.

Kinome Yaki

PREPARATION: 10 mins
COOKING: 700 watt – 6 mins
            650 watt – 8 mins
            500 watt – 11 mins
Times given here are for a
650 watt oven. Decrease time
by 15 seconds per minute for
a 700 watt oven. Increase time
by 20 seconds per minute for
500 watt oven.
KCAL 565
SERVES 4

300 g (10 oz) mackerel (*ikan
    tenggiri*)
2 × 2 cm (¾ × ¾ in) young ginger
½ tablespoon sugar
salt
1 tablespoon sweet sherry
2 tablespoons *tamari shoyu*
2 tablespoons *sake*

Garnish
cucumber slices, trimmed
    decoratively
pickled ginger
1 tablespoon sugar
1 teaspoon table salt
1 tablespoon vinegar
a few stalks spring onion to
    decorate dish

This is normally broiled – the Japanese term for it being yakimono *– and the pieces can be either served on skewers or loose.*

Preparation

Wash and cut fish into serving sized pieces. Pat dry with kitchen paper.

Pound ginger to extract juice. Add sugar and salt to juice and soak fish in this marinade.

Mix sherry, *shoyu* and *sake* together for a glaze. Brush glaze on fish, reserving some for later.

Microwave Cooking Method

Place fish on a shallow greased baking dish and microwave for 4 minutes on High (100%), covered loosely with plastic. Brush on more glaze.

Turn fish over and cook for 4 minutes more on High (100%), uncovered. Taste and correct for salt.

Remove and serve hot in its own dish with side plates of garnish, pickled radish, fresh chives and spring onions.

Note: Add chilli if you prefer a spicier dish.

Mohinga (Burmese Laksa)

PREPARATION: 25 mins
COOKING: 700 watt – 29 mins
            650 watt – 39 mins
            500 watt – 52 mins
Times given here are for a
650 watt oven. Decrease time
by 15 seconds per minute for
a 700 watt oven. Increase time
by 20 seconds per minute for a
500 watt oven.
KCAL 2168
SERVES 6

**400 g (14½ oz) shad (Burmese use
nga shwe)**

Blend A
200 g (6⅔ oz) shallots
3-4 cloves garlic
2 × 2 cm (¾ × ¾ in) ginger
1 stalk lemon grass
2 red chillies

¾ coconut, grated
**8 cm (3¼ in) length young banana
stem**
100 g (3½ oz) fish sauce
¼ teaspoon turmeric
4 stalks lemon grass, bruised
4 red chillies, bruised
2 tablespoons oil
**2 tablespoons rice flour, mixed to
a smooth paste with water**
8 shallots, quartered
2 eggs, hardboiled
salt
pepper
**1 packet fine rice noodles (mo),
precooked**

Garnish
lemon wedges
chilli oil
onion crisps
garlic crisps

An extremely tasty national dish. Traditionally, freshwater fish is cooked for Mohinga but in some areas sea fish is used.

Preparation

Clean fish and remove gills and eyes. Leave the rest intact.

Peel and cut, then blend together ingredients in 'Blend A'.

Work grated coconut with ¼ cup water and extract milk.

Peel green skin from banana stem and slice thinly into rings with a very sharp knife.

Microwave Cooking Method

Place fish in a casserole with ½ cup water, fish sauce, turmeric and bruised lemon grass and chillies. Cook on High (100%) for 6 minutes. Turn fish and cook for 2 minutes on High (100%).

Remove fish from casserole and flake flesh from bones carefully. Discard bones. Strain liquid in casserole and set aside.

Heat a browning dish for 7 minutes on High (100%). Add 2 tablespoons oil and cook on High (100%) for 1 minute.

Add Blend A and cook on High (100%) for 3 minutes until it gives up a pleasant aroma. Add flaked fish, mix well and keep aside.

Mix strained fish liquid with coconut milk and 3½ cups water in a heatproof bowl. Cover with plastic wrap and bring to a boil in about 10 minutes on High (100%). Add rice flour paste, stirring well to ensure lumps do not form. Cook for 2 minutes on High (100%).

Add thin banana stem slices, quartered shallots and eggs. Cook for 4 minutes on High (100%). A vent in the plastic wrap will allow a stirring spoon to be inserted. Stir twice during the cycle.

Add spiced flaked fish mixture, salt and pepper to taste. Cook for another 4 minutes on High (100%).

Serving

To serve hinga, divide precooked rice noodles into individual serving bowls. Each person ladles boiling hot hinga over the noodles, sprinkles some chilli oil, onion and garlic crisps, and squeezes some lime juice over the food. This is similar to a Laksa meal in Malaysia or Singapore.

Paul's Har Loke (87)

Ceylonese Prawn Patties (92)

Pattaya Pomfret (Pla Chalamet)

PREPARATION: 15 mins
COOKING: 700 watt – 16 mins
                 650 watt – 21 mins
                 500 watt – 28 mins
Times given here are for a
650 watt oven. Decrease time
by 15 seconds per minute for
a 700 watt oven. Increase time
by 20 seconds per minute for a
500 watt oven.
KCAL 1262
SERVES 6

1 kg (2 ¼ lb) black pomfret (*pla chalamet*)
½ teaspoon turmeric
salt
pepper
4 shallots
4 cloves garlic
3 stalks coriander leaves with roots
6 red chillies, ground fine
2 tablespoons fish sauce (*nam pla*)
½ cup thick coconut milk
1 teaspoon palm sugar
1 tablespoon oil
raffia twine

The Pattaya Pomfret, stuffed with shallots, garlic and coriander leaves and roots – cooked in record time in your microwave oven.

Preparation

Scale and gut fish, and remove gills and eyes. Wash well. Pat dry with kitchen paper and rub inside of fish with turmeric, salt and pepper. Cover the tail with foil. (Make sure foil does not touch sides of the oven.)

Peel and dice shallots and garlic. Cut coriander leaves and roots into small pieces. Blend together or pound till fine. (This is the stuffing.)

Mix together ground chilli, fish sauce, coconut milk and palm sugar.

Microwave Cooking Method

Preheat browning dish for 6 minutes on High (100%). Add oil and heat on High (100%) for 1 minute.

Brown stuffing mixture on High (100%) for 2 minutes. Remove and stuff fish with this mixture. Brush fish with turmeric and bind with raffia twine to hold stuffing together.

Cook fish on a greased platter for 6 minutes on High (100%). Turn fish over.

Add ground chilli mixture to fish and stir. Cook for 6 minutes on High (100%).

Decorate eye socket with a carrot slice. Serve hot.

Steamed Pegu Fish (Nga Yahn Tha)

PREPARATION: 15 mins
COOKING: 700 watt – 13 mins
650 watt – 18 mins
500 watt – 23 mins
Times given here are for a
650 watt oven. Decrease time
by 15 seconds per minute for
a 700 watt oven. Increase time
by 20 seconds per minute for a
500 watt oven.
KCAL 900
SERVES 4

500 g (1 lb) *nga yahn tha*
(or any firm white fish)
¼ coconut, grated
6 shallots
2 cloves garlic
2 stalks lemon grass
1 × 1 cm (½ × ½ in) galangal
1 red chilli
salt
pepper
2-3 large banana leaves
wooden skewers

It should not surprise that some dishes in parts of Asia should be duplicated: the same spices are available in most of Asia. I have tasted at least four forms of this dish from Burma – the other three in Thailand, Malaysia, and a spicier version in Southwest Kerala, all equally popular.

Preparation

Fillet fish and chop or blend till well minced.

Work grated coconut with a little water to extract ¼ cup thick coconut milk.

Blend or pound together shallots, garlic, lemon grass, galangal and chilli till fine.

In a bowl, mix minced fish, coconut milk and the ground spices with salt and pepper. Mould into 12 marbles and flatten.

Soften banana leaves by microwaving for 1½ minutes on High (100%). Cut into 10 cm (4 in) squares.

Place a fish patty on each banana leaf square and fold over twice, securing open ends with wooden skewers.

Microwave Cooking Method

Arrange 6 bundles at a time on a heatproof dish and microwave on High (100%) for 8 minutes.

Remove and repeat for the second lot of bundles.

Serve hot as a snack or hors d'oeuvre.

Tomato Fish Fillets

PREPARATION: 6 mins
COOKING: 700 watt — 9 mins
650 watt — 10 mins
500 watt — 13 mins
Times given here are for a
650 watt oven. Decrease time
by 15 seconds per minute for
a 700 watt oven. Increase time
by 20 seconds per minute for a
500 watt oven.
KCAL 982
SERVES 4-6

500 g (1 lb) fish fillets
1 teaspoon salt
1 teaspoon pepper
2 teaspoons cornflour
3 tablespoons tomato sauce
1 teaspoon oyster sauce
½ teaspoon sugar
2 cloves garlic
2 × 2 cm (¾ × ¾ in) ginger
oil
2 large tomatoes, sliced

A quick Chinese dish adapted to modern tastebuds.

Preparation

Rub fish fillets with salt and pepper.

Mix cornflour with ½ cup water, tomato sauce, oyster sauce and sugar.

Peel and cut garlic and ginger into thin slices.

Microwave Cooking Method

Heat casserole. Cook ginger and garlic in ½ tablespoon oil for 1 minute on High (100%).

Add fish fillets and pour cornflour sauce liquid over. Cook fillets for 9 minutes on High (100%), covered with plastic wrap or a glass lid.

Remove cover and garnish with tomato slices. Serve hot with a bowl of rice and Chinese greens.

Tandoori Machi (Fish in Yogurt)

PREPARATION: 10 mins
COOKING: 700 watt – 11 mins
          650 watt – 14 mins
          500 watt – 19 mins
Times given here are for a
650 watt oven. Decrease time
by 15 seconds per minute for
a 700 watt oven. Increase time
by 20 seconds per minute for a
500 watt oven.
KCAL 793
SERVES 4-6

600 g (1⅓ lb) red snapper (*ikan merah*)
2 lemons for juice
3 cloves garlic
2 × 2 cm (¾ × ¾ in) ginger
3 dried red chillies
¼ cup yogurt
1 tablespoon coriander powder
1 teaspoon *garam masala*
2 teaspoons cummin powder
orange colouring
½ teaspoon sugar
salt
1 tablespoon ghee

Garnish
1 lemon, sliced thin
mint leaves

Tandoori is named for the clay tandoor or oven that bakes bread, chicken, meat or fish in the northern Indian style. The blend of lemon juice and yogurt helps tenderise the fish, giving it an ambrosia-like quality.

Preparation

Clean and gut fish, removing gills and eyes. Cut some slits on both sides and rub with lemon juice. Cover the tail with foil (do not allow foil to touch sides of microwave oven).

Peel and slice garlic and ginger and break dried chilli into bits. Blend or grind together. Mix this blend with yogurt, spices, colouring, sugar and salt.

Rub inside of fish with some of this mixture, covering fish with the rest. Refrigerate wrapped in plastic wrap for 3-4 hours.

Microwave Cooking Method

Heat ghee in a shallow casserole for 2 minutes on High (100%).

Place fish in casserole, cover with plastic wrap and cook on High (100%) for 4 minutes. Baste with gravy that collects in casserole. Uncover, turn over and cook, uncovered, for 8 minutes on High (100%), basting it once more.

Garnish with thin lemon slices and crumbled mint leaves.

Paul's Har Loke

PREPARATION: 15 mins
COOKING: 700 watt – 10 mins
650 watt – 13 mins
500 watt – 17½ mins
Times given here are for a
650 watt oven. Decrease time
by 15 seconds per minute for
a 700 watt oven. Increase time
by 20 seconds per minute for a
500 watt oven.
KCAL 1065
SERVES 4

300 g (10 oz) prawns
2 cloves garlic
2 × 2 cm (¾ × ¾ in) ginger
1 stalk spring onion
1 tablespoon Chinese wine
½ teaspoon sugar
½ teaspoon salt
2 tablespoons tomato sauce
1 tablespoon thick soy sauce
1 teaspoon cornflour
2 tablespoons oil

A night trip in an outboard motor sampan to a kelong, *with the wind whipping up a storm, is no journey for the fainthearted. The ascent up slimy ropes is dangerous and traditionally no* kelong *owner welcomes women. Paul, however, not only welcomed us, he dredged up a glittering haul of flashing live king prawns which he deftly cooked over a kerosene stove into the best tasting Har Loke I have ever eaten. The salty tang still remains whenever I eat this dish.*

Preparation

Shell prawns, leaving tails intact. Devein and wash. Pat prawns dry with kitchen paper.

Peel and chop garlic. Shred ginger. Wash and cut spring onion into 2 cm lengths.

In a bowl, mix Chinese wine, sugar, salt, tomato sauce, thick soy sauce and cornflour.

Microwave Cooking Method

Preheat a browning dish for 7 minutes on High (100%). Add oil and cook 30 seconds on High (100%).

Add chopped garlic and ginger shreds which will sizzle at once.

Add prawns, stirring quickly into oil. Cook for 2 minutes, uncovered, on High (100%).

Add mixed sauces, stirring well into prawns. Cook for 3 minutes on High (100%), uncovered, stirring just once.

Add spring onion lengths and remove from heat.

Serve hot, on a bowl of rice.

Radha's Masala Raal

PREPARATION: 20 mins
COOKING: 700 watt – 14 mins
             650 watt – 18 mins
             500 watt – 24 mins
Times given here are for a
650 watt oven. Decrease time
by 15 seconds per minute for
a 700 watt oven. Increase time
by 20 seconds per minute for a
500 watt oven.
KCAL 925
SERVES 4

500 g (1 lb) king prawns
3 cloves garlic
6-8 shallots
2 × 2 cm (¾ × ¾ in) ginger
2 teaspoons tamarind paste
1 tablespoon tomato sauce
2 tablespoons chilli sauce
½ tablespoon cornflour
2 tablespoons ghee or butter
½ teaspoon *garam masala*
½ teaspoon sugar
salt
3 sprigs coriander leaves (*dhania*),
   chopped

The Indian Muslims from Kerala man little makeshift food stalls from the Gulf countries to the Malay archipelago. And some of the tastiest meals come from their little 'kitchens'. This recipe is named after a friend who makes the best version of this dish outside Kerala.

Preparation

Shell prawns, leaving head and tail intact. Devein and trim legs and feelers. Wash in cold water and drain in a colander.

Peel and dice garlic and shallots. Chop ginger.

Mix tamarind with 2 tablespoons water, working with the fingers to produce thick brown tamarind juice. Strain and set aside.

Marinate prawns in a mixture of tomato and chilli sauces and refrigerate for an hour.

Mix cornflour to a smooth paste with ¼ cup water.

Microwave Cooking Method

Heat a browning dish on High (100%) for 6 minutes. Add ghee or butter and cook garlic, shallots and ginger on High (100%) for 2 minutes. Stir once during the browning.

Lift prawns out of the marinade and add to browning dish with *garam masala*. Cook on High (100%) for 5 minutes. Stir once during the cooking cycle.

Add remaining marinade, cornflour paste, sugar and salt to taste, and finally the tamarind, very sparingly. Cook on High (100%) for 5 minutes. Stir well and garnish with chopped coriander leaves.

Serve with rice and pickled vegetables.

Note: There is an easy way to clean prawns, leaving the heads intact: use a very sharp pair of kitchen scissors to cut shell at head, lifting off the vein.

Chim Baung Prawns

PREPARATION: 20 mins
COOKING: 700 watt – 11 mins
          650 watt – 15 mins
          500 watt – 20 mins
Times given here are for a
650 watt oven. Decrease time
by 15 seconds per minute for
a 700 watt oven. Increase time
by 20 seconds per minute for a
500 watt oven.
KCAL 750
SERVES 4

400 g (14½ oz) medium prawns
200 g (6⅔ oz) *chim baung*
  (Burmese sorrel)
4 shallots
2 cloves garlic
4 green chillies
2 tablespoons groundnut oil
salt
pepper

Because of the hilly nature of Burma's terrain, there are so many itinerant travellers who carry packs of food with them as they travel long distances. This prawn dish is popular because it preserves well and is commonly given with good wishes, to speed a traveller on his way.

Preparation

Shell and devein prawns, washing once in water. Drain.

Strip *chim baung* leaves from their stems. Clean and cut shallots and garlic into thin slices. Chop green chilli into tiny bits.

Microwave Cooking Method

Preheat browning dish for 6 minutes. Add oil and heat for another minute.

Add garlic, which will sizzle at once. Add shallots and cook for 2 minutes on High (100%), stirring once. Shallots should be golden brown.

Add prawns, stir and continue cooking for 4 minutes on High (100%).

Add *chim baung* leaves, chillies, salt and pepper. Stir well into the prawn mixture. Cook for 2 minutes on High (100%). Stir and remove from heat.

Cool and refrigerate in a jar. Reheat and serve hot with rice when required.

Koi Gung

PREPARATION: 15 mins
COOKING: 700 watt – 6 mins
                 650 watt – 8 mins
                 500 watt – 11 mins
Times given here are for a
650 watt oven. Decrease time
by 15 seconds per minute for
a 700 watt oven. Increase time
by 20 seconds per minute for a
500 watt oven.
KCAL 1110
SERVES 2-4

300 g (10 oz) large prawns
3 limes
100 g (3½ oz) minced pork
2 stalks lemon grass
10 mint leaves
6-8 citrus leaves
1 × 1 cm (½ × ½ in) tamarind
   paste
2 eggs
salt
pepper
salad greens
1 tablespoon palm sugar
1 tablespoon fish sauce (*nam pla*)
1 teaspoon roasted curry paste
   (*nam prik pao*)
4 tablespoons thick coconut milk
   from ½ coconut, grated

Although this dish is Thai, it is similar to a Laotian-Burmese dish, the prawns being pounded in a wooden mortar instead of being chopped. The lime juice marinade cooks the prawns, rather like vinegared fish from Japan.

Preparation

Shell and devein prawns, then chop them. Extract juice from limes and strain over prawns. Leave for 10 minutes, then drain and set aside. Reserve juice for sauce.

Cook minced pork for 3 minutes on High (100%), stirring once during the cycle.

Chop lemon grass, mint and citrus leaves.

Add a little water to tamarind paste and work with fingers to extract 2 tablespoons juice.

Beat eggs with a little salt and pepper.

Microwave Cooking Method

Grease a pie plate and cook eggs into an omelette on High (100%) for 3 minutes, moving liquid centre to sides as egg cooks on edges of pie plate. Give 30 seconds more if egg is runny. Remove and cut into thin strips.

In a salad bowl, mix prawns, lemon grass, mint and citrus leaves with pork and egg strips. Tightly pack mixture into a greased Chinese bowl and invert quickly over a plate. Surround pork-prawn mould with salad greens.

Mix prawn marinade with palm sugar, tamarind juice, fish sauce, curry paste and coconut cream. Cook on Low (30%) for 2 minutes.

Serve Koi Gung prawn salad with the sauce.

Pinais

PREPARATION: 15 minutes
COOKING: 700 watt – 11 mins
650 watt – 14 mins
500 watt – 19 mins
Times given here are for a
650 watt oven. Decrease time
by 15 seconds per minute for
a 700 watt oven. Increase time
by 20 seconds per minute for a
500 watt oven.
KCAL: 1060
SERVES 4-6

1 kg (2⅓ lb) small prawns
2 coconuts, grated
2 small onions
salt
pepper
***gabi* or banana leaves**
wooden skewers
2 red chillies (*sili labuyo*), slit
** lengthwise**

A Filipino prawn dish (pronounced pee-nah-is*) simmered in coconut milk. If* gabi *leaves are not available, wrap Pinais in banana leaves for a similar effect.*

Preparation

Shell, devein and chop prawns.

Reserve 2 tablespoons grated coconut. Add ¾ cup water to the rest to extract 2 cups thick coconut milk. Refrigerate for 15 minutes to allow cream to rise to the top. Separate cream for later use.

Chop reserved grated coconut and onions. Mix prawns, onions, coconut, salt and pepper to taste.

Wilt leaves by microwaving on High (100%) for 1½ minutes.

Wrap Pinais in leaves (see illustrations) and secure with skewers.

Microwave Cooking Method

Arrange leaf-wrapped Pinais in the bottom of an earthenware pot or *belanga*. Add chillies and the thick coconut milk. Cover the pot with plastic wrap and cook for 10 minutes on Medium (70%).

Remove plastic wrap and add thick separated cream. Cook for 3 minutes on High (100%) and you will find mixture has thickened a little.

Remove from heat and serve with rice.

  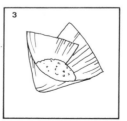

Ceylonese Prawn Patties

PREPARATION: 20 mins
COOKING: 700 watt – 20 mins
           650 watt – 27 mins
           500 watt – 36 mins
Times given here are for a
650 watt oven. Decrease time
by 15 seconds per minute for
a 700 watt oven. Increase time
by 20 seconds per minute for a
500 watt oven.
KCAL 1310
MAKES 20 patties

500 g (1 lb) medium prawns
6 dried chillies (less if you prefer
   patties mild)
2 tablespoons fennel seeds
1 cup grated coconut
6 shallots
2 egg yolks, beaten
1 stalk curry leaves, stripped from
   stalk and chopped
salt
pepper
juice of 1 lime
2 tablespoons flour
2 egg whites, beaten
breadcrumbs
2 tablespoons oil

A traditional prawn cutlet that I watched being made under the palmyra palms of Jaffna. In that dry and arid land, seafood and vegetable tastes are particularly exciting. Slightly salty yet sparkling water drawn from deep wells adds to the flavour of cooked food in northern Sri Lanka where the people pride themselves on being discerning eaters.

Preparation

Shell and devein prawns. Add ½ cup water to prawns and dried chillies and cook for 6 minutes on High (100%), stirring once to distribute heat. Allow to cool then blend prawns with chilli.

Roast fennel for 1 minute on High (100%). Roast grated coconut in a shallow plate for 8 minutes on High (100%), stirring halfway through the cycle. Grind coconut and fennel with a little water to a fine paste.

Peel and chop shallots finely.

Microwave Cooking Method

Mix prawn-chilli mixture with coconut-fennel paste, egg yolks, chopped curry leaves, salt, pepper and lime juice. You may need a little flour to bind the mixture if it is too runny.

Divide mixture into 20 small oval cakes the size of small hen's eggs. Flatten slightly, dip in egg white and roll in breadcrumbs.

Preheat a browning dish for 6 minutes on High (100%). Add 2 tablespoons oil and heat for 1 minute on High (100%). Cook patties for 3 minutes on High (100%). Turn. Cook a further 2 minutes on High (100%). Let them stand before serving.

Note: Contrary to microwave beliefs, this recipe proves that patties may be made in a microwave browning dish, using very little oil. The end-product is the same as the deep-fried version, with one difference – minus the oil it is a decided dieter's delight.

Satay Prawns

PREPARATION: 20 mins
COOKING: 700 watt – 14 mins
          650 watt – 18 mins
          500 watt – 24 mins
Times given here are for a
650 watt oven. Decrease time
by 15 seconds per minute for
a 700 watt oven. Increase time
by 20 seconds per minute for a
500 watt oven.
KCAL 1050
SERVES 4-6

400 g (14½ oz) large prawns
2 tablespoons thick coconut milk
  from ¼ coconut, grated
1 teaspoon sesame oil
2 large onions
2 cloves garlic
1 tablespoon oil
1 teaspoon five-spice powder
2 tablespoons satay sauce
1 teaspoon curry powder
2 teaspoons Chinese wine
  (optional)
½ teaspoon sugar
salt

This popular dish can be prepared quite easily with the use of a commercially prepared satay sauce.

Preparation

Shell and devein prawns. Season with coconut milk and sesame oil.

Peel and quarter onions. Cut into wedges. Chop garlic.

Microwave Cooking Method

Heat a browning dish on High (100%) for 6 minutes. Add oil and heat on High (100%) for 1 minute.

Add onions and garlic, browning on High (100%) for 2 minutes.

Cook prawns quickly on High (100%) for 4 minutes, stirring once to turn prawns over.

Add all other ingredients. Stir to mix and correct for salt. Cook on Medium (70%) for 3 minutes. Stir and cook on Medium (70%) for another 2 minutes.

Serve with rice and two crisp microwaved vegetables.

Amah's Sambal Udang

PREPARATION: 20 mins
COOKING: 700 watt – 19 mins
650 watt – 25 mins
500 watt – 33 mins
Times given here are for a
650 watt oven. Decrease time
by 15 seconds per minute for
a 700 watt oven. Increase time
by 20 seconds per minute for a
500 watt oven.
KCAL 1000
SERVES 4-6

500 g (1 lb) medium prawns
1 teaspoon turmeric
10 shallots
2 × 2 cm (¾ × ¾ in) ginger
4 cloves garlic
4-6 red chillies, seeded
   (depending on your chilli-
   tolerance)
4 candlenuts (buah keras)
1 cm (½ in) square dried shrimp
   paste (belacan)
1 tablespoon oil
1 tablespoon vinegar
1 teaspoon sugar
1 tablespoon tomato sauce
salt
pepper
1 tablespoon natural coconut
   cream powder

My Cantonese amah *was nanny to me when I was little but gradually took over other responsibilities, eventually organising our family with characteristic Chinese efficiency. She was a remarkably good cook and our guests learned to ask for this particular* sambal *which she served with Nasi Lemak and a cucumber salad or pickle.*

Preparation

Shell and devein prawns. Rub with turmeric.

Peel and blend together shallots, ginger, garlic and chillies. Add candlenuts and pound with the mixture.

Roast *belacan* for 3 minutes on High (100%), turning once in the cycle. Add to blended ingredients and pound till well mixed.

Microwave Cooking Method

Preheat a browning dish for 7 minutes on High (100%). Add 1 tablespoon oil and heat for 1 minute on High (100%).

Brown blended mixture in oil for 2 minutes on High (100%). Add prawns, vinegar, sugar and tomato sauce, stir to mix, and fry for 4 minutes on High (100%), stopping cycle a few times to stir. As you stir, distribute food toward the edges of the dish.

Cover with a lid and cook for 2 minutes on High (100%).

Make a paste of coconut cream powder and 1 tablespoon water. Stir it into hot prawn *sambal* evenly. Move prawns to edges of the dish.

Cook for another 6 minutes on High (100%), removing lid 3 minutes from start of cycle.

Remove, stir and garnish with pickled cucumber.

Note: Pickled cucumber is cucumber slices marinated in vinegar and sugar and refrigerated for 4 hours before the meal, preferably overnight. The drained vinegar and sugar liquid may be bottled and refrigerated and re-used.

'Car Park' Ho Chien (Oyster Omelette)

PREPARATION: 15 mins
COOKING: 700 watt – 16 mins
650 watt – 21 mins
500 watt – 28 mins
Times given here are for a
650 watt oven. Decrease time
by 15 seconds per minute for
a 700 watt oven. Increase time
by 20 seconds per minute for a
500 watt oven.
KCAL 1300
SERVES 2

3 eggs, separated
⅓ cup mayonnaise
salt
pepper
1 tablespoon light soy sauce
12 plump oysters
2 tablespoons butter, margarine
** or oil**
2 cloves garlic, chopped
2 shallots, chopped
3 stalks spring onion, sliced
1 tablespoon rice flour

The 'Ho Chien' has its humble origins in the foodstalls of Singapore and Malaysia. The hiss of carbide lamps, the stinging pungent smells of chilli frying, the tang of roasting pork and the delight of sinking one's teeth into plump oysters surrounded by crisp egg crusts are all part of a bygone era of 'carpark food stalls'. Orchard Road, eat your heart out – my gastronomic soul will always remain in your past.

Preparation

Beat egg whites till stiff, adding a pinch of salt. Set aside.

In another bowl, beat yolks till frothy, adding mayonnaise and 2 tablespoons water gradually, till mixture is creamy.

Fold both egg mixtures together, adding salt, pepper and light soy sauce.

Wash oysters, arrange them on the outer edges of a plate and microwave on High (100%) for 6 minutes to open. Discard any unopened oyster.

Microwave Cooking Method

Preheat a browning dish for 6 minutes on High (100%). Add butter, chopped garlic and shallots and cook for 2 minutes on High (100%). Add oysters and cook on High (100%) for 1 minute.

Add spring onion and rice flour to beaten egg. Pour egg mixture into the browning dish. Correct for salt.

Cook for 4 minutes on Medium (70%). Stir cooked egg from edges to the centre, as edges cook faster. Lift omelette to let uncooked egg flow underneath. Rotate dish 180° once. Cook for another 2 minutes on Medium (70%).

Serve with hot chilli/vinegar sauce.

Hong's Oyster Dish (Kyang Samrok Kroeung)

PREPARATION: 6 mins
COOKING: 700 watt – 16 mins
          650 watt – 22 mins
          500 watt – 29 mins
Times given here are for a
650 watt oven. Decrease time
by 15 seconds per minute for
a 700 watt oven. Increase time
by 20 seconds per minute for a
500 watt oven.
KCAL 490
SERVES 4

3 dozen oysters
2 cloves garlic
3 stalks lemon grass
2 × 1 cm (¾ × ½ in) galangal
½ tablespoon groundnut oil
1 tablespoon fish sauce (*tuk trey*)
**1 tablespoon crunchy peanut
  butter**
pepper
salt

Hong is a Cambodian student who had great difficulty extracting this recipe from his mother and translating it, for he was only just learning English. The final version I secured was no mean triumph.

One of the reasons for cooking oysters and cockles in Asia is that most rivers are silt-laden and the cooking of bivalves ensures safe eating.

Preparation

Wash and scrub oysters. Place on the outer edges of a plate to cook a dozen at a time. Heat on High (100%) for 3 minutes. Remove oysters as shells open. Discard unopened shells. Extract oysters from the rest and reserve empty shells for later use.

Chop garlic, lemon grass and galangal. Blend or pound together.

Microwave Cooking Method

Preheat a browning dish for 6 minutes on High (100%). Add 2 tablespoons oil and continue heating for 30 seconds on High (100%).

Add blended ingredients to the oil. Cook for 2 minutes on High (100%), stirring once during the cycle.

Stir oysters into the mixture in the browning dish and cook for 2 minutes on High (100%). Add fish sauce, crunchy peanut butter, pepper and salt. Stir well. Cook for a further 2 minutes on High (100%). Remove from heat.

Serve on flat side plates, in oyster shells, garnished with dotted chilli sauce or a vinegar and soy sauce combination.

Note: Cockles or mussels may be used in place of oysters.

Hua Hom Sod Sai

PREPARATION: 20 mins
COOKING: 700 watt – 18 mins
650 watt – 24 mins
500 watt – 32 mins
Times given here are for a
650 watt oven. Decrease time
by 15 seconds per minute for
a 700 watt oven. Increase time
by 20 seconds per minute for a
500 watt oven.
KCAL 1139
SERVES 8

8 large onions
1 teaspoon coriander roots
3 cloves garlic
½ teaspoon peppercorns
200 g (6⅔ oz) minced pork
170 g (6 oz) crabmeat
1 tablespoon oil
1 teaspoon brown sugar
1 teaspoon fish sauce (*nam pla*)
parsley
salt

Thai cooking is the only one I have encountered that uses the roots of the coriander plant. It has a not unpleasant flavour that adds to the authenticity of the dish.

Preparation

Peel onions and cut bases so they sit upright. Cut a section about 1 cm (½ in) from the top and scoop out the inside using a melon baller. Leave 3-4 of the outer layers. Immerse shells in icy water until needed.

Using a blender, or a mortar and pestle, clean, chop and then pound coriander roots, garlic and peppercorns. Add minced pork and crabmeat and stir or blend till well integrated.

Microwave Cooking Method

Heat a browning dish for 6 minutes on High (100%). Add 1 tablespoon oil and fry crab and meat mixture for 3 minutes on High (100%), stirring once during the cycle. Add sugar and fish sauce at this stage.

Drain onion cups and pat dry with a kitchen paper. Stuff with crab mixture, dividing equally.

Arrange onion cups on a shallow dish and cook, covered loosely with plastic wrap, for 15 minutes on High (100%). The stuffing should be firm and slightly solid.

Garnish with sprigs of parsley.

Ferringhi Seafood Satay

PREPARATION: 10 mins
COOKING: 700 watt – 17 mins
                     650 watt – 23 mins
                     500 watt – 31 mins
Times given here are for a
650 watt oven. Decrease time
by 15 seconds per minute for
a 700 watt oven. Increase time
by 20 seconds per minute for a
500 watt oven.
KCAL 1083
SERVES 4

16 medium prawns
16 Tasmanian scallops or other
shellfish
8 large fishballs, halved, or 16
small ones
16 squid balls

Marinade A
1 tablespoon oyster sauce
1 teaspoon pepper
1 teaspoon light soy sauce
1 tablespoon tomato sauce
a few drops sesame oil

Marinade B
juice of ½ lemon or lime
2 cloves garlic, pounded
1 teaspoon shredded ginger,
pounded
1 tablespoon oil
1 large onion, chopped

16 wooden skewers
100 g (3½ oz) bacon rashers, cut
into strips, or beef sausages

'Ferringhi', a North Indian name for the white foreigner, today refers to a picturesque expanse of beach on Pulau Pinang – Batu Ferringhi.

Preparation

Shell and devein prawns. Clean scallops, removing 'beard' or vein and leaving coral part intact. If using mussels or other shellfish, open by placing on a paper in the microwave oven and heating on High (100%) for 30 seconds per shellfish.

Marinate all seafood in either Marinade A or Marinade B. Let this stand for 2 hours at least, in the refrigerator.

Soak skewers in a dish of water and oil.

Microwave Cooking Method

Thread one of each variety of food on each wooden skewer. If using rashers, wrap a strip around the fishball.

Heat a browning dish on High (100%) for 7 minutes. Open the oven door. Add ½ teaspoon oil. Place 4 satay sticks onto dish and press down to obtain contact with hot dish. (They will sizzle as bacon or sausage provides oil.)

Close door and cook on High (100%) for 2 minutes. Turn over and cook a further 2 minutes on High (100%). Remove and keep under foil.

Continue till all skewers of Satay have been cooked and removed to a warm foil-covered tray.

Serve with rice and hot vegetables, or as a starter to a meal.

Top right to bottom left: Nonya Otak Otak (68), Ferringhi Seafood Satay (98), Johor Satay Lamb (130), Kajang Satay Sauce (220)

Hong's Oyster Dish (96)

Macau Baked Crab

PREPARATION: 25 mins
COOKING: 700 watt – 31 mins
          650 watt – 42 mins
          500 watt – 55 mins
Times given here are for a
650 watt oven. Decrease time
by 15 seconds per minute for
a 700 watt oven. Increase time
by 20 seconds per minute for a
500 watt oven.
KCAL 1000
SERVES 6

**6 medium crabs or 250 g (½ lb)
   crabmeat and 6 crab shells**
**100 g (3 ½ oz) dried Chinese
   mushrooms**
6 water chestnuts
1 tablespoon oil
2 cloves garlic, chopped
1 teaspoon shredded ginger
2 eggs, beaten
1 teaspoon light soy sauce
1 teaspoon sesame oil
salt
pepper
1 tablespoon cornflour
butter
flour
**a few stalks Chinese coriander
   leaves**

This dish microwaves well when coated with butter and a light dusting of flour.

Preparation

Steam crabs singly in a microwave oven, cooking each on High (100%) for 4 minutes. (It is quicker to steam conventionally: all together in a *wok* or *kuali* on a stove top.)

Extract meat and clean shells for re-use. Discard shells from claws and legs.

Chop water chestnuts coarsely. Cook mushrooms with 1 tablespoon water for 1 minute on High (100%) to plump them. Slice thinly.

Microwave Cooking Method

Heat a browning dish for 6 minutes on High (100%). Add oil and heat for another 30 seconds on High (100%).

Brown garlic and ginger in hot oil. This happens at once as garlic especially heats up fast.

Add crabmeat, mushrooms and chestnuts and cook for 2 minutes on High (100%), stirring thoroughly.

Add beaten eggs. Stir and cook for 1 minute on High (100%).

While eggs are cooking, mix light soy sauce, sesame oil, salt, pepper and cornflour with 2 tablespoons water. Add seasoning to dish, stir and cook for 50 seconds on High (100%). Remove from the oven and stir.

Stuff shells with the mixture. Brush surface with butter and dust with some flour, coating evenly.

Arrange on a shallow casserole. Cover loosely and cook for 6 minutes on Medium (70%), removing plastic wrap after 3 minutes.

Garnish with Chinese coriander leaves. Serve hot with rice.

BEEF, LAMB & PORK

Microtips on Cooking Beef, Lamb and Pork

Beef. Asian-style beef cuts are ideally cooked in the microwave oven. Larger roasts cannot be dry-roasted in a microwave oven as the marbling of fat needs liquid and slow cooking to break up the fibres and tenderise the meat.

Firm, fine-grained beef should be bought and the meat always cut across the grain. The meat should be pierced deeply with a fork or pounded with a meat mallet to tenderise it. Alternatively, marinating the meat with sauces as in Asian cooking imparts flavour and a succulent texture to beef.

Standing time specified in most meat recipes is essential as once the meat reaches a certain temperature it continues cooking. This tenderises the meat further, allowing the flavours to blend and the juices time to settle.

For Chinese and other recipes, a few minutes of cooking on High (100%) is all that is needed to cook beef. If a longer period is needed, however, the beef will go through two stages, first toughening then becoming tender and succulent after the initial cooking process.

Lamb. Cooking lamb in a microwave oven is also very successful as it is a tender meat and has sufficient fat in it to cook with or without liquid. Curried lamb cooked in the microwave oven is excellent provided the lamb is cooked on a Medium or Roast (70%) setting and the meat is covered to prevent drying out. Thinner areas should be shielded with foil and standing time allowed for, as in cooking beef.

Microwave times for roasting lamb in a 650 watt oven are:

	TIME (450 g/1 lb)	STANDING TIME	
Rare	10-12 mins	10 mins	Cover with foil to stand
Medium	13-15 mins	10 mins	Cover with foil to stand
Well done	16-18 mins	10 mins	Cover with foil to stand

Pork. Pork is a tender, rich meat that can be cooked, frozen and thawed with no loss of flavour.

Baba Beef (Braised Star Anise Beef)

PREPARATION: 15 mins
COOKING: 700 watt – 20 mins
           650 watt – 26 mins
           500 watt – 35 mins
Times given here are for a
650 watt oven. Decrease time
by 15 seconds per minute for
a 700 watt oven. Increase time
by 20 seconds per minute for a
500 watt oven.
KCAL 775
SERVES 6

250 g (8 oz) rump steak
1 clove garlic
2 onions
2 × 2 cm (¾ × ¾ in) ginger
1 lemon or lime
1 tablespoon oyster sauce
4 tablespoons light soy sauce
2 teaspoons dark soy sauce
½ teaspoon star anise powder
2 tablespoons Chinese wine or dry
  sherry
1 tablespoon oil
pepper to taste

A simple Chinese beef dish that has been a favourite of my son's who cooks it to perfection. Choose only the best cut and you will find it works as well for you.

Preparation

Slice meat wafer-thin across the grain, removing gristle and fat. (Meat is easier to slice while still a little frozen.)

Peel and slice garlic, onions and ginger. Extract lemon or lime juice.

Marinate meat for 2-3 hours in the lemon/lime juice, oyster sauce, light and dark soy sauces and star anise powder. Add sliced ginger and Chinese wine (or dry sherry) at the end of 2 hours.

Microwave Cooking Method

Preheat a browning dish for 6 minutes on High (100%). Add oil and garlic and stir. Garlic will brown as soon as it touches the hot oil. Twenty seconds later, add onion slices and cook on High (100%) a further 2½ minutes.

Add 3-4 slices of the seasoned meat and brown on High (100%) 1 minute on each side. Remove and keep warm. Cook all slices till done.

Place beef slices back in the pan, add marinade and pepper and continue cooking for another 2 minutes on High (100%). Cover loosely with plastic wrap and cook for 10 minutes on Medium (70%), as meat could toughen if cooked too long on High.

Remove dish from the oven and cover with foil to stand for 8 minutes to finish cooking in its own heat.

Serve with rice and vegetables.

Note: Beef cooked this way does not need salting as meats have their own salts which are heightened with the addition of sauces. The standing time suggested at the end of the recipe is essential as meats cooked in the microwave oven reach very high temperatures and continue to cook for a few minutes. When covered with foil, shiny side inside, the heat is retained longer in the meat.

Saigon Surprise

PREPARATION: 20 mins
COOKING: 700 watt – 28 mins
650 watt – 37 mins
500 watt – 49 mins
Times given here are for a
650 watt oven. Decrease time
by 15 seconds per minute for
a 700 watt oven. Increase time
by 20 seconds per minute for a
500 watt oven.
KCAL 1411
SERVES 4-6

Meatballs
500 g (1 lb) minced beef
8 water chestnuts, chopped
1 tablespoon ginger juice
1 tablespoon light soy sauce
1 egg yolk
1 teaspoon salt
1 teaspoon five-spice powder
1 teaspoon pepper
1 teaspoon chilli powder
1 teaspoon garlic powder
1 tablespoon *nuoc mam*
   (fish sauce)
1½ cups uncooked Quaker
   cooking oats

2 large onions
2 cloves garlic
oil

Sauce
1 tablespoon honey
1 tablespoon vinegar
2 tablespoons cornflour
1 tablespoon tomato sauce
4 tablespoons water

Meatballs are common to most Asian cuisines, but these are distinctive with their blend of chilli and fish sauce. I suspect that it has been anglicised a trifle for I first tasted it at the home of a Vietnamese refugee family in Sydney. In spite of the American influence in Vietnam, tomato sauce did not penetrate Vietnamese cuisine, especially that of the north, and it is for this reason that I call it the Saigon Surprise.

Preparation

Mix meat with all the other ingredients listed under 'Meatballs'. Leave for 20 minutes to settle.

Shape seasoned meat into large marble-sized balls using wet palms. Roll meatballs in a plate of oats.

Peel and slice onions and chop garlic into tiny pieces.

Microwave Cooking Method

Preheat a browning dish on High (100%) for 6 minutes. Add 1 tablespoon oil and heat for 30 seconds on High (100%) to grease the dish.

Place a layer of meatballs (they must not be piled up) in the browning dish. Cook on High (100%) for 12 minutes, turning them over and stirring slightly once during the cycle. Cook until all meatballs are done. (There should be 25.)

In a heatproof jar, combine sauce ingredients, mixing well so that cornflour is not lumpy. Cook sauce on High (100%) for 2½ minutes, stirring to prevent lumpiness.

Add sliced onions and chopped garlic to thickened sauce and pour the sauce over meatballs. Check seasoning, adding more ginger juice and soy sauce if preferred.

Microwave on High (100%) for 3-4 minutes to heat through.

Note: Saigon Surprise may be served as savoury cocktails or as the main meat accompaniment to a meal.

Tokyo Garlic Beef Steak

JAPANESE

PREPARATION: 5 mins
COOKING: 700 watt – 11 mins
650 watt – 14 mins
500 watt – 19 mins
Times given here are for a
650 watt oven. Decrease time
by 15 seconds per minute for
a 700 watt oven. Increase time
by 20 seconds per minute for a
500 watt oven.
KCAL 1054
SERVES 3-4

300 g (10 oz) rump steak
4 cloves garlic
6 shallots
1 tablespoon groundnut oil
1½ tablespoons pounded
black beans
2 teaspoons ginger juice
1 tablespoon *tamari shoyu*
1 tablespoon *sake* **or dry sherry**
½ teaspoon sugar
1 teaspoon vinegar
2 teaspoons cornflour
salt
pepper

I have memories of a dimpled Japanese waitress coyly pleased at my husband's war-vintaged Japanese compliments and the fragrance of smoky tea, gleaming coal hibachi *and garlic beef cooked to perfection. This unforgettable experience can also be yours, when this is cooked – minus the smoke and heat – in your microwave oven.*

Preparation

Slice beef thinly. Peel and slice garlic and shallots finely.

Microwave Cooking Method

Preheat a browning dish on High (100%) for 5 minutes. Add 1½ tablespoons oil and brown garlic and black beans instantly.

Cook steak on High (100%) for 4 minutes. Stir beef, turning slices, about halfway through the cycle.

Add shallots and ginger juice to meat, cover with plastic wrap and cook on Medium (70%) for 5 minutes.

Add remaining ingredients, mixing cornflour to a smooth paste with a little *sake* first. Test for seasoning.

Note: A browning dish is not essential but useful. A heatproof pyrex dish may be used but need not be preheated.

Brandy 'Bifstik'

PREPARATION: 10 mins
COOKING: 700 watt – 11 mins
650 watt – 15 mins
500 watt – 20 mins
Times given here are for a
650 watt oven. Decrease time
by 15 seconds per minute for
a 700 watt oven. Increase time
by 20 seconds per minute for a
500 watt oven.
·KCAL 820
SERVES 6

250 g (8 oz) rump steak

Marinade
1 teaspoon soda bicarbonate
1 teaspoon ginger juice
2 tablespoons brandy
2 green chillies, slit and seeds
**   discarded**
2 teaspoons sesame oil
1 tablespoon water

2 large onions
2 ripe but firm tomatoes
3 cloves garlic
groundnut oil
1 teaspoon cornflour
salt

My Cantonese amah used brandy as a panacea for all ills. In my antiseptically Methodist home, the brandy was produced by sleight of hand whenever anyone was ill and especially for this versatile dish.

Preparation

Cut slightly frozen beef into wafer-thin slices across the grain, removing gristle. Soak in the marinade and refrigerate, covered, for at least 6 hours.

Peel and slice onions into fine rings. Quarter tomatoes, and peel and chop garlic finely.

Microwave Cooking Method

Preheat a browning dish for 6 minutes on High (100%). Add 1 tablespoon groundnut oil and heat on High (100%) for 30 seconds.

Add steak slices, cooking on High (100%) for 1 minute on each side. Remove steak and wrap in foil to keep warm.

In the same dish, cook onions, tomatoes and marinade juices with cornflour, stirring well to prevent lumps. Cook on High (100%) for 3 minutes, stirring once during the cycle to 'even out' the sauce.

Add steak to marinade, test for salt. Cook covered with a plastic wrap on Medium (70%) for 4 minutes or until heated through. Spoon thick sauces over steak to serve.

Note: Salt should be added only if necessary as it may toughen the meat.

Microwaves are attracted to moisture, and while this helps cook the meat, it also dries it out. Cover meat with plastic to retain moisture and to create a steamy surround.

Songkla Soured Beef

PREPARATION: 15 mins
COOKING: 700 watt – 20 mins
650 watt – 27 mins
500 watt – 36 mins
Times given here are for a
650 watt oven. Decrease time
by 15 seconds per minute for
a 700 watt oven. Increase time
by 20 seconds per minute for a
500 watt oven.
KCAL 1460
SERVES 6

500 g (1 lb) beef
2 cm (¾ in) square tamarind paste

Grind together:
8 dried chillies
2 cm (¾ in) dried shrimp paste
   (kapee)
2 cloves garlic
10 shallots
2 × 2 cm (¾ × ¾ in) galangal
½ teaspoon fresh turmeric

oil
salt
sugar
1 teaspoon cornflour

Preparation

Remove gristle from beef. Slice into thin layers across the grain. Tenderise by pounding meat with the back of a knife.

Work tamarind with 1 cup water and strain to remove pulp and seeds.

Add ¼ cup water to dried chillies in a bowl. Cook on High (100%) for 1½ minutes to soften. Roast shrimp paste for 3 minutes on High (100%), turning once during the cycle to roast evenly.

Peel and wash garlic, shallots and galangal. Grind or blend these with dried chillies, shrimp paste and turmeric.

Microwave Cooking Method

Preheat a browning dish for 6 minutes on High (100%). Add 2 teaspoons oil and heat for 30 seconds on High (100%).

Add ground ingredients. Stir-fry on High (100%) for 1 minute. Stir and cook on Medium (70%) for 2 minutes.

Add beef and cook on Medium (70%) for 4 minutes, turning meat to cook on both sides.

Add tamarind juice to beef. Cook 4 minutes on Medium (70%). Stir once during cooking. Taste for seasoning and add some sugar and salt if necessary.

Blend cornflour with a little water to get a smooth paste. Stir into the contents of the dish and cook a further 5 minutes on Medium (70%).

Note: Beef toughens with lengthy cooking but will tenderise if cooking is continued.

Neva Pad Prik (Chilli Beef)

PREPARATION: 20 mins
COOKING: 700 watt – 13 mins
650 watt – 17 mins
500 watt – 23 mins
Times given here are for a
650 watt oven. Decrease time
by 15 seconds per minute for
a 700 watt oven. Increase time
by 20 seconds per minute for a
500 watt oven.
KCAL 1820
SERVES 6

500 g (1 lb) lean beef
2 × 2 cm (¾ × ¾ in) ginger
3 cloves garlic
1 tablespoon palm sugar
1 tablespoon soy sauce
30 g (1 oz) dried Chinese
  mushrooms
2 large onions
4 red chillies
oil
100 g (3½ oz) sweetcorn (canned
  if fresh is not available)
1 beef stock cube
1 tablespoon cornflour
2 tablespoons *nam pla* (fish
  sauce)
salt

A Thai dish that can be hot or mild, depending on taste. Use fresh sweetcorn if available – it is far superior to the canned variety.

Preparation

Remove gristle from meat and cut into thin slices across the grain.

Peel and blend or pound together ginger and garlic. Marinate beef in a mixture of ginger, garlic, palm sugar and soy sauce, coating beef thoroughly.

Soak mushrooms in hot water and slice thinly when soft. Slice onions into slivers. Slice chillies, removing seeds.

Microwave Cooking Method

Preheat a browning dish for 6 minutes on High (100%). Add 1 tablespoon oil and heat for 30 seconds on High (100%).

Add beef strips without marinade and press into the sizzling oil. Cook for 2 minutes on High (100%). Turn and cook for 3 minutes on High (100%), stirring after the cycle.

Add sweetcorn, mushrooms, chillies, stock cube, the marinade and ¼ cup water. Stir well and cook for 3 minutes on High (100%).

Mix cornflour to a smooth paste with fish sauce and 2 table-spoons water. Add to meat and stir to mix evenly.

Cook for 2 minutes on High (100%), stirring once during the cycle.

Serving

The Thais serve rice in a mound – pressed and moulded in a pudding basin while still hot, and inverted over a plate – with the Chilli Beef spread around it, rather like a volcano with hot coals at its foot. The best garnish to go with this dish would be thin slices of pineapple, arranged decoratively around the beef.

Thai Chilli Beef (108)

Rendang Indonesia (111)

Rendang Indonesia

PREPARATION: 20 mins
COOKING: 700 watt – 39-48 mins
           650 watt – 52-64 mins
           500 watt – 69-85 mins
Times given here are for a
650 watt oven. Decrease time
by 15 seconds per minute for
a 700 watt oven. Increase time
by 20 seconds per minute for a
500 watt oven.
KCAL 1250
SERVES 4

500 g (1 lb) beef
6 shallots
3 cloves garlic
2 × 2 cm (¾ × ¾ in) ginger
3 stalks lemon grass
3 × 3 cm (1¼ × 1¼ in) galangal
1 tablespoon coriander powder
2 teaspoons cummin powder
1 teaspoon fennel powder
½ teaspoon black pepper
1 teaspoon chilli powder
1 large onion
1 coconut, grated
½ tablespoon oil
1 stick cinnamon
6 cloves
2 screwpine leaves
1 × 1 cm (½ × ½ in) palm sugar
salt
pepper

'Rendang', runs one definition, 'is a dark beef curry with that subtle blend of spices cooked painstakingly over a slow fire . . .' Well, thanks to modern technology, a traditional Rendang can now be produced professionally in less than an hour with no loss of flavour.

Preparation

Cut meat into cubes, removing gristle.

Peel and clean shallots, garlic, ginger, lemon grass and galangal. Pound or blend together to a paste. Mix meat with this paste, coriander, cummin, fennel, black pepper and chilli.

Slice onion into thin pieces.

Toast 3 tablespoons of the grated coconut on High (100%) for 8-10 minutes, stirring once during the cycle to distribute heat evenly.

Extract ½ cup thick coconut milk from the rest. Add ¼ cup water to the coconut residue and extract ¼ cup thin coconut milk from this.

Microwave Cooking Method

Preheat a browning dish for 6 minutes on High (100%). Heat ½ tablespoon oil on High (100%) for 30 seconds. Add sliced onion, cinnamon and cloves and cook for 2 minutes on High (100%) until onion slices are soft.

Add meat, thin coconut milk and screwpine leaves. Stir, then move meat to the edges of the dish to cook, uncovered, for 15 minutes on Medium (70%).

Stir well, add thick coconut milk and continue to cook on High (100%) for 10 minutes.

Add toasted coconut and palm sugar, stir well and continue cooking on High (100%) for another 10 minutes.

Correct for salt and pepper. If beef is still tough, cook with a little more coconut milk for 10 minutes on High (100%).

Serve hot or cold with rice and sliced wedges of cucumber.

Note: Rendang can be preserved for over a week if it is not handled too much.

Rama's Bath

PREPARATION: 20 mins
COOKING: 700 watt – 28 mins
             650 watt – 38 mins
             500 watt – 50 mins
Times given here are for a
650 watt oven. Decrease time
by 15 seconds per minute for
a 700 watt oven. Increase time
by 20 seconds per minute for a
500 watt oven.
KCAL 1035
SERVES 6

600 g (1⅓ lb) beef

Blend A
8 dried chillies
5 shallots
4 cloves garlic
2 × 2 cm (¾ × ¾ in) ginger
2 × 2 cm (¾ × ¾ in) galangal
2 stalks lemon grass

1 coconut, grated
200 g (6⅔ oz) *pak bung* (green Thai spinach)
2 teaspoons *nam pla* (fish sauce)
1 × 1 cm (½ × ½ in) palm sugar
2 tablespoons peanut butter
1 tablespoon flour
salt
pepper

This recipe, discovered in an old YMCA cookbook, always intrigued me because of its romantic name, as I could picture the heroic Hindu figure of Rama wallowing in waterfalls of icy cool coconut milk, rather reminiscent of Cleopatraesque scenes. Although 'Rama' remains an enigma (probably named after King Rama), the dish was traced to the Royal Thai Embassy. It adapts well to microwave cooking, provided the beef is allowed to simmer gracefully on a Roast (Medium) cycle at first before finishing off on High.

Preparation

Remove gristle from beef and cut beef into thin strips across the grain.

Plump chillies in ¼ cup water for 1½ minutes on High (100%). Drain liquid.

Peel and clean shallots, garlic, ginger, galangal and lemon grass. Blend these with softened chillies. (Add a little water to facilitate blending.)

Work coconut with fingers or in a blender and extract ¾ cup thick coconut milk. Add 1 cup water to extract 1 cup thin coconut milk.

Wash and chop spinach into 5 cm (2 in) lengths. Drain and reserve for use.

Microwave Cooking Method

Mix beef with fish sauce, palm sugar, peanut butter and 1 cup thin coconut milk in a 2-litre casserole. Cook on Medium (70%) for 12 minutes, covered loosely with plastic wrap.

To the thick coconut milk, add Blend A. Stir and cook for 2 minutes on High (100%), making sure the mixture does not boil as oil would then separate from the coconut cream.

Add this blend to the cooking beef, stirring well. Cook on High (100%) for 10 minutes. Stir well.

Mix flour with a little curry liquid till smooth, then add to the dish. Correct for salt and pepper. Cook a further 10 minutes on High (100%), stirring twice during the cooking cycle. Most of the liquid should have evaporated by this time, thickening the curry.

Remove from the oven and cover with foil to stand while greens are being prepared.

Place greens on a plate and cover loosely with plastic wrap. Cook on High (100%) for 2½ minutes. Remove wrap and drain liquid (which can be added to any soup dish).

To serve, arrange greens on a platter, pour beef on top and serve hot, surrounded with fluffy hot rice.

Note: The advantage of microwaving this dish is that cheaper cuts of beef can be quickly and effectively cooked. This dish would take at least double the cooking time using conventional methods.

When heating up this curry, add a little coconut milk or water to the dish, cover with plastic wrap and heat on Low or Medium for 5 (with water) or 10 minutes (with coconut milk).

Cucumber and Beef Peony

PREPARATION: 10 mins
COOKING: 700 watt – 9 mins
650 watt – 12 mins
500 watt – 16 mins
Times given here are for a 650 watt oven. Decrease time by 15 seconds per minute for a 700 watt oven. Increase time by 20 seconds per minute for a 500 watt oven.
KCAL 1094
SERVES 4

100 g (3½ oz) rump steak
1 tablespoon light soy sauce
1 tablespoon sesame oil
½ teaspoon chilli powder
½ teaspoon honey
3 medium cucumbers
1 clove garlic
2 tablespoons sesame seeds
oil
salt
pepper

Preparation

Cut beef into thin slices after removing gristle and fat. Season with soy sauce, sesame oil, chilli powder and honey.

Peel cucumbers, scoop out and discard pulp and cut cucumbers into 2 × 4 cm (¾ x 1½ in) strips.

Peel and dice garlic.

Toast sesame seeds on an ovenproof dish for 2 minutes on High (100%). Stir once during the cycle.

Microwave Cooking Method

Preheat a browning dish for 5 minutes on High (100%). Add oil and heat for 1 minute on High (100%).

Add beef and garlic and stir while oil is hot. Cook on High (100%) for 2 minutes. Stir at the end of the cycle.

Add cucumber strips, stir well and add salt and pepper. Cook for 2 minutes on High (100%). Cucumbers will be crisp.

Serve hot, garnished with toasted sesame seeds.

Bangkok Beef

PREPARATION: 5 minutes
COOKING: 700 watt – 13 mins
              650 watt – 17 mins
              500 watt – 23 mins
Times given here are for a
650 watt oven. Decrease time
by 15 seconds per minute for
a 700 watt oven. Increase time
by 20 seconds per minute for a
500 watt oven.
KCAL 1137
SERVES 6

500 g (1 lb) rump steak
1 teaspoon soda bicarbonate

Blend A
5 dried chillies
2 shallots
2 cloves garlic
2 stalks lemon grass
2 × 2 cm (¾ × ¾ in) tender
  galangal

oil
2 tablespoons blackbean paste
¼ cup thick coconut milk
2 stalks coriander, chopped
1 tablespoon cornflour
salt

The Chinese influence in Thailand, no doubt, accounts for the distinctive combination of blackbean and chilli flavours. Use a tender cut of beef and for quick microwave cooking, substitute powdered galangal and lemon grass for the fresh variety.

Preparation

Slice rump steak into thin slices, across the grain. Rub soda bicarbonate onto meat.

Plump dried chillies in ¼ cup water on High (100%) for 1½ minutes.

Peel and clean shallots, garlic, lemon grass and galangal. Pound or blend these together (using some oil to facilitate blending) till fine.

Microwave Cooking Method

Preheat a browning dish on High (100%) for 6 minutes. Add oil, blackbean paste and blended ingredients. Cook on High (100%) for 1 minute.

Cook half the beef pieces for 3 minutes on High (100%). Remove and keep warm. Continue cooking the other half for 3 minutes on High (100%). Stir once during the cycle each time.

Add coconut milk, most of the chopped coriander and cornflour which has been mixed to a smooth paste with 2 tablespoons water. Add salt to taste. Cook for 2 minutes on High (100%), stir and serve.

Note: Chill the meat in the freezer for a short time before preparation to make slicing easier. Gristle and fat can also be removed more easily this way.

Fred's Favourite (Hamburger Casserole)

PREPARATION: 25 mins
COOKING: 700 watt – 33 mins
          650 watt – 44 mins
          500 watt – 59 mins
Times given here are for a
650 watt oven. Decrease time
by 15 seconds per minute for
a 700 watt oven. Increase time
by 20 seconds per minute for a
500 watt oven.
KCAL 2000
SERVES 6

2 cloves garlic
2 large onions
1 teaspoon oil
500 g (1 lb) hamburger meat
1 cup diced celery
1 can cream of mushroom soup
2 teaspoons chilli sauce (optional)
1 teaspoon five-spice powder
1 teaspoon pepper
½ cup cooked rice
1 packet potato chips
onion crisps

Fred, my husband's ex-professor and a friend, made our lives in Canada interesting and exciting. He sent me this recipe, created by his lovely wife, Faye. I include it with pride.

Preparation

Peel and chop garlic and onions till fine.

Microwave Cooking Method

Heat a browning dish on High (100%) for 6 minutes. Heat oil for 30 seconds on High (100%).

Brown garlic in the hot dish instantly. Add meat and stir to mix with garlic. Cook on High (100%) for 6 minutes. Stir halfway through cooking cycle. Drain fat from meat.

Return dish to the microwave oven. Add onions and celery. Cook on High (100%) for 4 minutes. Stir well. Continue to cook on High (100%) for another 6 minutes.

Add soup to meat mixture, rinsing can with ¼ cup hot water into the mixture. Add all spices and rice and stir well.

Spread neatly in a browning dish and cook on Medium (70%) for 20 minutes, covered loosely with plastic wrap.

Uncover plastic wrap away from you. Garnish with onion crisps and potato chips browned under a hot grill for 2-3 minutes. Serve with a green salad of cucumber, lettuce and green capsicums.

Note: This 'meal in a dish' casserole can be cooked earlier and frozen. You could vary the vegetables and substitute canned soup with a packet of soup mix instead. Its versatility is ideal for innovative cooks.

Autumn Joy

PREPARATION: 10 mins
COOKING: 700 watt – 9½ mins
650 watt – 12½ mins
500 watt – 16½ mins
Times given here are for a
650 watt oven. Decrease time
by 15 seconds per minute for
a 700 watt oven. Increase time
by 20 seconds per minute for a
500 watt oven.
KCAL 1370
SERVES 4

300 g (10 oz) lean beef
½ teaspoon five-spice powder
1 teaspoon soda bicarbonate
1 teaspoon dark soy sauce
1 teaspoon cornflour
2 cloves garlic
3 × 3 cm (1¼ × 1¼ in) ginger
1 medium red capsicum
2 tablespoons vegetable oil
1 tablespoon chilli-black bean
sauce

A black bean and beef dish that leans on a chilli-bean sauce for extra flavour. This dish is colourful and popular but should be prepared just before it is served, as beef toughens if left too long to cool.

Preparation

Trim off fat and gristle from beef. Slice into thin strips across the grain.

Mix beef strips with five-spice powder, soda bicarbonate, dark soy sauce and cornflour. Leave beef to marinate for 30 minutes.

Peel and pound garlic and ginger together.

Slice capsicum thinly, discarding seeds.

Microwave Cooking Method

Preheat a browning dish for 7 minutes on High (100%). Add oil and heat for 30 minutes on High (100%).

Brown garlic and ginger in oil for 30 seconds on High (100%). Add chilli-black bean sauce and cook for another 20 seconds on High (100%).

Stir in beef, tossing through sauces.

Cook, covered, for 4 minutes on High (100%). Stir in capsicum and cook a further minute on High (100%), stirring once more before dishing onto a serving plate.

Beef with Green Peppers

PREPARATION: 10 mins
COOKING: 700 watt – 10½ mins
650 watt – 14 mins
500 watt – 18½ mins
Times given here are for a
650 watt oven. Decrease time
by 15 seconds per minute for
a 700 watt oven. Increase time
by 20 seconds per minute for a
500 watt oven.
KCAL 1280
SERVES 4

250 g (8 oz) beef fillet
1 tablespoon light soy sauce
1 tablespoon green bean flour
1 tablespoon Chinese wine
1 green pepper
2 red chillies
2 cloves garlic
1 tablespoon preserved soy beans
1 tablespoon oil
¼ teaspoon sugar

Preparation

Slice beef thinly across the grain into thin strips. Tenderise by laying on a flat surface and pounding with the back of a knife.

Mix marinade ingredients (light soy sauce, green bean flour and wine) with beef strips.

Slice green pepper into squares and chilli into strips, discarding seeds.

Peel garlic and pound with preserved soy beans.

Microwave Cooking Method

Heat a browning dish for 7 minutes on High (100%). Add oil and heat for 30 seconds on High (100%).

Add garlic-soybean mixture and cook for 1 minute on High (100%), stirring well.

Add beef, turning and stirring it in the paste till well coated. Cover loosely with plastic wrap and cook on High (100%) for 2 minutes.

Remove plastic wrap carefully to prevent scalding. Stir in green pepper pieces, chilli strips and sugar.

Cook, covered, for 4 minutes on Medium (70%).

Beef is best served rare as meat toughens with prolonged cooking.

Kebab Massalam

PREPARATION: 20 mins
COOKING: 700 watt – 17 mins
          650 watt – 22 mins
          500 watt – 29 mins
Times given here are for a
650 watt oven. Decrease time
by 15 seconds per minute for
a 700 watt oven. Increase time
by 20 seconds per minute for a
500 watt oven.
KCAL 2290
SERVES 3-4

3 cloves garlic
4 shallots
2 × 2 cm (¾ × ¾ in) ginger
3 green chillies
4 stalks coriander
500 g (1 lb) minced lamb
2 teaspoons cummin powder
½ teaspoon turmeric powder
2 tablespoons yogurt
½ cup breadcrumbs
1 tablespoon lemon juice
salt
pepper
2 tablespoons butter

All countries with a Middle Eastern influence serve some form of kebab –
*the Lebanese have the Sheek Kebab and the Turks the Shish Kebab.
The Pakistani* kebab *is very spicy but simple enough to cook with
minced lamb pierced on thick wooden skewers and served with* roti
(Indian unleavened bread) and a range of select chutneys and pickles.

Preparation

Peel garlic, shallots and ginger, then blend or pound to a fine
paste.

Chop green chillies and washed coriander leaves into tiny
pieces.

Mix minced lamb with all the ingredients except butter, working
meat in a blender or by hand so that the spices penetrate
thoroughly.

Cover meat and allow it to season for at least 30 minutes.

Microwave Cooking Method

Preheat a browning dish for 6 minutes on High (100%).

Meanwhile, with wet hands, form mince into 30-36 marble-sized
lumps and flatten into banana shape. Thread 3 of these onto
each skewer. Makes about 12 skewers.

Add 1 tablespoon butter to the heated browning dish and grill 6
skewers of *kebabs* at a time, pressing meat down onto plate so
that all surfaces are seared.

Cook every 6 skewers for 5 minutes on High (100%), turning
once and brushing with butter during the cycle. Drain liquid that
collects.

Repeat process till all *kebabs* are done, brushing them with
butter as they cook.

The browning dish may become ineffective if there is too much fat
or grease in it. You may need to wash the dish after one lot of
kebabs and preheat for 5 minutes on High (100%) once more.
Each set of *kebabs* needs at least 4 minutes cooking time on
High (100%).

Serve on *roti*, with a yogurt sauce and some chutneys.

Note: Kebabs can be made earlier and frozen, then defrosted
and reheated on the day they are required. Defrost 6 skewers for
8 minutes on Defrost or Low (30%), then heat for 6 minutes on
Medium (70%). Cover loosely with plastic wrap to prevent
excessive drying out of meat.

Beef with Green Peppers (117)

Lamb Peretal (121)

Lamb Peretal

PREPARATION: 15 mins
COOKING: 700 watt – 30 mins
650 watt – 40 mins
500 watt – 53 mins
Times given here are for a
650 watt oven. Decrease time
by 15 seconds per minute for
a 700 watt oven. Increase time
by 20 seconds per minute for a
500 watt oven.
KCAL 2420
SERVES 6

600 g (1⅓ lb) lamb
2 cloves garlic
2 × 1 cm (¾ × ½ in) ginger
6 shallots
1 large onion
2 tablespoons mixed curry
powder
1 teaspoon cummin powder
1 tablespoon chilli powder
1 teaspoon rice flour
juice of 1 lime
½ teaspoon sugar
pepper
1 tablespoon ghee
2 star anise
4 cardamoms (seeds extracted
from pods, pod skin discarded)
5-6 cloves
4 cm (1½ in) cinnamon stick
1 cup thick coconut milk
1 stalk curry leaves
salt

Every Jaffna Tamil household has its own version of this dry tasty curry which normally takes hours of painstaking stirring and slow simmering. The microwave method certainly reduces the time spent cooking the meat.

Preparation

Trim gristle and some fat off meat. Cut into small cubes.

Peel and chop garlic and ginger. Slice shallots thinly. Peel and cut large onion into wafer-thin slices.

Season meat with curry, cummin and chilli powders and rice flour, lime juice, sugar and pepper. (Do not salt meat till after it is cooked.)

Microwave Cooking Method

Preheat a browning dish for 6 minutes on High (100%). Heat ghee, garlic, ginger and shallots with star anise, cardamom seeds, cloves and cinnamon. Cook for 3 minutes on High (100%).

Add meat, stir and cook uncovered for 6 minutes on High (100%), stirring twice during the cycle to brown meat in the dish.

Add thick coconut milk and stir meat. Cook, covered, for 15 minutes on Medium (70%).

Uncover, stir well and add thin onion slices. Cook for 10 minutes on High (100%). Stir once or twice during the cooking cycle to make sure liquid has evaporated. If, however, meat dries up too much, a spoonful of ghee could be added to the meat to keep it moist while cooking. Add salt to taste.

Note: This recipe is traditionally cooked using goat meat. Testing for this recipe was done using both lamb and goat meat. If goat meat is used, add ½ cup thin coconut milk and 10 minutes cooking time on High (100%) at the end. If you are not used to chilli-hot food, use less chilli powder, about one teaspoonful.

Mandalay Meatballs

PREPARATION: 20 mins
COOKING: 700 watt – 29 mins
650 watt – 38 mins
500 watt – 51 mins
Times given here are for a
650 watt oven. Decrease time
by 15 seconds per minute for
a 700 watt oven. Increase time
by 20 seconds per minute for a
500 watt oven.
KCAL 3050
SERVES 6

A
500 g (1 lb) minced mutton
½ cup fresh breadcrumbs (from 1
  slice bread)
1 large onion, chopped fine
2 eggs, beaten
1 teaspoon cinnamon powder
1 teaspoon curry powder
½ tablespoon chilli powder
1 tablespoon light soy sauce
1 teaspoon ginger juice
salt
pepper

flour
4-5 shallots
4 cloves garlic
2 tablespoons margarine
1 tablespoon oil
2 tablespoons curry powder
1 tablespoon chilli powder
  (optional)
½ cup thick coconut milk (from ½
  coconut, grated)
salt
pepper
lemon juice

The Indian and colonial influence in Burma is obvious in the make-up of these meatballs. The sauce is my old grandpa's recipe, equally good on its own with rice as it is with the meatballs.

Preparation

Combine all ingredients listed under 'A' in a large bowl, mixing well. Form into 20 large marble-sized balls. Roll these in flour.

Peel and chop shallots and garlic.

Microwave Cooking Method

Heat a browning dish for 7 minutes on High (100%). Add margarine and heat on High (100%) for 1 minute.

Add meatballs, pressing onto hot surface for better contact. Cook on High (100%) for 5 minutes, turning balls over twice during cooking. (If the browning dish is coated with baked-on grease, it becomes ineffective and you should remove the meatballs and clean the dish before starting afresh.) You may need to cook meatballs in 2 or 3 lots for 5 minutes each time.

Clean and heat the dish again on High (100%) for 7 minutes. Add oil and heat on High (100%) for 1 minute.

Brown garlic, then shallots on High (100%) for 2 minutes. Stir.

Make a paste of curry and chilli powder with ½ cup water. Add to dish and cook for 2 minutes on High (100%).

Stir then add thick coconut milk and seasoning. Cook on Medium (70%) for 5 minutes.

Add meatballs, spoon sauce over them and heat on Medium (70%) for 8 minutes.

Season with lemon juice and serve hot as an entrée or as a party snack.

Note: Mandalay Meatballs go equally well with a plate of hot rice and a mango pickle. The dish can be made well in advance of a dinner party, frozen and defrosted on the night of the party. It is best to freeze the meatballs only and to make a fresh sauce when needed.

The Flores Meatloaf

PREPARATION: 10 mins
COOKING: 700 watt – 11 mins
                650 watt – 14 mins
                500 watt – 19 mins
Times given here are for a
650 watt oven. Decrease time
by 15 seconds per minute for
a 700 watt oven. Increase time
by 20 seconds per minute for
500 watt oven.
KCAL 1750
SERVES: 6-8

2 large onions
3 cloves garlic
3 slices white bread
500 g (1 lb) crushed pineapple
3 teaspoons mixed curry powder
1 teaspoon five-spice powder
1 egg, beaten
½ cup milk
salt
pepper
500 g (1 lb) minced lamb or beef
1 cup green peas (optional)

This is a real budget stretcher with a Filipino flavour. Cut into thin slices, it could fill sandwiches or pancakes. Served in thicker slices, it takes the place of steak or chops.

Preparation

Peel and chop onions and garlic finely. Break up bread into crumbs, discarding crusts.

Drain syrup from canned pineapple and mix 1 teaspoon of the curry powder with crushed pieces.

Mix all ingredients (other than the pineapple), adding green peas if preferred. The mixture should be sticky and wet.

Microwave Cooking Method

Line the base of a buttered ovenproof casserole with pineapple-curry mixture. Spread spiced meat over the pineapple layer, pressing down to compact the layer. Cover loosely with plastic wrap.

Cook for 8 minutes on High (100%). Turn dish 180° and cook for 6 minutes more on High (100%).

Take casserole out of oven and let it stand, covered with foil, for 5-6 minutes.

Cut into slices with a sharp knife and serve with garlic bread.

Note: The meatloaf can be made, frozen and served when needed. It keeps up to 4 weeks in the freezer. Defrost on Low (30%) for 15 minutes, covered with a chilli and tomato sauce thickened with cornflour-water paste, as reheating meatloaf without a sauce could dry it up unnecessarily.

Sequiera Succulent Lamb

PREPARATION: 10 mins
COOKING: 700 watt – 23 mins
             650 watt – 31 mins
             500 watt – 41 mins
Times given here are for a
650 watt oven. Decrease time
by 15 seconds per minute for
a 700 watt oven. Increase time
by 20 seconds per minute for a
500 watt oven.
KCAL 4490
SERVES: 6-8

1 leg of lamb (1½ kg/3⅓ lb)
1 clove garlic
1 teaspoon pepper

Sauces
4 red shallots, pounded fine
1 tablespoon dark soy sauce
½ tablespoon Worcestershire
    sauce
1 tablespoon ginger juice
1 teaspoon chilli powder
1 beef stock cube
¼ cup water

1 can apricots
2 tablespoons sultanas
¼ cup cornflour mixed smoothly
    with ¼ cup water
salt
pepper

The Portuguese in their Asian bastions of Macau, Goa and Melaka have managed through the years to maintain their distinctive culture and style of cooking. This lamb dish is especially easy as it halves the time taken to roast a leg of lamb.

Preparation

Cut off gristle and some fat from the leg. Score remaining fat on top of the leg. Make slits in the meat with a knife and insert slivers of garlic in the thicker areas of meat. Rub pepper over the leg.

Combine sauces in the list given and brush some sauce on the leg of lamb. Cover loosely with plastic wrap.

Drain syrup from apricots.

Microwave Cooking Method

Use a casserole with a rack inside (or place an upturned saucer under meat so that the juices will drain away from the leg). Arrange apricots and sultanas on the dish so meat juices will penetrate fruit and partly cook them.

Cook the leg on High (100%) for 8 minutes. Baste with some more sauce. Turn the leg over and cook for 16 minutes on Medium (70%) – 24 minutes altogether.

Remove lamb and cover with foil to stand for 10-15 minutes, then uncover and place on a platter. Arrange apricots and sultanas around the leg of lamb.

Drain pan juices into a bowl and skim off fat. Stir in cornflour mixture and remaining sauce mixture. Cook on High (100%) for 2 minutes. Stir well and continue cooking for 5 minutes. Test for seasoning and add more salt and pepper if needed.

Serve leg of lamb with sauce and mint jelly, baked sweet potato or Malaysian style fluffy white rice and microwaved green vegetables.

Note: The sauce should be heated just before the meal and served in a gravy boat.

Mee Lai Lamb

PREPARATION: 10 mins
COOKING: 700 watt – 15 mins
650 watt – 20 mins
500 watt – 27 mins
Times given here are for a
650 watt oven. Decrease time
by 15 seconds per minute for
a 700 watt oven. Increase time
by 20 seconds per minute for a
500 watt oven.
KCAL 1082
SERVES 3-4

250 g (8 oz) lamb fillet
1 teaspoon soda bicarbonate or
meat tenderiser
1 tablespoon light soy sauce
2 teaspoons plum sauce
1 teaspoon chilli sauce
½ teaspoon sugar
2 cloves garlic
2 capsicums, one red and one
green
1 teaspoon oil
1 tablespoon cornflour, mixed
with ¼ cup water
salt
pepper

A succulent lamb dish that has long been a favourite of the Chinese in Vietnam. Lamb is not common in Vietnam. This dish tastes especially good when microwaved.

Preparation

Remove any fat or gristle from meat. Cut lamb into thin slices across the grain.

Marinate lamb in soda bicarbonate, soy sauce, plum sauce, chilli sauce and sugar.

Peel and pound garlic. Slice capsicums thinly.

Microwave Cooking Method

Heat oil in a browning dish for 3 minutes on High (100%), adding garlic at the end of the cycle.

Add meat, turning to brown on all sides. Cover loosely with plastic wrap and cook on High (100%) for 1 minute on each side.

Add marinade and cook meat on High (100%) for 6 minutes. Remove plastic wrap and stir meat well. Cook for 6 minutes on Medium (70%).

Add capsicum slices and cornflour mixture, stirring well into meat. Cook on High (100%) for 3 minutes or till meat is tender. (The soda bicarbonate may foam into the sauce but a good stir will settle it.) Season to taste.

Serve as a main dish with rice and green vegetables.

Dhansak (Mutton with Lentils)

PREPARATION: 20 mins
COOKING: 700 watt – 44 mins
          650 watt – 59 mins
          500 watt – 79 mins
Times given here are for a
650 watt oven. Decrease time
by 15 seconds per minute for
a 700 watt oven. Increase time
by 20 seconds per minute for a
500 watt oven.
KCAL 3054
SERVES 6-8

500 g (1 lb) mutton

Lentils
100 g (3½ oz) *toor dhal*
25 g (1 oz) *moong dhal*
25 g (1 oz) *channa dhal*
50 g (2 oz) *masoor dhal*

1 medium brinjal
200 g (6⅔ oz) pumpkin
2 onions
3 cloves garlic
2 × 2 cm (¾ × ¾ in) ginger
150 g (5 oz) spinach
2 tomatoes
2 green chillies
2 tablespoons ghee

Curry Ingredients
2 cm (¾ in) cinnamon stick
5 cardamoms, bruised
3 cloves
1 tablespoon coriander powder
1 teaspoon turmeric powder
1 teaspoon chilli powder

salt
pepper
coriander leaves, chopped

This famous Parsee dish combines meat and lentils (dhal) into a tasty pureed curry. The Parsees brought their culture from Persia and have kept it intact. Although their cooking has an Indian influence, it remains distinctively Parsee. Traditionally, four kinds of lentil are used for this dish, but these can be substituted with small red and yellow lentils.

Preparation

Remove fat and gristle from meat and cut up into large 4 cm (1½ in cubes.

Pick grit from lentils and wash. Place all four kinds in a bowl, add water to level of lentils and cover loosely with plastic wrap. Cook for 15 minutes on High (100%) till lentils are soft. Drain off scum that collects at the top and stir once during the cooking cycle.

Cook brinjal and pumpkin in a shallow bowl, without peeling, for 10 minutes on High (100%). Remove from oven and scoop out flesh of pumpkin. Skin brinjal carefully as it may be very pulpy at this point.

Peel and chop onions, garlic and ginger. Cut spinach into 5 cm (2 in) lengths, halve tomatoes and split chillies lengthwise.

Microwave Cooking Method

Preheat a browning dish for 6 minutes on High (100%). Add ghee, chopped onions, garlic and ginger and cook (covered so oil does not splatter) on High (100%) for 1 minute.

Stir in lamb and cook on High (100%) for 3 minutes, stirring once during the cooking cycle.

Stir in all curry ingredients and cook for 20 minutes on High (100%).

Add pureed lentils, and cooked and raw vegetables. Correct for salt, pepper and chilli. Cook on Medium (70%) for 10 minutes, adding ½ cup boiling water if puree is too thick. Stir well.

Sprinkle with chopped coriander before serving with *roti, puri* (Indian breads) or rice.

Note: The meat can be cooked and frozen until needed. The lentils and vegetables should be cooked just prior to serving as lentils do not freeze well.

Curry Devil

PREPARATION: 20 mins
COOKING: 700 watt – 21 mins
            650 watt – 28 mins
            500 watt – 37 mins
Times given here are for a
650 watt oven. Decrease time
by 15 seconds per minute for
a 700 watt oven. Increase time
by 20 seconds per minute for a
500 watt oven.
KCAL 1780
SERVES 4-6

500 g (1 lb) lamb
10 shallots
2 large cloves garlic
1 teaspoon mustard
1 tablespoon vinegar
1 tablespoon chilli powder or
**   10 fresh red chillies, ground**
2 teaspoons thick soy sauce
2 tablespoons tomato sauce
salt
pepper
2 cm (¾ in) square dried shrimp
**   paste (*belacan*)**
1 tablespoon oil
5-6 cloves

The Portuguese settlement in Melaka meant the salty tang of sea breezes blowing across little stilted homes perched amidst neat gardens of bougainvillea and hibiscus. One rather special home belonged to a beautiful old lady we called 'Mama' who always had food enough to feed yet another guest. Her curries reflect the colourful personality of the Portuguese with the heat of chillies, the tartness of tomatoes and the spice of belacan – combined to create a Curry Devil so spicy that one perspires as the curry is enjoyed.

Preparation

Cut meat into thin slices across the grain, trimming off the fat.

Peel shallots and garlic. Slice shallots into thin rings and pound garlic.

Mix meat, mustard, vinegar, chilli, garlic, soy sauce, tomato sauce, salt and pepper.

Roast *belacan* on High (100%) for 2 minutes, turning over once during the cycle.

Microwave Cooking Method

Place oil and sliced shallots in a shallow dish and cook on High (100%) for 3 minutes. Crumble in roasted *belacan*, stir and cook for 1 minute on High (100%).

Add lamb and its marinade, and cloves, then stir well. Cover loosely with plastic wrap.

Cook on Medium (70%) for 18 minutes. Remove plastic wrap and stir well, then cook on High (100%), uncovered, for 4 minutes.

Correct for salt.

Serve hot with rice or baked potatoes.

Mem Sahib's Lamb Raan

PREPARATION: 20 mins
COOKING: 700 watt – 19-26 mins
650 watt – 25-35 mins
500 watt – 33-47 mins
Times given here are for a
650 watt oven. Decrease time
by 15 seconds per minute for
a 700 watt oven. Increase time
by 20 seconds per minute for a
500 watt oven.
KCAL 3400
SERVES 6

1 kg (2¼ lb) shoulder or leg of lamb
4 cloves garlic
6 large onions
2 × 2 cm (¾ × ¾ in) ginger
3 green chillies
1 tablespoon cummin powder
2 teaspoons cardamom powder
1 teaspoon clove powder
1 lime

Almond Coating
3 tablespoons ground almonds
1 × 1 cm (½ × ½ in) palm sugar
½ teaspoon turmeric powder
½ cup yogurt

Deboning Lamb

With a
sharp
knife cut
meat
away
from
bone.

Scraping
away as
much
meat
from
bone as
possible,
remove
bone.

Cut thick
parts of
meat to
open it
out flat.

I grew up in Colonial Malaya where the British mem sahibs kept tight rein over their mini empires in rubber estates all over the country. Sunday lunch at one of these houses was a special event, my appetite sharpened by the long bumpy ride down bamboo hedged lateritic driveways, finally arriving at a double-storeyed estate house, its doors and windows darkened by green mosquito netting. 'Tiffin' almost always consisted of a leg or shoulder of lamb coated with spices and almonds, for our mem sahib, I now suspect, must have had a North Indian past. This recipe faithfully reproduces the tastes from memory, while it employs a quick microwave method of roasting.

Preparation

Ask the butcher to debone the leg or shoulder of lamb. Remove gristle from meat and stab all over with a sharp skewer so that marinade will penetrate.

Peel garlic, onions and ginger. Blend or grind these with green chillies to a paste, and mix with cummin, cardamom and clove powder. Squeeze in the juice of 1 lime.

Coat lamb with this marinade, spreading it all over the meat in a thick coating. Refrigerate for 3 hours. A plastic wrap may be used to keep the flavours in the meat.

Mix ground almonds with palm sugar, turmeric powder and yogurt. Coat meat in almond paste and cover with plastic wrap. Refrigerate for another 3-4 hours.

Microwave Cooking Method

Unwrap lamb and place in a greased casserole. Cook on High (100%) for 8 minutes, turning lamb over carefully once.

Cook lamb on Medium or Roast (70%) for 17 minutes, turning meat once to cook evenly. (If meat is darker in colour, it may be hogget or older lamb, in which case give it another 10 minutes on High to make sure meat is well cooked.)

Remove from the microwave oven and cover with foil, shiny side within, so that meat will continue cooking in its own heat.

If some yogurt and almond coating has dropped off during the cooking, re-coat it onto meat carefully so that the finished product looks neat.

Garnish with Chinese coriander and top each serve with a little almond coating.

Lamb Sakura

PREPARATION: 10 mins
COOKING: 700 watt – 14 mins
                650 watt – 19 mins
                500 watt – 25 mins
Times given here are for a
650 watt oven. Decrease time
by 15 seconds per minute for
a 700 watt oven. Increase time
by 20 seconds per minute for a
500 watt oven.
KCAL 2650
SERVES 6

8 lamb chops or cutlets (600 g/1⅓ lb)
1 tablespoon baking soda

Sauces
2 tablespoons golden syrup
2 tablespoons tomato sauce
2 tablespoons light soy sauce
1 tablespoon *hoisin* sauce
1 tablespoon plum sauce
1 tablespoon ginger powder

1 tablespoon sesame seeds
1 tablespoon cornflour
salt
pepper

Garnishes
strips of cucumber soaked
   overnight in vinegar and sugar
mint leaves

Preparation

Coat cutlets with baking soda and refrigerate for 2 hours.

In a mixing bowl, combine sauces given in the list.

Toast sesame seeds for 2 minutes on High (100%), stirring once during the cycle so they are evenly golden.

Microwave Cooking Method

Dip and coat cutlets in sauce mixture, covering meat evenly with sauces.

Drain cutlets and place on a shallow casserole. Cover loosely with plastic wrap and cook for 6 minutes on High (100%).

Turn cutlets over and cook, uncovered, for 8 minutes on High (100%). Remove from the oven and cover with foil to finish cooking.

Put remaining sauce in the casserole. Stir in cornflour and ½ cup water till smooth. Cook for 3 minutes on High (100%) to thicken sauce.

Spoon sauce over cutlets and sprinkle with sesame seeds just before serving. Garnish with cucumber pickle and mint leaves.

Note: Cutlets prepared this way ensures that the meat is cooked through. To reheat cutlets, add a little water and cover dish with plastic wrap.

Johor Satay Lamb

PREPARATION: 20 mins
COOKING: 700 watt – 18 mins
650 watt – 25 mins
500 watt – 33 mins
Times given here are for a
650 watt oven. Decrease time
by 15 seconds per minute for
a 700 watt oven. Increase time
by 20 seconds per minute for a
500 watt oven.
KCAL 1600
MAKES 24

24 wooden satay skewers
500 g (1 lb) lamb
2 × 2 cm (¾ × ¾ in) ginger
1 × 1 cm (½ × ½ in) galangal
3 shallots
3 cloves garlic
2 stalks lemon grass
1 cm (½ in) fresh turmeric
1 teaspoon coriander powder
1 teaspoon cummin powder
1 teaspoon fennel powder
salt
1 tablespoon sugar
1 tablespoon coconut oil

Basting Mixture
1 tablespoon coconut oil mixed
  with ½ cup water

2 onions, quartered

Preparation

Soak skewers in water overnight.

Strip gristle and fat off lamb. Drain all visible signs of blood and cut meat into thin strips across the grain, then into small squares.

Peel and dice ginger, galangal, shallots, garlic, lemon grass and turmeric. Blend the lot together in a blender to a smooth paste.

Marinate meat in the powdered spices and blended ingredients for 4-6 hours, adding salt and sugar to taste at the end of this period.

Drain liquid marinade before piercing meat onto skewers, allowing 5-6 pieces to each skewer.

Microwave Cooking Method

Heat a flat browning dish for 6 minutes on High (100%). Add 1 tablespoon coconut oil and heat for 30 seconds on High (100%).

Cook 6 skewers of satay on one side, then on the other – 2 minutes on High (100%) for each side. Satay will not brown but will be cooked through. Baste with coconut oil and water mixture while cooking. Repeat this with the other skewers of satay. You may need to wash and heat browning dish again as a dirty browning dish is ineffective.

Keep satay warm under foil till ready.

Add quartered onions to pan juices and cook for 10 minutes, covered.

Place cooked onions on a plate and arrange satay skewers on top. Serve with satay sauce.

Note: This is an easy way of making satay. It can be prepared without the fire hazard in the kitchen and the conventional grill can be used to char-grill the meat before satay is served to guests at the table. Quick and novel, if not traditional.

The Singha Roast (Crown Roast Lamb)

PREPARATION: 20 minutes
COOKING: 700 watt – 33 mins
650 watt – 44 mins
500 watt – 59 mins
Times given here are for a
650 watt oven. Decrease time
by 15 seconds per minute for
a 700 watt oven. Increase time
by 20 seconds per minute for a
500 watt oven.
KCAL 3620
SERVES 6

1 crown roast, about 1½ kg (3⅓ lb)
2 cm (¾ in) square Chinese
**   roast pork (*char siew*)**
2 teaspoons butter
1 clove garlic, chopped
1 can button mushrooms, drained
salt
pepper
1 teaspoon cinnamon powder
½ cup cooked rice
1 teaspoon chilli/tabasco sauce

Glaze
2 cloves garlic, crushed
pepper
soy sauce

rosemary for garnish

The old Prince's Hotel in Singapore used to serve an excellent crown roast of lamb and when as a struggling $20-a-week student I was invited to dinner at this Mecca of food gourmands, I knew I'd arrived! I still recall the awe with which I approached the gleaming silver and crystal. This recipe attempts to recreate part of that exotic past that was Singapore in the 1950s.

Preparation

Cover bone tips of crown roast with foil. Dice or shred roast pork.

Melt butter in a bowl on High (100%) for 30 seconds. Sauté garlic, mushrooms and roast pork on High (100%) for 2 minutes. Stir once.

Add salt, pepper, cinnamon, rice, and chilli/tabasco sauce. Stir and cook on medium (70%) for 1 minute. Keep aside.

Microwave Cooking Method

Place roast in a shallow casserole and pile rice stuffing into the centre. Brush with glaze of garlic, pepper and soy sauce.

Cook on High (100%) for 10 minutes. Reduce heat to Medium (70%) and cook for 20 minutes.

Take roast out of the oven and cover with foil. Let it stand for 15 minutes to cook in its own heat.

Prepare cutlet frills (see illustrations) and place on bone tips before serving.

Garnish with rosemary.

 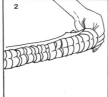 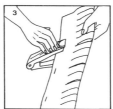  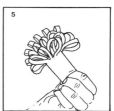

Trade Winds Lamb or Pork Chops

PREPARATION: 20 mins
COOKING: 700 watt – 31-32 mins
650 watt – 41-43 mins
500 watt – 55-57 mins
Times given here are for a
650 watt oven. Decrease time
by 15 seconds per minute for
a 700 watt oven. Increase time
by 20 seconds per minute for a
500 watt oven.
KCAL 2980
SERVES 4

500 g (1 lb) lamb or pork chops

Marinade
**2 tablespoons blended mixture of
    garlic, onion and ginger
1 teaspoon pepper
2 tablespoons tomato sauce
1 tablespoon light soy sauce
1 teaspoon fennel powder
1 teaspoon sesame oil
salt
sugar**

**4 potatoes (about 300 g/10 oz)
4 large brown onions
2 cloves garlic
5 tomatoes
1 tablespoon oil
1 teaspoon ground almonds**

Indonesia, with its diverse islands, has been the melting pot for several nationalities, each one contributing its culinary heritage to the whole. This dish, obviously Dutch in origin, uses potato and tomato with the spices of the East – a blend that has made Indonesian cuisine distinctive.

Preparation

Cut off any visible fat from the chops. Mix marinade and season chops in this for at least 4 hours or overnight, refrigerated.

Cook potatoes in the microwave oven for 12-14 minutes on High (100%).

Peel onions. Slice two and quarter the rest. Peel and chop garlic.

Cook tomatoes for 30 seconds each on High (100%) then skin them.

Microwave Cooking Method

Heat a browning dish for 6 minutes on High (100%). Add oil and garlic. Cook for 30 seconds on High (100%).

Add sliced onions and cook on High (100%) for 3 minutes, stirring once.

Drain marinade from meat and set aside. Cook meat on High (100%) for 2 minutes. Turn chops and cook for another 2 minutes on High (100%).

Add the marinade and cook for 5 minutes, covered, on Medium (70%), stirring and adding a little water if necessary.

Cook on Medium (70%) for another 5 minutes, uncovered, then add quartered onions, tomatoes and cooked potatoes. Test for seasoning and continue to cook, uncovered, for 5 minutes on Medium (70%).

Garnish with ground almonds.

Vinegared Goan Pork

PREPARATION: 15 mins
COOKING: 700 watt – 19 mins
           650 watt – 25 mins
           500 watt – 33 mins
Times given here are for a
650 watt oven. Decrease time
by 15 seconds per minute for
a 700 watt oven. Increase time
by 20 seconds per minute for a
500 watt oven.
KCAL 2315
SERVES 6-8

500 g (1 lb) pork
2 × 3 cm (¾ × 1¼ in) ginger
4 green chillies
4 cloves garlic
3 large onions

Curry Paste
1 tablespoon coriander powder
1 teaspoon cinnamon powder
1 teaspoon cardamom powder
1 teaspoon turmeric powder
1 teaspoon chilli powder
½ teaspoon clove powder

1 cup vinegar
2 tablespoons oil
salt
pepper

The little colony of Portuguese Goa on the west coast of India has a distinctive cooking style. Pork features a great deal in this cooking, while in the rest of India, because of Muslim and Brahmin taboos, it is avoided.

Preparation

Clean and cut pork into bite-size cubes.

Clean and chop ginger, chillies and garlic. Mix with the pork.

Peel and slice onions.

Mix curry ingredients with some vinegar to obtain a smooth curry paste.

Microwave Cooking Method

Preheat a browning dish for 6 minutes on High (100%). Add 2 tablespoons oil and sauté thin onion slices for 2 minutes on High (100%) till brown.

Stir in curry paste and cook for 2 minutes on High (100%).

Add pork pieces and stir. Cook for 5 minutes on High (100%), stirring well after 2 minutes of the cycle.

Correct for salt and pepper and cook, covered, for 10 minutes on High (100%) when oil will have separated from the meat.

Serve with *naan/roti* (Indian breads) or hot rice and a grated coconut garnish.

Makati Pork Terrine

PREPARATION: 10 mins
COOKING: 700 watt – 13 mins
           650 watt – 17 mins
           500 watt – 23 mins
Times given here are for a
650 watt oven. Decrease time
by 15 seconds per minute for
a 700 watt oven. Increase time
by 20 seconds per minute for a
500 watt oven.
KCAL 3236
SERVES 4-6

1 cucumber
2 tablespoons sugar
½ cup vinegar
200 g (6⅔ oz) ham
500 g (1 lb) minced pork
1 teaspoon oil
2 tablespoons diced onion
2 slices bread soaked in
    ½ cup milk
½ teaspoon nutmeg powder
½ teaspoon cinnamon powder
2 teaspoons oyster sauce
½ teaspoon five-spice powder
juice of 2 small limes (*calamansi***)**
pepper
salt

butter
1 egg yolk, beaten
1 stalk spring onion or Chinese
    chives, chopped

A terrine with the flavours of Spain and the Philippines combined.

Preparation

Peel and cut cucumber into 3 cm (1¼ in) strips, about ½ cm (¼ in) thick. Discard soft core. Pickle cucumber strips overnight in sugar and vinegar, then drain.

Chop ham and mix well with pork.

Microwave Cooking Method

In a heavy casserole dish, heat 1 teaspoon oil for 2 minutes on High (100%). Add diced onion and brown in sizzling oil, for 2 minutes on High (100%), stirring often during the cycle.

Mix all ingredients together except egg and spring onion/chives. Do not forget to include the drained pickled cucumber and the sautéed onion.

Pile into a small shallow buttered casserole or pie dish and smooth top with the back of a spoon. Brush the top with beaten egg yolk and a little butter. Garnish with chopped spring onion or chives.

Cover loosely with plastic wrap and cook for 13 minutes on Medium (70%). Rotate dish twice during the cooking cycle. Uncover away from your body and leave to stand, covered with foil, before serving.

Serve on toast, sliced into thin wafers, or in thicker slices with rice and a vegetable soup.

Note: Seasoning may be varied according to personal tastes, e.g., a teaspoon of tabasco sauce could be added if you prefer a sharper taste.

Makati Pork Terrine can also be served cold as a luncheon dish, with a crisp green salad of lettuce, green peppers, apple chunks and green olives.

Koo's Char Siew

PREPARATION: 3 mins
COOKING: 700 watt – 15 mins
          650 watt – 20 mins
          500 watt – 27 mins
Times given here are for a
650 watt oven. Decrease time
by 15 seconds per minute for
a 700 watt oven. Increase time
by 20 seconds per minute for a
500 watt oven.
KCAL 1642
SERVES 6

**250 g (8 oz) pork fillet or tender
  shoulder**

Marinade
**2 tablespoons light soy sauce
1 teaspoon thick soy sauce
1 teaspoon cornflour
1 teaspoon sesame oil
1 teaspoon red food colouring
½ teaspoon pepper
½ teaspoon salt
2 teaspoons sugar**

Chinese roast pork or Char Siew has always been last on my list of cooking priorities, as the variety available at hawker stalls was superior to any I could make at home. This simple recipe created by my talented sister-in-law takes the myth out of Char Siew cooking, and adapts well to the microwave oven.

Preparation

If using fillet, do not cut meat. If any other cut of pork is used, slice into thick strips across the grain. Prick meat all over with a fork.

Mix marinade ingredients and steep pork in it, making sure marinade penetrates meat. Refrigerate a few hours, preferably overnight, covered with plastic wrap so that meat does not dry out.

Microwave Cooking Method

Remove pork from the marinade and place in an ovenproof dish to cook, covered with kitchen paper to prevent splatters, for 10 minutes on Medium (Roast or 70%). Turn over pieces and cook a further 5 minutes on Medium (70%).

Turn meat over once more, baste with some marinade and cook for 5 minutes on High (100%).

Cool and serve with slices of cucumber, garnished with sprigs of Chinese coriander.

Note: A tasty alternative would be to serve Char Siew rolled in sesame seeds. (See 'Microwave Cooking at a Glance' for toasting sesame seeds.)

Babi Pong Tay (Nonya Stewed Pork)

PREPARATION: 15 mins
COOKING: 700 watt – 38 mins
650 watt – 51 mins
500 watt – 67 mins
Times given here are for a
650 watt oven. Decrease time
by 15 seconds per minute for
a 700 watt oven. Increase time
by 20 seconds per minute for a
500 watt oven.
KCAL 3170
SERVES 4

500 g (1 lb) shoulder pork
200 g (6⅔ oz) pig's trotters
10 shallots
4 cloves garlic
1 tablespoon oil
5 cm (2 in) cinnamon stick
2 tablespoons preserved soy
beans, pounded
1 tablespoon sugar
1 teaspoon salt
2 teaspoons thick soy sauce
1 tablespoon cornflour

My earliest memories of our visits to my mother's Straits Chinese friends in Penang are of the feasts. Noisy exchanges delivered a few decibels higher as more friends arrived mingled in my recollection of a festive spirit with the tender, melt-in-the-mouth Babi Pong Tay served with steaming bowls of rice and a choice Nonya fare.

Preparation

Dice pork into bite-size pieces. Scrape hair and skin trotters wherever possible.

Peel and pound shallots and garlic coarsely.

Microwave Cooking Method

Preheat a browning dish for 6 minutes on High (100%). Heat oil for 30 seconds on High (100%) then add shallots, garlic and cinnamon. Brown for 1 minute on High (100%).

Add preserved soybean paste, sugar and salt and stir. Cook for 2 minutes on High (100%), stirring once during the cycle.

Add meat and soy sauce, stir and cook, uncovered, for 6 minutes on High (100%).

Add 1 cup water and cook, covered loosely with plastic wrap, for 20 minutes on High (100%), stirring twice during the cycle. While stirring, adjust for taste and move heavier pieces to the edge of the dish to cook faster.

Cook for 15 minutes on High (100%), uncovered, for liquid to evaporate slightly. After the first 5 minutes of this cycle, add cornflour mixed to a smooth paste with some liquid from the dish.

Note: The advantage of cooking this dish in a microwave oven is that the cooking time is cut by a third.

Mem Sahib's Lamb Raan (128)

Left to right: Makati Pork Terrine (134)
and Ma Uon (139)

Ma Uon

PREPARATION: 20 mins
COOKING: 700 watt – 12 mins
           650 watt – 16 mins
           500 watt – 21 mins
Times given here are for a
650 watt oven. Decrease time
by 15 seconds per minute for
a 700 watt oven. Increase time
by 20 seconds per minute for a
500 watt oven.
KCAL 1122
SERVES 4-6

100 g (3½ oz) minced pork
100 g (3½ oz) minced chicken
100 g (3½ oz) crabmeat
3 stalks spring onion, chopped
3 stalks Chinese coriander,
  chopped
3 cloves garlic, chopped
2 × 2 cm (¾ × ¾ in) ginger,
  chopped
2 tablespoons fish sauce (*nam*
  ***pla*)**
2 tablespoons thick coconut milk
1 cm (½ in) cube palm sugar
2-3 chopped chillies
1 egg yolk
pepper
salt

1 egg white, beaten
banana leaves
wooden skewers/toothpicks

A delicious Thai mixed meat hors d'oeuvre steamed in plastic patty-moulds or conical banana leaf cups. Delightful served on a bed of rice, surrounded by curls of spring onions and chilli flowers.

Preparation

Blend pork, chicken and crabmeat to obtain a smooth consistency.

Mix blended meat with all ingredients but egg white.

If using banana leaves, cut into 20 × 15 cm (8 × 6 in) pieces, dampen and cook on High (100%) for 1 minute to soften leaves. Fold into conical cups, skewering in place with toothpicks.

Press mixture into these banana cups, folding over banana leaf to cover (see illustrations), or straight into small greased pyrex bowls and brush beaten egg white over the top.

Microwave Cooking Method

Cook for 15 minutes on Medium (70%), then take out from the oven to stand, covered with foil, for 10 minutes.

Unmould onto the serving dish, garnish with chilli flowers (chillies, slit many times lengthwise, stalk end intact, and left in iced water to curl).

Filipina Adobo

PREPARATION: 20 mins
COOKING: 700 watt – 26-29 mins
          650 watt – 35-38 mins
          500 watt – 47-51 mins
Times given here are for a
650 watt oven. Decrease time
by 15 seconds per minute for
a 700 watt oven. Increase time
by 20 seconds per minute for a
500 watt oven.
KCAL 3100
SERVES 6

300 g (10 oz) pork
300 g (10 oz) chicken
6 cloves garlic
2 tablespoons olive oil
¼ cup vinegar
2 bay leaves
6 peppercorns
pepper
salt
½ cup chicken stock
***achuete*, or a few drops red food**
  colouring
1 tablespoon rice flour
½ cup thick coconut milk

Although this particular dish is Filipino, my husband Selva and I tasted an almost identical one (called Piquet) in a tiny offbeat eating house in Bogota, Colombia some 12 years ago. I remember the bongo drummer and the taste of this absolutely lovely Creole dish and can only assume that the Spanish influence in both places has spread more than a superficial cultural net over the two diverse countries.

Preparation

Dice pork and chicken into bite-size pieces. Peel and bruise or crush garlic roughly.

Microwave Cooking Method

Preheat a browning dish for 7 minutes on High (100%). Add 2 tablespoons olive oil and heat for 1 minute on High (100%).

Add meat pieces and brown in dish for 6 minutes on High (100%), stirring twice during the cycle.

Add garlic, vinegar, bay leaves, peppercorns, pepper and salt to taste. Stir the meats, then add stock. Cook, uncovered, for 15 minutes on Medium (70%).

Stir twice during the cycle, adding *achuete* or red food colouring.

Stir in rice flour mixed smoothly with coconut milk and cook on High (100%) for another 6 minutes. Remove from the oven and check if meat is tender. If not, give pork another 3 minutes on High (100%).

Allow 10 minutes standing time, covered with foil.

Lou Jo

PREPARATION: 10 mins
COOKING: 700 watt – 22-23 mins
650 watt – 29-30 mins
500 watt – 39-40 mins
Times given here are for a
650 watt oven. Decrease time
by 15 seconds per minute for
a 700 watt oven. Increase time
by 20 seconds per minute for a
500 watt oven.
KCAL 1562
SERVES 4

250 g (8 oz) pork
1 tablespoon thick soy sauce
2 tablespoons flour
½ teaspoon five-spice powder
1 teaspoon pepper
1 teaspoon salt
2 shallots
1 clove garlic
1 tablespoon oil
1 teaspoon brown sugar
2 tablespoons plum sauce
1 tablespoon tomato sauce

My friend Ina from Hongkong was the most exotic of Chinese cooks. This is Ina's recipe for keeping the heat in and the cold out.

Preparation

Remove gristle and dice pork into 1 × 1 cm (½ × ½ in) pieces. Add soy sauce and mix well.

Combine flour, five-spice powder, pepper and salt in a paper bag. Add pork and shake to coat the pieces thoroughly.

Peel and slice shallots, and chop garlic.

Microwave Cooking Method

Preheat a browning dish for 6 minutes on High (100%). Add oil and sauté shallots and garlic for 1 minute on High (100%).

Reheat browning dish for 3-4 minutes, add floured pork and brown for 4 minutes on Medium (70%), tossing and turning meat after 2 minutes of the cycle. Continue cooking on High (100%) for 4 minutes. Remove from oven and cover with foil to let meat cook in its own heat.

In a bowl, mix brown sugar, plum sauce and tomato sauce. Heat till boiling, 3 minutes on High (100%). You may need to add a little water to the mixed sauces.

Pour boiling sauce over pork and cook the whole dish for 8 minutes on Medium (70%).

Serve hot with rice and vegetables.

Banh La (Banana Leaf Cake)

PREPARATION: 20 mins
COOKING: 700 watt – 17 mins
650 watt – 23 mins
500 watt – 31 mins
Times given here are for a
650 watt oven. Decrease time
by 15 seconds per minute for
a 700 watt oven. Increase time
by 20 seconds per minute for a
500 watt oven.
KCAL 4375
SERVES 6

150 g (5 oz) prawns
400 g (13 oz) minced pork
4-5 stalks spring onion
1 tablespoon fish sauce (*nuoc
mam*)
½ teaspoon pepper
3 cloves garlic
4 shallots
4 banana leaves
1 tablespoon oil

Batter
2 cups rice flour
¼ cup tapioca flour
salt
2 cups water

Serving Sauce
2 cloves garlic
2 tablespoons fish sauce
2 tablespoons lime juice
2 tablespoons water
1 teaspoon chilli sauce
1 teaspoon sugar

This snack is from Central Vietnam. The banana leaves give the batter a delicate flavour and colour. Banh La is traditionally served with a shrimp paté.

Preparation

Shell and devein prawns and cut into thin pieces.

Combine pork and cleaned spring onions. Season both prawns and pork with fish sauce and pepper.

Peel and chop garlic and shallots till fine.

Cut banana leaves into 20 × 10 cm (8 × 4 in) pieces. Wash and steam on High (100%) for 1 minute to make them pliant.

Microwave Cooking Method

Preheat a browning dish on High (100%) for 5 minutes. Add oil and garlic and shallots. Cook for 2 minutes on High (100%), stirring once.

Add seasoned prawns and pork and cook on High (100%) for 3 minutes, stirring twice during the cycle.

In a casserole, mix batter and whisk with a fork till an even mixture is obtained. Cook batter for 2 minutes on High (100%), in short bursts of 30 seconds each, stirring in between till mixture thickens to a thick dropping consistency. Continue to whisk to smoothen batter.

Lay banana leaves flat and spread 2 tablespoons batter on each. Spread some filling on top and fold the packet envelop-style. Skewer banana leaf in place. You should have 20 packets.

Place 10 packets on a platter with ridges on its base so that air circulates around the top and bottom of the packets. An upturned rattan tray would be ideal. Steam on Medium (70%) for 10 minutes. Repeat till all packets are steamed.

Serve with fish sauce or a special serving sauce.

The serving sauce is made by pounding garlic first, then blending this with all other ingredients listed till quite well integrated.

Middle Country Steamed Pork

PREPARATION: 10 mins
COOKING: 700 watt – 7 mins
650 watt – 9 mins
500 watt – 12 mins
Times given here are for a
650 watt oven. Decrease time
by 15 seconds per minute for
a 700 watt oven. Increase time
by 20 seconds per minute for a
500 watt oven.
KCAL 2240
SERVES 4

6 shallots
6 cloves garlic
4 eggs
500 g (1 lb) minced pork
150 g (5 oz) shrimps
1 lime
1 large banana leaf
1 teaspoon light soy sauce
1 teaspoon oyster sauce
salt
pepper

Traders travelling between the Shan plateau and the rice plains of Burma carried steamed packets of food. Banana and yam leaves used to wrap these were pliant, aromatic and could be slipped easily into the colourful shoulder bags.

Preparation

Peel and blend or pound together shallots and garlic.

Beat eggs and mix pork with eggs and shallot-garlic blend.

Shell and devein shrimps and squeeze lime juice over them.

Mix pork and shrimp mixtures, adding all seasonings.

If using a banana leaf, dampen and soften in the oven by heating for 1 minute on High (100%).

Microwave Cooking Method

Press pork mixture into a greased pie plate. If using banana leaf, pat into a pancake-like shape on the leaf and fold over, envelope fashion, skewering leaf in place with wooden skewers.

Microwave on High (100%) for 8 minutes, turning meat mixture once during the cycle.

Serve with rice and green vegetables.

CHICKEN

Microtips on Cooking Chicken

Chicken cooks very quickly and with excellent results in the microwave oven. It retains all the tender and juicy flavours of conventional cooking. Because it cooks so quickly, however, it has no time to crisp or to brown, so it should be basted with a browning agent to give a pleasing colour. Soy sauce, a mixture of soy sauce and tomato sauce or Parisian essence are all good browning agents as their flavours do not clash with the herbs normally used in chicken recipes.

Ways to Cook Chicken.   Chicken can be cooked in various ways:

PLAIN	Microwave cooking does not brown meat which remains pale.
COATED	Usually with flour and crumbs, then braised in the browning dish. Chicken browns beautifully this way.
BASTED	With a paste of 1 egg yolk, 1 tablespoon flour and ¼ teaspoon baking powder. This gives a crisp outer skin.
BROWNED	By brushing with a blend of 1 teaspoon dark soy sauce to 2 teaspoons tomato sauce for a browning effect.
MILKED	When chicken is dipped in milk and then in seasoned breadcrumbs before being cooked in a browning dish, a crisp skin is formed.
CURRIED	This is chicken rolled in a mixture of curry powder and flour, and cooked as a normal curry.

Cooking Time.   As with other meats, the size and number of pieces cooked determines the cooking time. Always bring frozen chicken to room temperature before cooking, and turn the pieces over halfway through the cycle. Times given below are for a 650 watt oven.

NO. OF PIECES	COOKING TIME	MICROWAVE SETTING
2	6 minutes	High (100%)
4	10 minutes	High (100%)
8	20-22 minutes	High (100%)

(And following are times for a whole chicken)

½ kg	10-12 minutes	High (100%)
1 kg	20 minutes	High (100%)
1½ kg	30 minutes	High (100%)

Useful Tips. Use less salt to cook chicken. Salt toughens protein. In any case, microwaving releases natural salts present in meat and it cooks faster.

Chicken pieces should be placed in dishes with the meatier sides on the outer edges, the smaller pieces inside. Microwaves cook outer edges first therefore cooking is quicker and more even when meat is positioned this way.

Freezing Chicken. To freeze chicken for casseroles or curries, it is best to cut into pieces, then wash, pat dry and freeze in freezer bags. Separate each piece in the bag with plastic wrap so pieces separate easily when needed. Whole chickens should be cleaned inside and out, its inside dried with paper towels, and packed airtight. Do not pack in foil if you intend to defrost in your microwave oven.

Defrosting Chicken Pieces. Place chicken in its freezer bag in the microwave oven. Defrost on the Defrost or Low cycle (30%) for 10 minutes. Break up pieces, then heat for another 10 minutes on Defrost.

Defrosting a Whole Chicken. It may be necessary to shield the thinner and more vulnerable areas with foil, so that the bird is evenly defrosted. Cover wing tips and drumstick ends. Defrost in a casserole for 15 minutes on the Defrost or Low cycle (30%), then turn chicken over and continue on Defrost cycle for another 5 minutes. Pieces should remain cool and slightly icy. Allow 10 minutes standing time for chicken to arrive at room temperature naturally.

Chicken should not be over-defrosted as it will then begin to cook and flavours will be ruined.

Chicken Stock

PREPARATION: 5 mins
COOKING: 700 watt – 17-21 mins
650 watt – 23-28 mins
500 watt – 31-37 mins
Times given here are for a
650 watt oven. Decrease time
by 15 seconds per minute for
a 700 watt oven. Increase time
by 20 seconds per minute for a
500 watt oven.

**bones, giblets and some chicken
meat**
2 × 2 cm (¾ × ¾ in) ginger
4 stalks spring onion
salt

Preparation

Remove fat from bones, mix meat and bones with giblets.

Clean and shred ginger, bruise spring onions.

Microwave Cooking Method

Add 4 cups water to chicken and other ingredients in a deep casserole and cook, covered loosely with plastic wrap, on High (100%) for 8 minutes.

Reduce to Medium (70%) and cook for 15-20 minutes.

Remove plastic wrap carefully and allow stock to cool, adding salt at this stage.

Strain stock and freeze till required. Skim off fat that collects at the top before using it.

Note: Stock should keep for 2 months frozen.

Surprise Wraps

PREPARATION: 20 mins
COOKING: 700 watt – 16 mins
650 watt – 21 mins
500 watt – 28 mins
Times given here are for a
650 watt oven. Decrease time
by 15 seconds per minute for
a 700 watt oven. Increase time
by 20 seconds per minute for a
500 watt oven.
KCAL 1610
SERVES 6

2 cloves garlic
4 shallots
1 × 1 cm (½ × ½ in) ginger
1 tablespoon chilli garlic sauce
½ cup ghee or butter
2 tablespoons peanut butter
6 chicken breasts
2 teaspoons coriander leaves

Seasoned Flour
1 cup rice flour
½ teaspoon chilli powder
½ teaspoon pepper
½ teaspoon salt

wooden skewers
margarine
½ lemon or lime

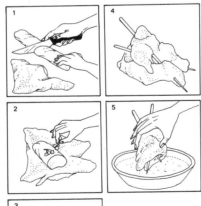

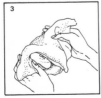

A surprising Burmese dish that my grandfather used to cook, using the old 'coal top 'n' below' ovens, a beautiful blend of shallots, garlic, peanut butter and ghee stuffed into tender chicken breasts. Serve them as a main course at an intimate dinner party and wait for those compliments!

Preparation

Peel and blend garlic, shallots and ginger to a paste. Add chilli sauce, ghee, peanut butter and salt. Cream till well blended.

Roll into a 2 cm (¾ in) thick long 'cigar' on plastic wrap, then freeze till hard.

Debone chicken breasts: holding chicken breast with one hand on a chopping board, remove central bone with the other hand. You may need to use a small knife to separate bone from meat.

Use a wooden mallet to pound breasts till thin.

Spread the tenderised breast. Cut 'ghee roll' into 6 parts. Place one portion with some chopped coriander leaves in the centre. Roll into a parcel and secure with wooden skewers. Make sure you enclose the 'ghee roll' as it melts during cooking and seeps out.

Roll each chicken parcel in seasoned flour.

Microwave Cooking Method

Preheat a browning dish for 7 minutes on High (100%). Add margarine which will sizzle, then place chicken parcels in the dish. Press each in hot margarine and turn to press down, so each parcel is coated in margarine.

Cook for 7 minutes on High (100%), then turn parcels and cook for 7 minutes on Medium (70%).

Arrange in a shallow platter, spooning pan juices over. Squeeze lemon juice over the wraps just before serving and garnish with a sprig of mint and a cut chilli.

Note: Serve as a main dish with honeyed ginger, carrots and little mounds of ghee rice. Press ghee rice while hot into buttered Chinese tea cups and invert onto a platter of Surprise Wraps, or onto individual serving plates.

Surprise Wraps (146)

Mawk Kai (149)

Mawk Kai

PREPARATION: 30 mins
COOKING: 700 watt – 15 mins
650 watt – 21 mins
500 watt – 27 mins
Times given here are for a
650 watt oven. Decrease time
by 15 seconds per minute for
a 700 watt oven. Increase time
by 20 seconds per minute for a
500 watt oven.
KCAL 1129
SERVES 4-6

500 g (1 lb) chicken pieces
6 dried chillies
10 shallots
4 stalks lemon grass
4-5 stalks spring onion
4-5 kaffir lime leaves
1 tablespoon fish sauce (*kapee*)
salt
pepper
4 large banana leaves
wooden skewers

Preparation

Cut and wash chicken pieces, drying well with kitchen paper.

Plump dried chillies in ¼ cup water on High (100%) for 1½ minutes. Peel shallots and shred lemon grass. Grind or blend the three ingredients together.

Chop spring onions and tear kaffir lime leaves after cleaning thoroughly.

In a bowl, mix chicken, ground ingredients, fish sauce, salt, pepper, chopped spring onions and kaffir leaves, checking for salt and spice sufficiency.

Trim banana leaves and sprinkle with water. Soften in the microwave by heating on High (100%) for 1 minute.

Divide chicken into 4 parts. Wrap in banana leaves, envelope-style, securing with wooden skewers.

Microwave Cooking Method

Steam chicken bundles for 18 minutes on Medium (70%).

Place on a plate, opened, garnished with fresh spring onion. Serve hot with rice.

Ayam Sioh (Tamarind Chicken)

PREPARATION: 20 mins
COOKING: 700 watt – 17 mins
650 watt – 23 mins
500 watt – 31 mins
Times given here are for a
650 watt oven. Decrease time
by 15 seconds per minute for
a 700 watt oven. Increase time
by 20 seconds per minute for a
500 watt oven.
KCAL 2300
SERVES 6

1 kg (2¼ lb) chicken
200 g (6⅔ oz) tamarind paste

Ground Ingredients
10-15 shallots
2 cloves garlic
2 teaspoons black pepper
2 tablespoons coriander powder
1 teaspoon five-spice powder
2 tablespoons sugar
2 tablespoons dark soy sauce
salt

oil
2 tablespoons cornflour

Melaka and Nonya food are synonymous. Ayam Sioh, served in a translucent pink and aqua-blue Nonya porcelain dish, was the highlight of some of our most interesting meals at Aunty Poh Siew's red-brick flat behind the old church and fort in Melaka. I remember scrambling around the government offices through rusty iron gates and coming back to steamy bowls of tasty Nonya or Straits Chinese food cooked by old Nenek, the grandmother of the house. This recipe combines microwave and traditional cooking techniques.

Preparation

Skin and cut chicken into large pieces. Wash in salt water to remove liquid beneath skin.

Add ¾ cup water to tamarind paste and work with fingers to extract juice. Strain.

Prepare and grind or blend ingredients listed under 'Ground Ingredients'.

Mix chicken with tamarind juice and ground ingredients. Marinate overnight in the refrigerator, in a porcelain or some other non-metallic bowl. (Tamarind is acidic and will tarnish metal.) Stir a few times so chicken is well mixed with marinade.

Microwave Cooking Method

Cover bowl with plastic wrap and cook chicken in marinade for 20 minutes on High (100%), stirring twice during the cycle. Uncover and let chicken cool.

In a heavy *kuali* (*wok*), heat oil and deep-fry each cooked piece over a low flame till golden.

Thicken remaining marinade in the microwave oven by adding cornflour and stirring well. Cook for 3 minutes on High (100%). Stir once. Adjust liquid for seasoning or sweetness according to preference.

Pour thick sauce over golden fried chicken pieces. Serve hot.

Note: To freeze Ayam Sioh successfully, cook and cool chicken and freeze before deep-frying stage. To serve, heat on a Defrost or Low cycle (30%) for 10-12 minutes, then deep-fry chicken and thicken gravy. Pour over chicken and serve.

Chicken in Mango

PREPARATION: 10-18 mins
COOKING: 700 watt – 15 mins
                 650 watt – 20 mins
                 500 watt – 27 mins
Times given here are for a
650 watt oven. Decrease time
by 15 seconds per minute for
a 700 watt oven. Increase time
by 20 seconds per minute for a
500 watt oven.
KCAL 1022
SERVES: 4

250 g (8 oz) chicken breasts
4 × 4 cm (1½ × 1½ in) ginger
1 clove garlic
2-4 shallots

Batter
½ cup flour
½ cup water
1 teaspoon salt

1 semi-ripe mango or
  1 can mango
2 tablespoons oil

Sauce
1 tablespoon sherry
1 tablespoon plum sauce
1 teaspoon sugar
1 teaspoon vinegar
1 chicken stock cube
2 teaspoons cornflour

This is an exotic taste using fruits not traditional to Chinese cooking flavours. It is delicate and exciting and my son Anand's favourite 'batching alone' dish.

Preparation

Cut chicken into 4 cm (1½ in) squares. Peel and pound ginger, garlic and shallots. Mix with chicken.

Mix batter in a bowl using a whisk. Coat chicken with batter.

Peel (if using fresh mango) and cut mango into thin slices.

Microwave Cooking Method

Heat a browning dish for 7 minutes on High (100%). Add 1 tablespoon oil. Do not remove from the oven.

Fry battered pieces of chicken in the hot dish, pressing them down in hot oil to sizzle. Then turn chicken to cook the other side, covering dish with kitchen paper, for 2 minutes on High (100%). Turn chicken pieces. Cook for another 2 minutes on High (100%).

Continue cooking till all pieces are cooked. The browning dish may have to be washed and reheated before frying another batch as a dirty browning dish is ineffective.

In a separate bowl, combine sauce ingredients, stirring well. Cook on High (100%) for 3 minutes, then stir and whisk. Add mango slices and cook for another 2 minutes on High (100%).

Pour hot sauce over chicken pieces. Serve at once on a bed of rice.

Gloria's Folly (Spicy Lemon Chicken)

PREPARATION: 12 mins
COOKING: 700 watt – 28 mins
                  650 watt – 37 mins
                  500 watt – 49 mins
Times given here are for a
650 watt oven. Decrease time
by 15 seconds per minute for
a 700 watt oven. Increase time
by 20 seconds per minute for a
500 watt oven.
KCAL 1290
SERVES 6

500 g (1 lb) chicken pieces
¼ cup rice flour
1½ teaspoons five-spice powder
3 cm (1¼ in) square dried shrimp
** paste**
20 dried chillies
6 shallots
3 cloves garlic
2 stalks lemon grass
1 tablespoon butter or ghee
juice of 3 limes
2 cinnamon sticks
salt
pepper
1 tablespoon brown sugar

Gloria was our talented Portuguese cook with a weight problem. This dish was certainly her pièce de résistance and her folly! It is typically Melakan in origin but adapts well to microwave cooking.

Preparation

Trim off chicken fat. Pat pieces dry with kitchen paper. Roll them in rice flour seasoned with five-spice powder. Reserve excess flour.

Roast dried shrimp paste for 2 minutes on High (100%), turning over once during the cycle.

Microwave dried chillies in ½ cup water for 3 minutes on High (100%).

Peel shallots, cloves and lemon grass. Blend these ingredients to a fine paste with softened chillies and roasted dried shrimp paste.

Microwave Cooking Method

Heat ghee or butter in a large shallow casserole on High (100%) for 3 minutes.

Add blended mixture and cook on High (100%) for 3 minutes. Stir and cook for another minute on High (100%) till it is fragrant.

Arrange chicken on top of the cooked mixture and add lime juice, cinnamon, salt and pepper. Cover with plastic wrap and cook on High (100%) for 15 minutes.

Meanwhile add sugar and ¾ cup water to remaining seasoned flour and stir till smooth.

Stir chicken carefully, turning pieces over. Pour flour mixture over chicken and stir well. Cover and cook for another 10 minutes on Medium (70%). Stir once during the cycle. Garnish with lime wedges and serve hot with rice.

Note: You may need to adjust salt and sugar to taste. Lime juice alters seasoning requirements and you may find you need more salt. Approach cautiously, however, adding a little at a time. Chilli content may also be varied.

Taj Murgh Tikka (Tender Chicken Kebabs)

PREPARATION: 15 mins
COOKING: 700 watt – 35 mins
　　　　　 650 watt – 46 mins
　　　　　 500 watt – 61 mins
Times given here are for a
650 watt oven. Decrease time
by 15 seconds per minute for
a 700 watt oven. Increase time
by 20 seconds per minute for a
500 watt oven.
KCAL 2382
SERVES 6-8

1 kg (2¼ lb) chicken breasts
6 shallots
3 cloves garlic
1 × 1 cm (½ × ½ in) ginger
1 teaspoon coriander powder
1 teaspoon chilli powder
1 teaspoon *garam masala*
¾ cup yogurt
juice of 1 lemon
a few drops red colouring
24 wooden skewers
½ tablespoon ghee

Indian and Pakistani cooks make delightful versions of this kebab. I managed to wrest this from the cook of one of the luxurious Taj hotels in India. It adapts well to microwave cooking as the splatters are contained within the oven and skewers remain cool while meat cooks.

Preparation

Dice chicken into pieces that can be skewered.

Peel and pound or blend together the shallots, garlic and ginger. Mix well with spices, yogurt, lemon juice and red colouring for a dull orange result.

Marinate chicken in this paste for 3-4 hours, then thread 5-6 pieces on each skewer. You should have 24 skewers.

Microwave Cooking Method

Heat a browning dish for 6 minutes on High (100%). Add ghee and heat another minute on High (100%).

Cook chicken, 3 skewers at a time, in the hot dish, pressing meat down for maximum contact. Cook for 2 minutes on High (100%), then turn and cook for another 2 minutes on High (100%).

Continue till all chicken has been cooked. You may have to clean the browning dish and heat it again if it becomes too dirty and hence inefficient.

Garnish with quartered onions and coriander leaves.

Dutch Eastern Delight

PREPARATION: ¾-1 hour
COOKING: 700 watt – 21 mins
              650 watt – 28 mins
              500 watt – 37 mins
Times given here are for a
650 watt oven. Decrease time
by 15 seconds per minute for
a 700 watt oven. Increase time
by 20 seconds per minute for a
500 watt oven.
KCAL 6390
SERVES 8

1 chicken, about 1½ kg (3⅓ lb)
500 g (1 lb) lean minced pork
200 g (6⅔ oz) pork luncheon meat
5 stalks spring onion
salt
pepper
butter
2 teaspoons ground almonds
½ cup sherry or sweet wine
⅓ cup vinegar
3 egg yolks

Glaze
1 tablespoon butter
1 teaspoon dark soy sauce

1 teaspoon cornflour
½ onion, sliced
pepper

Although they have long since left the islands, the Dutch Indonesians have maintained their ties with Indonesia through the food they serve in their homes. Boning a chicken requires some skill, a sharp boning knife, time and patience. This chicken galantine is delicious cold or hot.

Preparation

Working from the underside and using a very sharp knife inserted through the opening of chicken, carefully remove flesh and bones. If wing and neck areas cannot be removed, leave them in order to keep skin and fat intact. You may need a sharp pair of scissors to cut through bone and gristle.

Debone chicken meat. Chop or mince with pork, luncheon meat and spring onions.

Mix salt, pepper, 1 tablespoon butter, ground almonds, sherry or wine, vinegar and egg yolks. Add to meat and mix thoroughly to bind the mixture.

Stuff mixture into chicken skin, making sure all crevices are stuffed neatly, leaving skin intact. Sew up chicken, pulling skin over all openings.

Mix 1 tablespoon butter with 1 teaspoon dark soy sauce for a glaze. Heat for 20 seconds on High (100%).

Brush stuffed chicken with butter glaze.

Microwave Cooking Method

Place stuffed chicken in a buttered casserole and cook for 20 minutes on Medium (70%). Turn chicken over and cook a further 5 minutes on High (100%). Throughout cooking process, stop cycle often to spoon sauces over chicken to keep it moist.

Remove chicken from oven and give it 10 minutes of standing time, covered with foil.

Collect pan juices and add 1 teaspoon butter, 1 teaspoon cornflour and sliced onion. Cook on High (100%) for 3 minutes. Stir, adding pepper. Be sparing with the salt as luncheon meat and butter are often oversalted.

Serve slices of Dutch Eastern Delight on a large serving plate and decorate with boiled egg halves, their tops cut decoratively into a serrated edge. Serve sauce in a gravy boat and prepare a crisp salad with vinegar dressing to go with the dish.

Note: You may vary stuffing by adding chilli powder or soy/oyster sauce.

Spicy Chicken and Tomatoes

PREPARATION: 20 mins
COOKING: 700 watt – 21 mins
650 watt – 28 mins
500 watt – 37 mins
Times given here are for a
650 watt oven. Decrease time
by 15 seconds per minute for
a 700 watt oven. Increase time
by 20 seconds per minute for a
500 watt oven.
KCAL 2162
SERVES 4-6

500 g (1 lb) chicken
8 dried chillies
6 stalks spring onion
3 cloves garlic
3 shallots
2 × 2 cm (¾ × ¾ in) galangal
1 tablespoon coriander roots
2 stalks lemon grass
½ teaspoon white peppercorns
1 tablespoon coriander powder
1 teaspoon cummin powder
1 teaspoon dried shrimp paste
  (**kapee**)
1 coconut, grated
8 ripe tomatoes
1 tablespoon sugar
1 teaspoon fish sauce (nam pla)
salt

This delicate spiced blend of chicken cooked with tomatoes and chillies goes by this name: 'Gaeng Phed Gai Gub Makhua-Tes'.

Preparation

Clean and cut chicken into serving-size pieces.

Plump up dried chillies by adding ¼ cup water and cooking on High (100%) for 2 minutes. Blend or grind with spring onions, garlic, shallots, galangal, coriander roots and lemon grass.

Grind peppercorns (you may need a little water to facilitate grinding) and add this with coriander and cummin powder to blended ingredients, mixing well.

Roast dried shrimp paste for 2 minutes on High (100%). Crumble and set aside.

Blend grated coconut with ¾ cup water and strain for 1½ cups thick coconut milk.

Skin and chop tomatoes coarsely.

Microwave Cooking Method

Put chicken with coconut milk in a deep casserole and cook on High (100%) for 6 minutes, stirring once or till mixture is near boiling point.

Stir in blended herbs and spices and crumbled shrimp paste. Cover with plastic wrap and cook on Medium (70%) for 12 minutes, stirring once during the cycle.

Add chopped tomatoes, sugar and fish sauce. Continue cooking on High (100%) for 6 minutes. Chicken should be tender. Correct for salt.

Serve hot with rice.

Krispy Korean

PREPARATION: 10 mins
COOKING: 700 watt – 17 mins
              650 watt – 22 mins
              500 watt – 29 mins
Times given here are for a
650 watt oven. Decrease time
by 15 seconds per minute for
a 700 watt oven. Increase time
by 20 seconds per minute for a
500 watt oven.
KCAL 2000
SERVES 6-8

**500 g (1 lb) chicken pieces or
     wings**

Seasoning
1 tablespoon oyster sauce
1 tablespoon sugar
1 tablespoon honey
1 tablespoon light soy sauce
1 tablespoon sesame oil
1 teaspoon five-spice powder
pepper
salt
**2 teaspoons chilli powder or
     gochujang (Korean chilli paste)**

3 cups cornflakes
pepper

1 tablespoon margarine
2 eggs
**1 teaspoon chilli powder
     (for colour)**

½ tablespoon oil

*I have used a traditional Korean chicken dish, Tahk Chim, adding
cornflakes for a crispy layer that bakes well in the microwave oven.*

Preparation

Clean and skin chicken carefully. Drain pieces.

Mix seasoning ingredients and leave chicken to marinate in this
for 3-4 hours or overnight. (Refrigerate the chicken.) Turn pieces
in marinade and prick with a fork to allow marinade to permeate
meat.

Crush cornflakes between sheets of greaseproof paper with a
rolling pin, or use a blender. Add pepper to crushed cornflakes
and mix well.

Melt margarine in a dish for 30 seconds on High (100%). Beat
eggs till frothy, add melted margarine and chilli powder and mix
thoroughly.

Drain chicken pieces. (Marinade may be bottled in the freezer for
future use.)

Roll chicken in cornflake crumbs, dip in egg mixture, then roll in
cornflakes once more.

Microwave Cooking Method

Preheat a browning dish for 7 minutes on High (100%). Grease it
with ½ tablespoon oil and heat for another 30 seconds on High
(100%).

Arrange chicken pieces in the dish and cook on High (100%) for
9-10 minutes. Turn them once during the cycle. Do not cover
while cooking.

Cook on High (100%) for a further 5 minutes till crisp.

Note: The advantage of microwaving this dish is that it can be
cooked without the use of any oil. In fact, at the end of the
cooking cycle, chicken fat will have melted and seeped out,
leaving the chicken crisp and slightly crunchy.

Krispy Korean (156)

Salt 'n' Steam (159)

Salt 'n' Steam

PREPARATION: 5 mins
COOKING: 700 watt – 17 mins
650 watt – 22 mins
500 watt – 29 mins
Times given here are for a
650 watt oven. Decrease time
by 15 seconds per minute for
a 700 watt oven. Increase time
by 20 seconds per minute for a
500 watt oven.
KCAL 2800
SERVES 8

1 chicken, about 1½ kg (3⅓ lb)
2 teaspoons five-spice powder
2 teaspoons ginger juice
greaseproof paper
newspaper
3 kg (6½ lb) kitchen salt (the kind
obtained in bulk in the market,
not too coarse)

A Chinese recipe that utilises salt to encase then tenderise the chicken. The newspaper-wrapped chicken can be bundled into a parcel with sticking tape or raffia twine.

Preparation

Wash, clean and dry chicken thoroughly with kitchen paper. Rub insides with five-spice powder and ginger juice.

Wrap chicken in greaseproof paper, making sure there are 2 layers covering chicken. Tape or tie up with raffia into a parcel. Cover with a thick layer of salt and newspaper.

Half-fill a large casserole with salt, making a depression for chicken to sit on salt. Cover with more salt till chicken is encased. Cover with a lid (you may need to use an inverted plastic bowl). Make sure there are no gaps between lid and casserole: use masking tape to seal edges if necessary.

Microwave Cooking Method

Steam in the microwave oven for 22 minutes on Medium (70%). Stand chicken in salt for 10 minutes, covering with foil to allow it to cook further in its own heat.

Remove chicken carefully from salt and cut into serving-size pieces. Serve with chilli and garlic sauce and rice cooked in chicken stock.

Note: You may also steam the chicken without a casserole by wrapping in many layers of newspaper.

   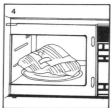

Pav's 20-Chilli Curry

PREPARATION: 15 mins
COOKING: 700 watt – 26 mins
650 watt – 35 mins
500 watt – 47 mins
Times given here are for a
650 watt oven. Decrease time
by 15 seconds per minute for
a 700 watt oven. Increase time
by 20 seconds per minute for a
500 watt oven.
KCAL 3050
SERVES 4-6

500 g (1 lb) chicken
20 dried chillies
1 teaspoon fennel
¼ cup flour
4 cloves garlic
20 shallots
1 large onion
1 coconut, grated
1 tablespoon oil
3 cloves
3 star anise
½ teaspoon sugar
salt
½ lime

I married into a family of excellent cooks and this is one of the recipes that was traditional at family gatherings. It is a Jaffna Tamil curry that young brides brought with them as they travelled to their new homes in Malaya. I have never been able to better my mother-in-law's curry, but this microwaved version is closest to the original. A little rice flour thickens it to a full-flavoured curry.

Preparation

Cut chicken into small serving-size pieces.

Plump up dried chillies by cooking with ½ cup water in a bowl for 3 minutes on High (100%). Drain water.

In a bowl, dry-roast fennel for 1 minute on Medium (70%), turning to distribute heat evenly. Grind into a paste with softened chillies.

Coat chicken well with chilli-fennel paste and flour.

Peel and slice garlic and shallots. Peel and slice onion into thin rings.

Blend grated coconut with ½ cup water and strain to extract ¾ cup thick coconut milk.

Microwave Cooking Method

Preheat a browning dish for 6 minutes on High (100%). Add 1 tablespoon oil and heat for 1 minute on High (100%).

Brown sliced garlic, shallots, cloves and star anise for 2 minutes on High (100%). Stir once or twice during the cycle.

Add chilli-fennel coated chicken pieces, cloves and star anise. Cook for 4 minutes on Medium (70%) and stir well.

Add coconut milk, sugar and salt. Cover loosely with kitchen paper to prevent splatters. Cook for 8 minutes on Medium (70%), stirring twice. Add onion rings at this stage and mix well with the chicken.

Remove kitchen paper, stir and add juice of ½ lime. Cook for another 10 minutes on Medium (70%). When gravy reaches thick consistency, remove dish from the oven and test for salt.

Serve in the same dish.

Chicken Sesame Salad

PREPARATION: 5 mins
COOKING: 700 watt – 11 mins
650 watt – 14 mins
500 watt – 19 mins
Times given here are for a
650 watt oven. Decrease time
by 15 seconds per minute for
a 700 watt oven. Increase time
by 20 seconds per minute for a
500 watt oven.
KCAL 1060
SERVES 4-6

**3 whole chicken breasts,
about 300 g (10 oz)**
½ teaspoon salt
½ teaspoon five-spice powder
1 tablespoon sesame seeds
3 sticks celery
½ teaspoon pepper
1 teaspoon ginger juice
1 tablespoon sesame oil
½ tablespoon groundnut oil
2 teaspoons light soy sauce
½ tablespoon dark soy sauce

Served cold, this chicken salad is an inspired cold dish, an adjunct to any main Chinese meal. Microwaving makes it simple and quick.

Preparation

Cover breasts in water in a glass bowl. Add salt and five-spice powder. Cover bowl with plastic wrap and microwave on High (100%) for 5 minutes, turning once.

Let the chicken stand for 3 minutes in stock, then remove from stock and cool. Debone chicken and cut into bite-size wedges or slivers.

Toast sesame seeds on kitchen paper for 3 minutes on High (100%). Stir once during the cycle to ensure even toasting.

Cut celery into 2½ cm (1 in) pieces.

Microwave Cooking Method

Boil stock on High (100%) for 5 minutes. Add celery and cook on High (100%) for 1 minute. Drain celery.

In a large bowl, mix celery, chicken, pepper, ginger juice, sesame oil, groundnut oil, soy sauce and sesame seeds.

Arrange decoratively and serve in a clear glass bowl as an entrée. (Provide forks or toothpicks.)

Chicken and Pork Hotpot

PREPARATION: 30 mins
COOKING: 700 watt – 29 mins
               650 watt – 39 mins
               500 watt – 52 mins
Times given here are for a
650 watt oven. Decrease time
by 15 seconds per minute for
a 700 watt oven. Increase time
by 20 seconds per minute for a
500 watt oven.
KCAL 2554
SERVES 4-6

6 shallots
2 cloves garlic
1 cup radishes
2 tomatoes
2-3 dried chillies
2 tablespoons sesame seeds
300 g (10 oz) diced chicken
300 g (10 oz) diced pork
½ tablespoon oil
2 tablespoons thick soy sauce
1 tablespoon light soy sauce
pepper
salt
1 tablespoon cornflour

Toyaji-kogi Wa Tahk-kogi, as this chicken and pork hot-pot is called, goes well with rice. The Koreans have a large range of meaty dishes and this one combining chicken and pork is from North Korea. Korean food, like Japanese, is served decoratively, in lacquer and stainless steel ware.

Preparation

Peel and chop shallots and garlic. Peel radish and cut into wafer thin slices. Cut tomatoes into wedges and break dried chillies into pieces.

Roast sesame seeds for 3 minutes on High (100%), stirring once during the cycle to roast evenly.

Cook chicken and pork with ½ cup water, covered with plastic wrap, on High (100%) for 10 minutes. Stir through plastic vent once or twice during the cycle. Reserve stock and keep meat warm.

Microwave Cooking Method

Heat a browning dish for 5 minutes on High (100%). Add ½ tablespoon oil and heat for 1 minute on High (100%), then sauté shallots and garlic till brown for 2 minutes on High (100%).

Add cooked chicken and pork and brown for 3 minutes on High (100%).

Add tomatoes, radishes, dried chillies, soy sauces, pepper, salt and ½ cup stock. Stir well and cover with plastic wrap. Cook for 10 minutes on High (100%).

Blend cornflour with ½ cup of the remaining stock till smooth. Add this to the dish and cook for 5 minutes on High (100%), stirring once during the cycle.

Add salt and pepper to taste. Garnish with toasted sesame seeds and serve hot with rice and *kimchee*, the spicy Korean pickle.

Baked Chicken Mindanao

PREPARATION: 15 mins
COOKING: 700 watt – 16 mins
               650 watt – 22 mins
               500 watt – 29 mins
Times given here are for a
650 watt oven. Decrease time
by 15 seconds per minute for
a 700 watt oven. Increase time
by 20 seconds per minute for a
500 watt oven.
KCAL 2700
SERVES: 4-6

500 g (1 lb) chicken
1 tablespoon light soy sauce
1 teaspoon garlic salt
1 tablespoon tabasco
1 teaspoon ginger juice
½ teaspoon pepper
5 tablespoons flour
1 teaspoon chilli powder
1 egg, beaten
¾ cup grated coconut
1 teaspoon oil
lemon or lime wedges

This Filipino dish combines the Malay, American, Polynesian and Spanish influences that have gone into the making of the colourful nation. An elegant dish that may be served as an entrée or as part of the main course.

Preparation

Wash and clean chicken, and cut into serving-size pieces. Rub with soy sauce, garlic salt, tabasco and ginger juice so that flavours penetrate the meat. Refrigerate for 2 hours.

Mix pepper, flour and chilli powder together. Roll chicken in flour mixture.

Dip chicken in beaten egg and roll in fresh coconut flakes.

Microwave Cooking Method

Heat a browning dish for 6 minutes on High (100%). Add oil and heat for 30 seconds on High (100%).

Place chicken in dish, pressing down each piece so it sizzles on contact. Turn over to brown the other side. Continue till all pieces are done.

Bake, uncovered, for 15 minutes on High (100%), turning all pieces after each 5-minute cycle.

Serve garnished with lemon or lime wedges. This chicken can be served with baked sweet potatoes (4 minutes each on High/100%) and a fresh green salad.

Note: Microwaving this dish produces superior results. Baked Chicken Mindanao needs no grease or oil while baking. In fact, any fat in the chicken seeps out slowly, crisping the coconut layer and imparting a delicious nutty flavour to the chicken.

Murgh I Salaam

PREPARATION: 15 mins
COOKING: 700 watt – 24 mins
          650 watt – 32 mins
          500 watt – 43 mins
Times given here are for a
650 watt oven. Decrease time
by 15 seconds per minute for
a 700 watt oven. Increase time
by 20 seconds per minute for a
500 watt oven.
KCAL 4675
SERVES 6-8

1 chicken, about 1½ kg (3⅓ lb)
4 dried chillies
4 onions
6 cloves garlic
1 × 1 cm (½ × ½ in) ginger
150 g (5 oz) almonds
½ teaspoon cloves
6 cardamoms
2 star anise
3 tablespoons ghee
salt
pepper
1 tablespoon chickpea flour
   (besan)
4 stalks coriander

Pakistani dish traditionally roasted in clay ovens. Students living on far-flung campuses are often drawn together by common food ties. Roshni was a beautiful Pakistani girl whose husband was a graduate student. We were living together on campus in Canada and could only communicate through our daughters as Roshni spoke no English. My friend was a brilliant cook though she used the 'estimate' method and it was left to me to work out exact porportions. This was her favourite dish.

Preparation

Carefully skin chicken and prick all over with a skewer so that marinade will penetrate meat.

Plump up dried chillies in ¼ cup water by cooking on High (100%) for 1½ minutes.

Peel and blend or pound onions, garlic and ginger with softened chillies and almonds to form a paste.

Pound cloves, cardamoms and star anise and mix these spices with the wet blended mixture.

Melt ghee in 40 seconds on High (100%) and mix with the combined ingredients, salt and pepper. Bind the whole with chickpea flour.

Rub inside of chicken with a little of this marinade and cover chicken with the rest of it.

Microwave Cooking Method

Place chicken in a greased ovenproof dish and microwave on High (100%) for 15 minutes.

Turn chicken over, spoon marinade over chicken and cook for another 15 minutes on High (100%).

Lay chicken on its back and cover with foil to stand for 10 minutes.

Carve chicken, garnish with coriander leaves and serve with saffron rice.

Chicken Teriyaki

PREPARATION: 15 mins
COOKING: 700 watt – 18 mins
650 watt – 24 mins
500 watt – 32 mins
Times given here are for a
650 watt oven. Decrease time
by 15 seconds per minute for
a 700 watt oven. Increase time
by 20 seconds per minute for a
500 watt oven.
KCAL 4900
SERVES 6-8

1 kg (2¼ lb) chicken
1 × 1 cm (½ × ½ in) ginger
2 cloves garlic
4 tablespoons *tamari shoyu*
3 tablespoons sugar
4 tablespoons *sake* or *mirin*
½ teaspoon salt
1 tablespoon groundnut oil
1 teaspoon cornflour

No Japanese meal is complete without one of the Teriyaki dishes, beef or chicken being the popular choice. While the grilled effect is not achieved in a microwave oven, the result is just as tasty.

Preparation

Cut chicken into thin strips, removing fat from meat.

Peel and blend ginger and garlic to a paste. Mix this with *tamari shoyu,* sugar, *sake* or *mirin,* salt and oil (reserving 1 teaspoon to grease the browning dish). Marinate chicken in this mixture.

Microwave Cooking Method

Preheat a browning dish for 6 minutes on High (100%). Add 1 teaspoon oil. Place chicken in the greased dish and cook on High (100%) for 10 minutes.

Turn chicken over, baste with the sauce that collects in the dish and cook on Medium (70%) for 6 minutes.

Pour sauce into a separate dish and let chicken stand, covered with foil.

Add cornflour to sauce to thicken it and cook for 2 minutes on High (100%).

Arrange chicken decoratively on a flat platter and leave space for garnish. Pour thickened sauce over chicken and garnish with red pickled ginger and pickled radish so that there is a pleasant colour contrast of pickles and chicken.

Serve hot with rice.

Note: The microwave oven is best for Japanese cooking because it cooks instantly, cleanly and without heat. The cook is able to serve a dinner without the bother of fumes, smoke or sweat.

Tori No Kushiyaki

PREPARATION: 15 mins
COOKING: 700 watt – 9-17 mins
         650 watt – 12-23 mins
         500 watt – 16-31 mins
Times given here are for a
650 watt oven. Decrease time
by 15 seconds per minute for
a 700 watt oven. Increase time
by 20 seconds per minute for a
500 watt oven.
KCAL 639
SERVES 4

250 g (8 oz) chicken breasts
2 large onions
250 g (8 oz) red capsicum

Marinade
2 tablespoons *mirin* or sweet
  sherry
2 tablespoons *tamari shoyu*
1 teaspoon sugar
½ teaspoon grated ginger
½ teaspoon pounded garlic

16 wooden skewers
2 tablespoons oil

Sauce
soy sauce
sugar
mirin
grated ginger
red pickled ginger

This is chicken on skewers, a Japanese version of the kebab which can be varied by changing the accompanying vegetables. Use mushrooms or abalone, young corn, or even bamboo shoots if you want variety.

Preparation

Cut chicken into 3 cm (1¼ in) pieces.

Peel onions. Cut onions and capsicum into 3 cm (1¼ in) wedges.

Marinate chicken in a mixture of marinade ingredients, refrigerating for 2-4 hours, preferably overnight.

Soak wooden skewers in 1 tablespoon oil and ½ cup water for 4 hours before use.

Skewer chicken pieces, alternating with onion and capsicum wedges. Marinade may be poured off into a jar and re-used, if refrigerated properly.

Microwave Cooking Method

Heat a browning dish on High (100%) for 7 minutes.

Pour ½ tablespoon oil into the hot browning dish and place chicken on skewers on oil, pressing them into the oil to sear edges while the dish is still hot.

Cook on High (100%) for 2 minutes. Open oven door, baste chicken with marinade and turn skewers over to cook on High (100%) for 2 minutes more. Keep hot under foil till all skewers have been cooked. (Chicken does not take long to cook.) You may need to wash the browning dish and heat it again as a dirty browning dish is ineffective.

Serve with sauce and bowls of steaming hot rice.

Sauce: Combine sauce ingredients (except pickled ginger) in a bowl and cook on High (100%) for 1 minute to dissolve sugar. Add red pickled ginger and divide sauce into 4 sauce dishes as a dip for Kushiyaki.

Korean Pot Stew (Tahk Pok-Kum)

PREPARATION: 15 mins
COOKING: 700 watt – 23 mins
650 watt – 31 mins
500 watt – 41 mins
Times given here are for a
650 watt oven. Decrease time
by 15 seconds per minute for
a 700 watt oven. Increase time
by 20 seconds per minute for a
500 watt oven.
KCAL 1856
SERVES 4-6

600 g (1⅓ lb) chicken pieces
3 cloves garlic
8-10 shallots
1 × 1 cm (½ × ½ in) ginger
2 red chillies
100 g (3½ oz) straw mushrooms
2 tablespoons sesame seeds
oil
1 teaspoon five-spice powder
3 tablespoons light soy sauce
1 tablespoon sugar
salt
pepper
1 tablespoon cornflour
½ cup chicken stock
thin strips of pickled cabbage

This dish, made to be eaten on cold nights, is equally tasty eaten with rice on a warm night. The Koreans use chilli and soy sauce with great success and chicken cooked this way is particularly tasty.

Preparation

Wash chicken and pat dry with kitchen paper.

Peel and slice garlic, shallots and ginger into thin slices. Do not mix the three ingredients.

Slit chillies lengthwise and slice mushrooms.

Roast sesame seeds for 2 minutes on High (100%). Stir after 1 minute of the cycle to ensure even roasting.

Microwave Cooking Method

Heat 1 tablespoon oil on High (100%) for 2 minutes. Add garlic and ginger and cook on High (100%) for 30 seconds. Add shallots and cook on High (100%) for 1 minute.

Arrange chicken pieces over the hot mixture so larger portions are nearer the edge of the bowl.

Mix five-spice powder, slit red chillies, mushrooms, soy sauce, sugar, salt, pepper, cornflour and chicken stock till cornflour is even and smooth.

Stir sauce well and spoon over chicken, making sure meat is coated. Cover loosely with plastic wrap and cook on High (100%) for 15 minutes.

Stir carefully and rearrange pieces if necessary. Cook on Medium (70%) for 10 minutes. Add roasted sesame seeds.

Let dish stand, covered in foil, for at least 8 minutes. Test for salt and pepper sufficiency before garnishing with thin strips of pickled cabbage.

Green Thai Chicken

PREPARATION: 30 mins
COOKING: 700 watt – 19 mins
          650 watt – 25 mins
          500 watt – 33 mins
Times given here are for a
650 watt oven. Decrease time
by 15 seconds per minute for
a 700 watt oven. Increase time
by 20 seconds per minute for a
500 watt oven.
KCAL 2685
SERVES 4-6

1 kg (2¼ lb) chicken
salt

A
6 green chillies
1 teaspoon dried shrimp paste
(kapee)
1 shallot
2 cloves garlic
rind of ½ lemon
1 tablespoon coriander root
3-4 stalks coriander leaves
2 stalks lemon grass
2 stalks dried lesser galangal
(krachai)
2 cm (¾ in) dried galangal

1 coconut, grated

B
1 tablespoon coriander powder
1 teaspoon cummin powder
½ teaspoon turmeric powder
1 tablespoon fish sauce (nam pla)

salt
pepper
4 stalks coriander

Although the chilli in Thai food seems excessive, the blend of spices added to green curries tempers the 'heat', making Thai food a memorable experience for connoisseurs.

Preparation

Cut chicken into pieces and rub salt into skin to clean and remove some of the moisture.

Blend or grind all ingredients listed under 'A' till smooth.

Add ½ cup water to grated coconut and blend to extract coconut milk. Strain for 1½-2 cups thick coconut milk.

Microwave Cooking Method

Heat thick coconut milk uncovered on High (100%) for 6 minutes until it boils. Continue to boil on High (100%) for 2 minutes.

Add blended ingredients ('A'), mix well and cook on High (100%) for 3 minutes.

Stir chicken pieces into paste and cook on Medium (70%) for 4 minutes.

Add ingredients listed under 'B'. Stir well and cook on Medium (70%) for 10 minutes.

Stir and test for salt and pepper sufficiency. Add coriander leaves for garnish.

Note: This dish will have a thin, hot gravy which is slightly tart and chilli hot. For a hotter taste, add chopped chillies at the end.

Honey-braised Chicken

PREPARATION: 10 mins
COOKING: 700 watt – 21 mins
          650 watt – 28 mins
          500 watt – 37 mins
Times given here are for a
650 watt oven. Decrease time
by 15 seconds per minute for
a 700 watt oven. Increase time
by 20 seconds per minute for a
500 watt oven.
KCAL 3318
SERVES 6

1 chicken, about 1½ kg (3⅓ lb)
2 star anise
1 clove garlic
5 slices ginger
rind of ½ orange
1 tablespoon honey
2 tablespoons light soy sauce
1 tablespoon oyster sauce
½ teaspoon sesame oil

Chicken roasted in a microwave oven is tasty and moist as the meat cooks from inside so the whole bird is tender. The dark sauces create a beautiful golden colour, as inviting as when cooked in a conventional oven.

Preparation

Wash chicken and pat dry with a towel.

Pound star anise, garlic and ginger together. Bruise the orange rind.

Rub chicken, inside and out, with bruised orange rind, then coat with pounded mixture.

Mix honey, soy sauce, oyster sauce and sesame oil and brush chicken skin with this sauce mixture.

Microwave Cooking Method

Cook chicken in a casserole on High (100%) for 15 minutes. Stop cycle after 5-6 minutes to baste the chicken, then continue till cycle is complete.

Turn chicken and cook on High (100%) for another 13 minutes.

Cover with foil and leave to stand while preparing the rest of the meal. Carve into pieces and serve with slices of lemon, sweet red ginger and a mixture of salt and pepper roasted together.

Note: Size of chicken determines the cooking time required. Every 100 g (3½ oz) needs 1 minute on High (100%) for each side.

Sichuan Chicken and Cashew Nuts

PREPARATION: 10 mins
COOKING: 700 watt – 15 mins
650 watt – 21 mins
500 watt – 27 mins
Times given here are for a
650 watt oven. Decrease time
by 15 seconds per minute for
a 700 watt oven. Increase time
by 20 seconds per minute for a
500 watt oven.
KCAL 1314
SERVES 4-6

300 g (10 oz) chicken meat
100 g (3½ oz) cashew nuts
2 cloves garlic
2 × 2 cm (¾ × ¾ in) ginger
300 g (10 oz) cauliflower or
broccoli
1 tablespoon dark soy sauce
1 tablespoon light soy sauce
1 tablespoon sherry
1 tablespoon cornflour
2 tablespoons groundnut oil
2 dried red chillies
salt
pepper

A delicious blend of cashew nuts and dried chillies gives this dish a different flavour. It is quick and convenient when cooked in the microwave oven and can be frozen for later, as long as the nuts are added at the final warming stage.

Preparation

Skin chicken and slice meat into strips.

Toast cashew nuts on kitchen paper on High (100%) for 3 minutes, turning them once during the cycle.

Peel and chop garlic. Grate ginger and strain for juice. Cut vegetable into flowerettes.

Marinate chicken in a mixture of soy sauces, sherry, cornflour and ginger juice.

Microwave Cooking Method

Heat a browning dish for 7 minutes on High (100%). Add oil and cook on High (100%) for 30 seconds. Add dried chillies and chopped garlic and brown by stirring for a short time. Do not cook.

Drain chicken from marinade and add to the hot dish. Let it sizzle and brown in hot oil as you stir. Cook on High (100%) for 3 minutes, stopping cycle to stir once or twice.

Add vegetable and marinade. Cook, covered, on Medium (70%) for 7 minutes or till chicken is tender, stirring to prevent cornflour thickening unevenly. Test for seasoning, adding salt only if required. Let it stand for 3 minutes.

Sprinkle with roasted cashew nuts and serve with hot rice.

Enche Kabin (Spicy Roast Chicken)

PREPARATION: 12 mins
COOKING: 700 watt – 16 mins
           650 watt – 21 mins
           500 watt – 28 mins
Times given here are for a
650 watt oven. Decrease time
by 15 seconds per minute for
a 700 watt oven. Increase time
by 20 seconds per minute for a
500 watt oven.
KCAL 2429
SERVES 4

1 chicken, about 1 kg (2¼ lb)
2 tablespoons sugar
2 teaspoons five-spice powder
½ teaspoon pepper
salt

Marinade
1 tablespoon evaporated milk
2 tablespoons light soy sauce
2 cloves garlic, pounded
2 tablespoons ginger juice
1 teaspoon malt sugar
1 teaspoon dry sherry or Chinese
   wine

Kabin was probably a pidgin version of 'capon' but I prefer to link the name to some exotic personage from the past perhaps responsible for this famous Straits Chinese dish. (Enche is the old Malay spelling of Encik, which is equivalent to 'Mister'.) The best Enche Kabin chicken comes from a seaside restaurant in Batu Ferringhi where the senses are sharpened by the scent of frangipanni and the murmur of rippling waves.

Preparation

Clean chicken and cut into serving pieces. Pat dry with a paper towel and rub with a mixture of sugar, five-spice powder, pepper and salt.

Combine marinade ingredients. Place chicken in a large shallow casserole and pour marinade over chicken. Stir so chicken is well coated. Refrigerate for at least 4 hours. Chicken will taste better if left marinating in the refrigerator overnight.

Microwave Cooking Method

Drain off marinade and keep for basting. (Any marinade left over can be frozen for re-use.)

Cover casserole with kitchen paper and cook on High (100%) for 8 minutes. Turn chicken and baste with some marinade. Cook on High (100%) for another 8 minutes.

Turn chicken over and rotate casserole 180°. Cook for 5 minutes, covered with kitchen paper to prevent splatters.

If you prefer a darker roasted skin effect, place chicken under a conventional grill for 3-4 minutes.

Serve with sliced cucumber and a dip of soy sauce, vinegar and sugar combined.

Ginger Chicken

PREPARATION: 10 mins
COOKING: 700 watt – 16 mins
             650 watt – 21½ mins
             500 watt – 28½ mins
Times given here are for a
650 watt oven. Decrease time
by 15 seconds per minute for
a 700 watt oven. Increase time
by 20 seconds per minute for a
500 watt oven.
KCAL 970
SERVES 4

500 g (1 lb) chicken pieces
1 tablespoon Chinese wine
1 teaspoon dark soy sauce
1 teaspoon cornflour
2 cloves garlic
4 shallots
10 cm (4 in) length young ginger
2 tablespoons sesame oil
1 teaspoon salt
1 teaspoon pepper

I associate this chicken with babies, maternity leave and that special cloistered period when one is pampered by the family and fed the choicest herbs and viands – tender ginger for the womb, brandy and herbs for 'heat', sesame oil for baby's milk. This recipe, however, is adapted for everyday use as chicken cooked in sesame oil is succulent and delicious in any meal.

Preparation

Cut chicken into pieces and score skin wherever possible to allow marinade to penetrate.

Mix Chinese wine, soy sauce and cornflour to a smooth paste. Stir marinade into chicken and let it stand for a while to allow maximum absorption.

Peel and slice garlic and shallots. Peel and shred ginger into fine strips.

Microwave Cooking Method

Place chicken and marinade in a bowl. Cover with plastic wrap and cook for 6 minutes on High (100%). Stir chicken once during the cycle.

Preheat a browning dish for 7 minutes on High (100%). Add sesame oil and heat for another 30 seconds on High (100%).

Add sliced garlic, shallots and ginger shreds. Cook, uncovered, for 1 minute on High (100%).

Add chicken, salt and pepper. Stir well and cook, covered with plastic wrap, for 5 minutes on High (100%). Serve at once.

Ginza Sesame Chicken

PREPARATION: 6 mins
COOKING: 700 watt – 17 mins
          650 watt – 23 mins
          500 watt – 31 mins
Times given here are for a
650 watt oven. Decrease time
by 15 seconds per minute for
a 700 watt oven. Increase time
by 20 seconds per minute for a
500 watt oven.
KCAL 1175
SERVES 6

6 chicken breasts or thighs
¼ cup _miri_ or dry sherry
3 tablespoons _tamari shoyu_
1 teaspoon mustard powder
salt
pepper
2 tablespoons sesame seeds
6 stalks coriander or
**   Chinese coriander**

An ideal meal for weight watchers tired of bland, conscience-salving diets. Try this superb blend of spices and chicken cooked, without any oil, to perfection in the microwave oven.

Preparation

Wash and dry chicken pieces. Cut away skin.

Mix all seasoning together with chicken, leaving chicken to marinate for at least 6 hours or overnight in the refrigerator.

Toast sesame seeds for 3 minutes on High (100%), stirring once during the cycle.

Chop coriander leaves finely.

Microwave Cooking Method

Arrange chicken pieces on the rack or upturned plate in a shallow casserole. Cook for 15 minutes on High (100%), covered loosely with plastic wrap.

Brush with marinade and cook for 5 minutes on Medium (70%), uncovered.

Remove and roll in toasted sesame seeds.

Cut chicken into serving-size pieces before presenting at the table garnished with a few sprigs of coriander leaves.

Note: Japanese dishes are inspired in their subtle decoration. Arrange the slices of chicken alternately with sprigs of coriander on a light coloured compote for effect.

EGGS

Microtips on Cooking Eggs

Never attempt to boil an egg in its shell in the microwave oven. Microwaves enter the porous shell very quickly and heat up the air sac within. When air is heated rapidly, it expands and bursts the shell and the egg explodes.

Egg yolk cooks very fast because of its fat content, so if cooking an egg whole, prick the membrane of the yolk so that any gas built up can escape. Always undercook eggs, and let the heat built up within the egg finish the cooking process. Overcooked eggs are rubbery in texture. It is advisable to watch the microwave oven while cooking as times given are only an approximate guide.

It is possible to cook an egg whole without pricking the membrane of the yolk. Break the egg into a cup or bowl. Gently beat the egg white with the tip of a fork, then cook egg as usual.

Basic Scrambled Eggs

PREPARATION: 2 mins
COOKING: 700 watt – 1 min 44 secs
           650 watt – 2 mins 20 secs
           500 watt – 3 mins 6 secs
Times given here are for a 650 watt oven. Decrease time by 15 seconds per minute for a 700 watt oven. Increase time by 20 seconds per minute for a 500 watt oven.
KCAL 527
SERVES 4

3 eggs
4 tablespoons milk
salt
pepper
nutmeg
1 tablespoon butter

Preparation

Beat eggs together till creamy.

Add milk, salt, pepper and nutmeg and mix well.

Microwave Cooking Method

In a plastic or glass bowl, melt butter on High (100%) for 30 seconds – *not longer*.

Add creamed eggs and cook on High (100%) for 50 seconds. Whisk with a fork and return to the oven to cook on High (100%) for 50 seconds. Fluff it up with a fork and cook on High (100%) for another 10 seconds.

Left to right: Pulau Pinang Serikaya (178)
and Scrambled Eggs (174)

Top to bottom: Gingered Carrots (185), Vientianne Green Beans (183) and Mint Curried Potato Balls (186)

Variations:

1   Add 2 tablespoons chopped parsley or green chilli instead of nutmeg.

2   Add 1 small chopped tomato and chopped or sliced button mushrooms.

3   Add 1 chopped onion to melted butter and cook for 1 minute on High (100%) before adding eggs to the bowl.

4   Add 2 tablespoons grated cheese to eggs.

Note: You can stir, whisk or fluff egg while bowl sits in the microwave oven, as all these can be done by merely reaching into the oven. Remember to remove metal fork or whisk before resuming the cooking cycle.

Bacon and Eggs on Toast

PREPARATION: 2 mins
COOKING: 700 watt – 7 mins 30 secs
                650 watt – 10 mins
                500 watt – 13 mins 20 secs
Times given here are for a 650 watt oven. Decrease time by 15 seconds per minute for a 700 watt oven. Increase time by 20 seconds per minute for a 500 watt oven.
KCAL 611
SERVES 2

4 pieces bacon
2 eggs
1 tablespoon butter
2 slices toast
1 tomato, sliced

Microwave Cooking Method

Heat a browning dish for 7 minutes on High (100%). Place bacon in the hot dish. It will start cooking at once. Turn over and cook for 1 minute on High (100%).

Add butter which will melt. (You may prefer to leave out the butter and use bacon fat to cook eggs.)

Break eggs into fat, pricking yolk with a fork. Cook for 2 minutes on High (100%).

Slide an egg and 2 rashers onto each slice of toast and top with slices of tomato.

Pulau Pinang Serikaya

PREPARATION: 20 mins
COOKING: 700 watt – 18 mins
          650 watt – 24 mins
          500 watt – 32 mins
Times given here are for a
650 watt oven. Decrease time
by 15 seconds per minute for
a 700 watt oven. Increase time
by 20 seconds per minute for a
500 watt oven.
KCAL 3500
SERVES 10

1 coconut, grated
10 eggs
500 g (1 lb) castor sugar
1 teaspoon vanilla essence
2 screwpine leaves (*daun*
**   *pandan*), shredded**
**   lengthwise and knotted**

Serikaya is the Malaysian coconut custard that was used to sweeten bread long before western-style jams found their way into local homes. It was, and still is, possible to buy extra sweet, caramel-like kaya *packed into used condensed milk cans. It is difficult to match the experience of sinking one's teeth into a lightly toasted and buttered slice of bread spread thickly with* kaya.

Preparation

Extract ½ cup thick coconut milk from the grated coconut.

Break eggs into a deep ovenproof casserole and beat gently with a fork or whisk, making sure eggs do not turn too frothy.

Add sugar gradually while beating then add vanilla essence and screwpine leaves that have been torn into long shreds and tied into a knot.

Finally, add thick coconut milk and continue to beat till sugar has dissolved. Strain to remove dregs (use a fine-mesh sieve).

Microwave Cooking Method

Place 2 pieces of absorbent kitchen paper between casserole and lid to absorb moisture.

Cook for 15 minutes on Low (30%), stirring 2 or 3 times during the cycle.

Cook for 4 minutes on Medium (70%), then rotate the casserole.

Cook for 5 minutes more on Medium (70%).

When Serikaya is ready, there will be a frothy patch in the centre. This is normal.

Change the sheets of absorbent paper between the casserole and lid and cool before refrigerating in a sterilised jar.

Ekuri

PREPARATION: 5 mins
COOKING: 700 watt – 9 mins
650 watt – 12 mins
500 watt – 16 mins
Times given here are for a
650 watt oven. Decrease time
by 15 seconds per minute for
a 700 watt oven. Increase time
by 20 seconds per minute for a
500 watt oven.
KCAL 961
SERVES 4

4 eggs
1 onion
1 × 1 cm (½ × ½ in) ginger
2-3 stalks coriander
1 chilli
2 tomatoes
1 tablespoon butter
salt
pepper
4 slices toast

The Parsees are a religious community in India who are Persian in origin. They have adapted to many Indian cultural ways, and this Parsee egg recipe is one example. Ekuri converts well to microwave cooking as it needs only short bursts of power from the microwave oven to cook. Eggs cook quickly so it is best to watch the oven during the cooking.

Preparation

Beat eggs lightly. Peel onion and ginger and chop finely. Chop coriander leaves and chilli.

Peel and quarter tomatoes.

Microwave Cooking Method

Heat a browning dish for 7 minutes on High (100%). Add butter, onion, ginger and chilli and cook on High (100%) for 2 minutes, stopping cycle twice to stir.

Add tomatoes and cook on High (100%) for 1 minute.

Pour in eggs and stir into ingredients. Cook for 30 seconds on High (100%), then stir well.

Add salt and pepper. Cook for another 1½ minutes on High (100%), stopping halfway through the cycle to stir well.

Pile on buttered toast or serve with rice, garnished with chopped coriander leaves.

VEGETABLES

Microtips on Cooking Vegetables

Cook vegetables just before you need to serve them. Vegetables may be cooked in plastic bags, then taken out and seasoned. Check individual recipes and 'Basic Stir-fried Vegetables'. A general rule is that root vegetables need more cooking time than watery vegetables, as, for example, carrot and cauliflower would against tomato and zucchini.

Cut down on salt. Microwave cooking is fast and releases salts already present in food. Cut vegetables into pieces of equal size and place thicker parts such as stems on the outer edges of the dish so cooking is even.

Garlic, Ginger and Onion Mix. Use this 'starter' blend for sautéeing meats and vegetables to cut down on time spent in the kitchen and the need to peel or handle garlic or onion each day. Working women will realise that it is almost impossible to look glamorous and efficient at work while the whiff of garlic lurks at your fingertips!

You need 200 g (6⅔ oz) ginger, the same quantity of garlic and twice as much onion. Wash and dry thoroughly after peeling. Blend together using a little vinegar to facilitate blending. Add ½ teaspoon salt and freeze in sterilised bottles. Cover tightly or your freezer may reek of garlic.

To use this blend, merely chop off a piece and defrost on Low (30%) for 1 minute before using it. Do not throw a frozen piece of mix into hot oil as ice crystals will splatter oil.

Basic Stir-fried Vegetables

PREPARATION: 10 mins
COOKING: 700 watt – 12 mins
650 watt – 17 mins
500 watt – 22 mins
Times given here are for a
650 watt oven. Decrease time
by 15 seconds per minute for
a 700 watt oven. Increase time
by 20 seconds per minute for a
500 watt oven.
KCAL 482
SERVES 4

1 clove garlic
2 large onions
2 slices ginger
2 green peppers
1 large carrot
6 pieces cauliflower
2 tablespoons peas
a few pieces canned baby corn
1 tablespoon butter or oil
1 stock cube, crumbled

Alternatives:
snowpeas
mushrooms
celery
cabbage

This recipe is the basis for all vegetable cooking. Because vegetables cook so quickly in the microwave oven, they retain more of their natural goodness than when boiled.

Preparation

Peel and chop garlic. Peel and quarter onions.

Prepare peppers and carrot by slicing diagonally. Break cauliflower into bite-size pieces. Peas should be used straight from the freezer. Drain baby corn.

Microwave Cooking Method

Heat a browning dish for 6 minutes on High (100%). Add butter or oil which should sizzle. Heat for 30 seconds on High (100%).

Brown garlic, onions and ginger for 2 minutes on High (100%). Stir often during the cycle.

Add sliced carrot and cauliflower pieces. Cover loosely with plastic wrap and cook for 5 minutes on High (100%). Uncover by lifting plastic on the side away from you. Stir carefully.

Add softer vegetables and crumbled stock cube. Stir. Cook, covered, for 3 minutes on High (100%). Stir once during cycle.

Serve hot.

Note: If you wish to add a little prawn, crab, beef or pork, do so before you add softer vegetables and cook for 2 minutes on High (100%).

Sumatran Gado-Gado

PREPARATION: 20 mins
COOKING: 700 watt – 23 mins
                650 watt – 30 mins
                500 watt – 40 mins
Times given here are for a
650 watt oven. Decrease time
by 15 seconds per minute for
a 700 watt oven. Increase time
by 20 seconds per minute for a
500 watt oven.
KCAL 1916
SERVES 6

200 g (6⅔ oz) water convolvulus
  (kangkung)
200 g (6⅔ oz) tender long beans
2 cucumbers, peeled
1 small turnip, peeled
200 g (6⅔ oz) cabbage
2 firm soybean squares
300 g (10 oz) beansprouts
3 hardboiled eggs
3 potatoes

Sauce
20 red chillies
10 shallots
2 teaspoons sesame seeds
2 cm (¾ in) square dried shrimp
  paste (belacan)
3 cm (1¼ in) square tamarind
  paste
3 cm (1¼ in) square palm sugar
1 cup crunchy peanut butter
1 cup coconut milk
½ tablespoon black shrimp paste
  (haeko or petis)

The Gado-Gado may be Indonesian in origin but it is also served in Malaysia and Singapore. The distinctive peanut sauce dresses up even the plainest of vegetables and makes a festive centrepiece for the dinner table. It is a close relative to the unpretentious Rojak, a Malaysian salad.

Preparation

VEGETABLE PLATTER:

Wash and cut *kangkung*, long beans, cucumber and turnip into 5 cm (2 in) lengths. Reduce cucumber and turnips further to thin ½ cm (¼ in) strips. Cucumber and turnip do not require cooking.

Shred cabbage. Halve the soybean square, then cut each half into ½ cm (¼ in) thick slices, across the width. 'Top and tail' beansprouts and quarter eggs lengthwise.

Cook potatoes, allowing 4 minutes to cook each on High (100%). Peel and cube.

Put *kangkung*, long beans and cabbage into a plastic bag and cook for 3 minutes on High (100%) then drain.

Cook beansprouts in a plastic bag for 1 minute on High (100%), then drain.

Cool and arrange all vegetables and egg quarters on a platter, cover with plastic wrap and refrigerate until needed.

SAUCE:

Grind or pound red chillies and shallots together.

Toast sesame seeds for 2 minutes on High (100%). Stir once about halfway through the cycle for even toasting.

Toast dried shrimp paste for 3 minutes on High (100%), turning once during the cycle.

Work tamarind paste with ½ cup water. Strain. This should produce ½ cup thick tamarind juice.

Break up palm sugar and bring to a boil with ½ cup water in 4 minutes on High (100%). Do not overboil – the syrup should just begin to bubble. Strain.

In a deep bowl, mix all sauce ingredients together.

Microwave Cooking Method

Most of the cooking has been done, of course, and all that remains is to heat the combined sauce ingredients.

Cook sauce for 3 minutes on High (100%) and stir. Continue cooking for 2 minutes on Medium (70%), adding more water if mixture is too thick. Season to taste.

Remove from heat, cool and pour over prepared vegetables.

Vientianne Green Beans

PREPARATION: 4 mins
COOKING: 700 watt – 7 mins
          650 watt – 10 mins
          500 watt – 13 mins
Times given here are for a 650 watt oven. Decrease time by 15 seconds per minute for a 700 watt oven. Increase time by 20 seconds per minute for a 500 watt oven.
KCAL 294
SERVES 4-6

250 g (8 oz) french beans or snowpeas
1 clove garlic
1 tablespoon butter or oil
½ cup blanched almonds
salt

Green french beans take on glamour with almonds.

Preparation

String and cut beans into diagonal slices. If using snowpeas, string and use whole. Slice garlic.

Melt butter on High (30%) for 30 seconds on a flat plate. Toast almonds and garlic in butter on High (100%) for 3 minutes, turning once.

Microwave Cooking Method

In a buttered serving dish, microwave beans or snowpeas on High (100%) for 4 minutes, covered loosely with plastic wrap. Stir, add garlic, almonds and salt.

Cook, uncovered, for 2 minutes on High (100%).

Note: Vegetables should be eaten as soon as they are cooked, as standing changes their crisp and fresh appearance. Microwave vegetables in their serving dish while the table is being set for dinner.

Precious Jade Stir-Fry

PREPARATION: 10 mins
COOKING: 700 watt – 10 mins
              650 watt – 13 mins
              500 watt – 17½ mins
Times given here are for a
650 watt oven. Decrease time
by 15 seconds per minute for
a 700 watt oven. Increase time
by 20 seconds per minute for a
500 watt oven.
KCAL 825
SERVES 4-6

200 g (7 oz) chicken meat
2 × 2 cm (¾ × ¾ in) ginger
1 tablespoon soy sauce
2 tablespoons Chinese cooking
   wine
1 teaspoon honey
1 tablespoon cornflour
200 g (7 oz) snow peas
200 g (7 oz) french beans
1½ tablespoons vegetable oil
2 cloves garlic, sliced
50 g (2 oz) almond slivers

The microwave oven retains vegetable colours and flavours as cooking is fast. Normally a toss and a turn are all that is needed to cook the vegetables which contrast artistically with the pearly morsels of chicken.

Preparation

Remove skin from chicken and slice meat thinly across the grain.

Pound ginger to extract juice.

In a bowl, mix chicken meat with soy sauce, cooking wine, honey, ginger juice and cornflour. Leave chicken in marinade for 30 minutes.

String snow peas and french beans. Slice diagonally into 5 cm (2 in) lengths.

Microwave Cooking Method

Preheat browning dish for 7 minutes on High (100%).

Add oil and heat for 30 seconds on High (100%). Add garlic slices which will sizzle at once.

Add chicken, without marinade. Toss chicken in oil, uncovered, for 2 minutes on High (100%).

Stir, then add snow peas and french beans. Cook for 3 minutes on High (100%), covered with a plastic wrap.

Stir in marinade and cook for 1 minute more on High (100%).

Serve hot, sprinkled with almond slivers.

Gingered Carrots

PREPARATION: 4 mins
COOKING: 700 watt – 8-9 mins
650 watt – 10-12 mins
500 watt – 14-17 mins
Times given here are for a
650 watt oven. Decrease time
by 15 seconds per minute for
a 700 watt oven. Increase time
by 20 seconds per minute for a
500 watt oven.
KCAL 600
SERVES 4-6

500 g (1 lb) baby carrots
1 tablespoon butter
½ teaspoon honey
2 teaspoons ginger juice
1 wedge lemon
sprig of parsley

Simple and tasty as a vegetable on its own, and a quick and easy accompaniment for roasts or Chinese food.

Preparation

Scrape carrots. If they are too large, cut diagonally into long, thin slices.

Microwave Cooking Method

Cook carrots, covered in a bowl of water, on High (100%) for 8-10 minutes. Drain.

In a serving dish, melt butter on High (100%) for 30 seconds. Add honey and ginger juice and toss in carrots. Cook on Medium (70%) for 2 minutes.

Sprinkle with lemon juice and serve garnished with parsley.

Green Tomato Salad

PREPARATION: 10 mins
COOKING: 700 watt – 3-4 mins
650 watt – 4-6 mins
500 watt – 5-8 mins
Times given here are for a
650 watt oven. Decrease time
by 15 seconds per minute for
a 700 watt oven. Increase time
by 20 seconds per minute for a
500 watt oven.
KCAL 570
SERVES 4

½ cup peanuts
6 green tomatoes
2 large onions
4 stalks coriander
3 green chillies
1 tablespoon groundnut oil
2 teaspoons fish sauce
½ lime
1 tablespoon onion crisps

The peanut flavour of this recipe mingled with green tomatoes is distinctive and I have found that roasting peanuts in the microwave oven is relatively painless, making this a handy 'everyday' dish.

Preparation

Roast peanuts in a pie plate for 4 minutes on High (100%), turning nuts once during the cycle. Continue to roast for another 2 minutes if desired colour is not reached in that time. Keep turning as nuts could burn very quickly.

Pound peanuts. Slice tomatoes and onions into thin pieces. Chop coriander leaves and chillies into tiny pieces.

Just before salad is needed, mix all the ingredients together, adding groundnut oil and fish sauce alternately until desired taste is reached. Squeeze in lime juice and sprinkle with crispy onions and give salad a final toss.

Serve cold.

Tabouli Salad

PREPARATION: 5 mins
COOKING: 700 watt – 4 mins
              650 watt – 6 mins
              500 watt – 7 mins
Times given here are for a
650 watt oven. Decrease time
by 15 seconds per minute for
a 700 watt oven. Increase time
by 20 seconds per minute for a
500 watt oven.
KCAL 900
SERVES 4-6

½ cup burghul (Lebanese
    cracked-wheat)
2 large onions
2 large tomatoes
1 bunch Chinese coriander
2 large ripe limes
salt
pepper
½ teaspoon sugar
1 tablespoon olive oil
    or groundnut oil
1 tablespoon vinegar

A fresh tangy salad traditionally eaten rolled up in Lebanese bread. I have tasted variations of the salad in various parts of North India as burghul wheat is a staple in the drier regions of India and Pakistan. Tabouli goes well with hamburger buns or western-style meat dishes. Used with less vinegar, it complements any Asian meal.

Preparation

Heat burghul wheat in 1 cup water for 5 minutes on High (100%) until wheat puffs up. Let it soak for 30 minutes till fluffy, then drain.

Peel and chop onions finely. Chop tomatoes into very small pieces.

Wash and chop Chinese coriander finely, using some of the thinner stems as well.

Heat limes for 30 seconds on Medium (70%) to yield more juice. Squeeze and strain juice.

Mix all ingredients together, and toss lightly. Refrigerate till needed.

Note: Tabouli can be kept overnight but needs refreshing with new salad oil and vinegar. Drain off the old dressing before adding a new one.

Mint Curried Potato Balls

PREPARATION: 3 mins
COOKING: 700 watt – 6 mins
              650 watt – 9 mins
              500 watt – 11 mins
Times given here are for a
650 watt oven. Decrease time
by 15 seconds per minute for
a 700 watt oven. Increase time
by 20 seconds per minute for a
500 watt oven.
KCAL 726
SERVES 4-6

200 g (6⅔ oz) sweet potato
2 tablespoons butter or margarine
½ teaspoon curry powder
1 cup chopped mint
salt

Graceful traveller's palms, squeaky rattan chairs and lethargic fans are features of the past in Singapore's oldest hotel where dainty curried potato balls were once served with Sunday lunch just before the tea dance.

Preparation

Peel sweet potatoes. Using a melon baller, scoop out sweet potato balls.

Mix butter or margarine with curry powder.

Microwave Cooking Method

Place sweet potato balls in an ovenproof bowl and just barely cover with water. Cover bowl with plastic wrap and cook on High (100%) for 8 minutes. Stir carefully once or twice during the cycle.

Drain and cover balls with foil or a cloth to keep them warm.

Melt butter/margarine with curry powder mixture for 30 seconds on High (100%). Add mint and salt and mix well.

Roll sweet potato balls in this mixture and serve as a complement to a meat dish.

Glo's Brinjal Sambal

PREPARATION: 8 mins
COOKING: 700 watt – 7 mins
         650 watt – 9 mins
         500 watt – 12 mins
Times given here are for a 650 watt oven. Decrease time by 15 seconds per minute for a 700 watt oven. Increase time by 20 seconds per minute for a 500 watt oven.
KCAL 369
SERVES 4-6

2 large brinjals, about 300 g (10 oz)
2 shallots
2 cloves garlic
½ cup thick coconut milk
salt
juice of ½ lime
1 lemon slice
1 red chilli, chopped

The Jaffna Tamil community in Malaysia is renowned for its culinary expertise, especially in vegetable cooking. I include Glo's recipe because I am convinced she makes one of the best brinjal sambals east of Sri Lanka. This tastes good served hot, cold, or even as a vegetarian dip for potato chips.

Preparation

Cut stems and halve brinjals lengthwise.

Peel and chop shallots and garlic till very fine, or pound into a paste.

Microwave Cooking Method

Microwave brinjal pieces in a glass or plastic container, covered loosely with paper, for 8-9 minutes on High (100%). Brinjals should be soft to the touch at the end of the cycle.

Scoop out soft flesh and discard skin.

Mash brinjal with shallots, garlic and coconut milk, adding salt to taste. Squeeze in lime juice to complete the *sambal.*

Garnish with a twist of lemon or chopped red chilli.

This *sambal* tastes best served cold.

Kelangu Kootu (Potato Curry)

PREPARATION: 10 mins
COOKING: 700 watt – 27 mins
650 watt – 36 mins
500 watt – 47 mins
Times given here are for a
650 watt oven. Decrease time
by 15 seconds per minute for
a 700 watt oven. Increase time
by 20 seconds per minute for a
500 watt oven.
KCAL 880
SERVES 6

**5 medium potatoes, about
500 g (1 lb)**
3 shallots
2 cloves garlic
1 tablespoon tamarind paste
2 tablespoons oil
1 tablespoon chilli powder
2 tablespoons curry powder
salt
pepper
½ cup thin coconut milk
**½ cup thick coconut milk or
½ cup yogurt**
juice of ½ lime

A potato curry that adds vitality to a potentially bland vegetable. Use yogurt for a healthier version of the traditional coconut milk based recipe.

Preparation

Wash and pierce potatoes with a fork. Cook for 10 minutes on High (100%). They should be underdone so that they finish cooking in the curry.

Peel and quarter potatoes.

Peel and slice shallots and garlic thinly.

Mix tamarind with ½ cup water and work with fingers to make a thick paste. Strain tamarind juice.

Microwave Cooking Method

Heat a browning dish for 6 minutes on High (100%). Add oil and garlic at once, so garlic cooks in the hot dish.

Add shallots and cook on High (100%) for 3 minutes.

Add chilli and curry powder, salt and pepper mixed with tamarind juice and thin coconut milk. Cook on High (100%) for 6 minutes.

Add peeled and quartered potatoes, and cook, covered loosely with plastic wrap, for 10 minutes on Medium (70%). Add thick coconut milk or yogurt. Cook for 30 seconds, uncovered.

Test if potatoes are done and for seasoning. Add lime juice before removing from the oven.

Serve hot with rice.

Note: If you prefer a thicker curry, let it simmer for 10 minutes on a Simmer cycle (20%).

Cheese Cauliflower

PREPARATION: 7 mins
COOKING: 700 watt – 7 mins
                  650 watt – 10 mins
                  500 watt – 13 mins
Times given here are for a
650 watt oven. Decrease time
by 15 seconds per minute for
a 700 watt oven. Increase time
by 20 seconds per minute for a
500 watt oven.
KCAL 810
SERVES 6

500 g (1 lb) cauliflower
1 lime
½ tablespoon butter
1 tablespoon flour
½ cup milk
½ teaspoon chilli powder
salt
pepper
2 tablespoons grated Cheddar
1 tablespoon breadcrumbs or
**   shredded pickled turnip**
**   (*tungchye*)**
2 tablespoons yogurt

This is the traditional cheese and cauliflower dish 'lifted' with spice and pickle.

Preparation

Wash and cut cauliflower into pieces, squeezing lime juice over so it does not discolour.

Microwave Cooking Method

Cook cauliflower with ½ cup water in a deep dish, covered loosely with plastic wrap, on High (100%) for 7 minutes. Let it stand for 5 minutes, then drain. Keep vegetable warm.

In a deep bowl, melt butter in 30 seconds on High (100%). Whisk in flour, milk, chilli powder, salt and pepper. Cook for 2 minutes on High (100%), stirring once during the cooking cycle.

Add cheese to hot mixture. Stir well and microwave on High (100%) for 20 seconds. Add breadcrumbs or *tungchye* and yogurt at the end of this cycle. Do not cook further.

Pour sauce over warm cauliflower.

Note: The cauliflower can be cooked earlier and heated just before it is required. Substitute pickle for breadcrumbs for a different flavour.

Sambar Dhal

PREPARATION: 5 mins
COOKING: 700 watt – 24 mins
650 watt – 32 mins
500 watt – 43 mins
Times given here are for a
650 watt oven. Decrease time
by 15 seconds per minute for
a 700 watt oven. Increase time
by 20 seconds per minute for a
500 watt oven.
KCAL 1250
SERVES 6

**1 cup large yellow lentils
(*mysore dhal*)**
3 shallots
2 cloves garlic
**2 × 2 cm (¾ × ¾ in) tamarind
paste**
2 cm (¾ in) cinnamon stick
pinch of turmeric
1 tablespoon ghee or butter
2 dried chillies, broken into bits
½ teaspoon mustard seeds
1 stalk curry leaves
salt
½ cup thick coconut milk
½ teaspoon chilli powder

Indians use this as a staple gravy for meals served with mounds of rice spread on banana leaves. You have to sit cross-legged on the floor (ladies sit with legs folded beneath them, sideways) and use your fingers – it tastes better that way!

Preparation

Pick out grit and stones from lentils and wash and drain.

Peel and slice shallots and garlic.

Work tamarind paste with 2 tablespoons water to make a thick paste. Strain out dregs.

Microwave Cooking Method

In a deep casserole, cover lentils with water up to 2 cm (¾ in) over the lentil level. Cover loosely with plastic wrap and cook for 15 minutes on High (100%). Stir once or twice during the cycle. If the wrap is too tight, the lentils will boil over.

When lentils are softened, add half the sliced shallots, cinnamon and a pinch of turmeric. Cook for 5 minutes on High (100%) or until cooked.

To temper spices in a browning dish, heat dish for 6 minutes on High (100%), then add ghee which will sizzle and melt. Quickly add sliced garlic and remaining shallots and cook on High (100%) for 30 seconds. Stir, add broken chilli bits, mustard seeds and curry leaves stripped from their stalk. Cook for 30 seconds on High (100%) or till mustard seeds pop. If butter is used the spices will burn, so work quickly and stir often.

Stir tempered spices into boiled lentils, add ½ cup water to the browning dish and swirl around to wash up spices. Add this to the lentils.

Add salt, coconut milk, tamarind juice and chilli powder to the lentils. Stir well and cook on Medium (70%) for 5 minutes, stirring once during the cycle.

Serve Sambar Dhal with vegetables and rice.

Radha's Dhal Kootu

PREPARATION: 6 mins
COOKING: 700 watt – 12 mins
            650 watt – 17 mins
            500 watt – 22 mins
Times given here are for a
650 watt oven. Decrease time
by 15 seconds per minute for
a 700 watt oven. Increase time
by 20 seconds per minute for a
500 watt oven.
KCAL 600
SERVES 6

100 g (3½ oz) yellow or red
   lentils (mysore/toor dhal)
2 green chillies
2 cloves garlic
150 g (5 oz) cabbage
pinch of turmeric
1 teaspoon cummin powder
¾ teaspoon pepper
salt
1 teaspoon ghee
2 dried chillies, torn into bits
1 large onion, sliced
½ teaspoon mustard seeds

This South Indian recipe elevates the lowly cabbage to dinner table elegance. Lentils give this dish substance and take on the flavour of the vegetables. You can vary flavours by adding different vegetables.

Preparation

Pick grit out of lentils, wash and soak in warm water for 30 minutes.

Slice green chillies and peel garlic. Shred cabbage finely.

Microwave Cooking Method

Boil lentils with 1 cup water, green chillies, garlic and a pinch of turmeric for 10 minutes on High (100%), covered loosely with plastic wrap. When lentils are soft, drain off excess liquid.

Add cabbage, cummin, pepper and salt. Cook for 3 minutes on High (100%), uncovered. Stir well and remove from the oven.

In a dish, melt ghee in 30 seconds on High (100%). Add broken chilli bits, onion slices and mustard seeds. Cook for 3 minutes on High (100%) till oil boils or till onion and chilli are well browned.

Add spices to vegetable dish, stirring well.

Yong Dofu

PREPARATION: 30 mins
COOKING: 700 watt – 10½ mins
650 watt – 14 mins
500 watt – 18½ mins
Times given here are for a
650 watt oven. Decrease time
by 15 seconds per minute for
a 700 watt oven. Increase time
by 20 seconds per minute for a
500 watt oven.
KCAL 700
SERVES 4

300 g (10 oz) fish fillet
½ cup water mixed with
  1 teaspoon salt
4 dried soybean squares (*dofu pok*)
1 small bittergourd
2 large chillies
salt
pepper
2 teaspoons light soy sauce

Homemade Yong Dofu was something I tried to avoid as it was my job to pound the silvery flesh that would gradually turn into a sticky quagmire as the pestle dug deep into its crater. The more it is pounded, the smoother the texture, so one feverishly attacked the mortar, levering the pestle to allow for easy pounding. The end result often makes the effort worthwhile.

Preparation

Lay fish fillets on a flat surface. Holding one end, and using a downward motion, scrape out flesh with a spoon. It comes off easily. Reserve the skin and gristle for stock.

Place scraped flesh in a mortar and pound firmly, sprinkling with a few drops of salty water as you go along.

Prepare fish stock by cooking fish skin and gristle in 1 cup water on High (100%), covered with plastic wrap.

Slit *dofu pok*. Slice bittergourd and scrape out seeds. Slit and seed chillies. Stuff *dofu pok*, bittergourd slices and chillies with pounded fish.

Microwave Cooking Method

Strain fish stock into a deep casserole, bring to a boil, covered with plastic wrap, by cooking for 3 minutes on High (100%).

Add stuffed *dofu*, bittergourd and chilli to the stock.

Cook, covered with plastic wrap, on High (100%) for 5 minutes.

Remove plastic wrap and stir carefully, adding salt, pepper and soy sauce.

Cook for 1 minute, uncovered, on High (100%). Serve at once with hot bowls of rice and chilli sauce.

Yong Dofu (192)

Sumatran Gado-Gado (182)

Nara Dofu

PREPARATION: 8 mins
COOKING: 700 watt – 6 mins
            650 watt – 8 mins
            500 watt – 10 mins
Times given here are for a
650 watt oven. Decrease time
by 15 seconds per minute for
a 700 watt oven. Increase time
by 20 seconds per minute for a
500 watt oven.
KCAL 877
SERVES 4

200 g (6⅔ oz) spinach
2 medium carrots
1 piece bamboo shoot (from a
small can)
1 cup *dashi*
½ teaspoon *tamari shoyu*
½ teaspoon salt
1 teaspoon sugar

Sauce
3 tablespoons sesame seeds
1 soft soybean square
2 tablespoons sugar
1 teaspoon *tamari shoyu*

Dofu (soybean cakes and products of various forms) is probably the single Asian foodstuff best known in the west. It is very rich in protein and its delicate taste serves as a base for any flavour the cook wishes to impart.

Legend has it that during the Tang dynasty, there lived a very honest government official who refused to accept bribes and as a result could not afford to eat meat. To solve his dilemma, he created dofu from soy beans. From then on, the underpaid and overly honest government staff were called 'dofu officials'! This particular dofu recipe is from Japan.

Preparation

Clean and pick spinach leaves. Scrape and cut carrots and bamboo shoot into julienne strips.

Season *dashi* stock with *tamari shoyu*, salt and sugar. Add vegetables to stock.

Toast sesame seeds in an ovenproof plate for 2½ minutes on High (100%). Stir the seeds about halfway through the cycle for even toasting.

Microwave Cooking Method

Cook *dashi* and vegetables in a casserole, covered loosely with plastic wrap, for 5 minutes on High (100%). Drain and reserve for stock. Keep vegetables warm under foil.

Mash dofu and sesame seeds roughly in a mortar or blender. Add sugar and *tamari shoyu* and mix well.

Pour sauce over cooked vegetables and serve hot.

Macau Cabbage Rolls

PREPARATION: 10 mins
COOKING: 700 watt – 19 mins
650 watt – 25 mins
500 watt – 33 mins
Times given here are for a
650 watt oven. Decrease time
by 15 seconds per minute for
a 700 watt oven. Increase time
by 20 seconds per minute for a
500 watt oven.
KCAL 1080
SERVES 4-6

**1 medium cabbage, about
500 g (1 lb)**

A
**2 medium onions
2 cloves garlic
100 g (3½ oz) water chestnuts
100 g (3½ oz) canned bamboo
shoot
200 g (6⅔ oz) minced lamb, pork
or beef
1 teaspoon light soy sauce
1 teaspoon dark soy sauce
1 teaspoon pepper
1 teaspoon salt
1 teaspoon tomato sauce**

**2 tablespoons oil
toothpicks
1 cube chicken stock**

*The Portuguese influence in Macau has produced this culinary master-
piece, reflecting both eastern and western tastes and spices.*

Preparation

Core cabbage and place it in a casserole or ice cream container.
Pour water into the bottom of the container and cover loosely with
plastic wrap.

Cook for 7 minutes on High (100%). Cabbage will be pliable for
leaves to be removed and rolled. Pare down the thick part of the
stem of each leaf so that the leaf can be folded easily.

Peel and chop onions, garlic, water chestnuts and bamboo
shoots finely. Combine all ingredients listed under 'A' and mix
well.

Microwave Cooking Method

Heat a browning dish for 6 minutes on High (100%). Add oil and
brown meat mixture. Stir and cook for 4 minutes on High (100%).
Drain excess oil from meat.

Spread cabbage leaves and distribute meat evenly between
them. Fold into parcels and secure with toothpicks.

Pile rolls one on top of the other in a browning dish. Crumble
stock cube over rolls and cover loosely with plastic wrap.

Cook for 8 minutes on High (100%) to reduce gravy.

Let rolls stand for 5 minutes before serving with rice and
vegetables.

Empress Beancurd (Dofu)

PREPARATION: 8 mins
COOKING: 700 watt – 15 mins
650 watt – 20½ mins
500 watt – 27 mins
Times given here are for a
650 watt oven. Decrease time
by 15 seconds per minute for
a 700 watt oven. Increase time
by 20 seconds per minute for a
500 watt oven.
KCAL 1028
SERVES 4

250 g (8 oz) firm soybean squares
1 clove garlic
3 × 3 cm (1¼ × 1¼ in) ginger
4 prawns
4 dried Chinese mushrooms
¾ cup chicken stock
½ teaspoon salt
1 teaspoon sugar
1 tablespoon Chinese wine
1 teaspoon cornflour
½ teaspoon sesame oil
1 egg
3 lettuce leaves
2 tablespoons vegetable oil
150 g (5 oz) canned crabmeat

This takes me back to Chinese Cooking Classes when teacher-colleagues met once a week to learn Restaurant Dishes from long-suffering restaurateur, Mr Wong. Ivy, our mathematician, found it difficult to accept Mr Wong's 'pinch of salt' or 'finger-length of ginger'. 'That should be 2 inches' she would mutter while Mr Wong raised eyes heavenward in despair. In this recipe, however, add or subtract ingredients as you please, for dofu *is bland and adapts well to many flavours.*

Preparation

Cut soybean squares into 4 cm (1¾ in) cubes. Pat dry with a cloth.

Peel and chop garlic. Peel and shred ginger. Shell and devein prawns.

Cook mushrooms in ½ cup water, covered with plastic wrap, for 3 minutes on High (100%). Drain and slice caps thinly.

In a bowl, mix chicken stock, salt, sugar, wine, cornflour and sesame oil. Beat egg before adding to the stock and stir the mixture well.

Break up lettuce leaves roughly.

Microwave Cooking Method

Preheat a browning dish for 7 minutes on High (100%). Add oil and heat for 30 seconds on High (100%).

Brown *dofu* in hot oil and cook, uncovered, for 2 minutes on High (100%). Turn over and cook for another minute on High (100%). Carefully remove the *dofu* pieces.

Add garlic and ginger to the oil in the browning dish. Cook for 2 minutes on High (100%).

Add drained crabmeat, prawns and mushrooms. Toss with garlic and ginger, then cook for 2 minutes on High (100%).

Add chicken stock mixture. Stir well into crabmeat. Cook for 1 minute on High (100%), cautiously as egg may make mixture rubbery.

Stir well, then cook a further minute on High (100%). Add *dofu* pieces and lettuce leaves.

Stir and test for seasoning. Cook for 1 more minute on Medium (70%).

Serve hot with rice.

Saltfish Beansprouts

PREPARATION: 15 mins
COOKING: 700 watt – 8 mins
650 watt – 10½ mins
500 watt – 14 mins
Times given here are for a
650 watt oven. Decrease time
by 15 seconds per minute for
a 700 watt oven. Increase time
by 20 seconds per minute for a
500 watt oven.
KCAL 430
SERVES 4

200 g (7 oz) beansprouts
30 g (1 oz) saltfish
   (threadfin/*kurau*)
2 dried chillies
2 cloves garlic
2 tablespoons oil
1 teaspoon lime juice
1 teaspoon light soy sauce

Beansprouts should never be salted for they wilt easily, so this recipe is obviously an adaptation to accommodate Malaysian/Singaporean tastes. Chilli and dried fish do complement the bland beansprouts. If your priority is for the practical rather than the aesthetic, then skip the tailing of the beansprouts – a tiresomely slow process requiring nimble fingers.

Preparation

Wash and tail beansprouts. Drain well in a colander.

Shred saltfish and break up chillies roughly. Peel and chop garlic.

Microwave Cooking Method

Preheat a browning dish for 7 minutes on High (100%). Add oil and continue heating for another 30 seconds on High (100%).

Add shredded saltfish which will sizzle in oil. Stir to brown, then cook for 1 minute on High (100%). Remove saltfish.

Add the dried chilli bits and chopped garlic. Cook for 30 seconds on High (100%).

Add beansprouts and cook for 1 minute on High (100%). Stir and add lime juice and soy sauce. Cook for another 30 seconds.

Toss in fish shreds and dish out. Serve hot with rice.

RICE & NOODLES

Microtips on Cooking Rice

Rice cooks evenly without burnt crusts or dryness in the microwave oven. (So do pasta and noodles: notes on these follow below.) The proportion of water and the cooking time are about the same as in conventional cooking, but the texture is finer and the grains of rice emerge soft and separate.

Use a large ovenproof casserole or a firm plastic bowl. The cooking container (which may even be a cup) should be covered with a piece of kitchen paper to absorb moisture and prevent 'scum' or steam from fogging up the oven.

Rice can be stirred without spoiling it. The cooking cycle may be stopped at any stage to stir, to add ingredients or even some more water. The cooked product will not stick to the container and will not 'crust'. It may look dry when the cooking cycle is completed but if fluffed up with a fork and given standing time to finish cooking, it will soften and taste wonderful.

Rice reheats very satisfactorily with no loss of texture or flavour as occurs in reheating over a conventional stove.

It is not time-efficient, however, to cook more than 2½ cups of rice in the microwave oven.

Basic White Rice Recipe.   Here is a recipe for cooking 1 cup of white rice.

Wash rice as usual in water, rinsing 3 times. Add 1½ cups water to rice in a casserole, glass dish, earthenware or firm plastic container. Cover with kitchen paper (do not seal or rice will boil over). Cook on High (100%) for 12 minutes. Take out, fluff up and let rice stand for 3-4 minutes to absorb remaining water. Rice will separate beautifully.

For additional rice, allow 4 minutes and 1½ cups water more for every extra cup.

You may prefer not to use cup measurements. Place rice in a container. Add water up to 2½ cm (1 in) above rice level. Add a pinch of salt. Microwave on High (100%) for 12 minutes for the first cup of rice, and add 5 minutes for every additional cup.

Brown Rice Recipe.   Add 3 cups water to 1 cup rice and cover container with kitchen paper. Cook on High (100%) for 29 minutes. Loosen grains with a fork and let rice stand for 3-4 minutes.

Microtips on Cooking Noodles and Pasta

The following method for cooking spaghetti may be used for cooking the same quantity of any noodles: rice vermicelli (meehoon), yellow noodles, etc. However, you will need about ½ litre more water.

Cooking Spaghetti and Other Pasta. This recipe is for 250 g (8 oz) spaghetti. Pour 1-1½ litres (3½-5¼ cups) boiling water into a deep casserole or bowl. Add salt and ½ tablespoon oil or butter. Break spaghetti so it fits into the bowl. Slip into boiling water. Cover loosely with plastic wrap, leaving a vent for steam to escape. Cook on High (100%) for 12 minutes. Stir to separate spaghetti strands. Wash under cold water and drain.

Nasi Lemak

PREPARATION: 10 mins
COOKING: 700 watt – 15 mins
          650 watt – 20 mins
          500 watt – 26 mins
Times given here are for a 650 watt oven. Decrease time by 15 seconds per minute for a 700 watt oven. Increase time by 20 seconds per minute for a 500 watt oven.
KCAL 2520
SERVES 4-6

2 cups long-grained rice
1 white coconut, grated
  or 1 can coconut milk diluted
  to 3½ cups liquid
2 screwpine leaves (*daun pandan*)
1 onion
½ teaspoon salt

I lived in a winding, lateritic lane in Klang where early morning was punctuated by the musical call of the Nasi Lemak boy who peddled squat banana-leaf packets of aromatic rice topped with a generous sunshine of egg, cucumber and sambal. Food needs to be both a visual and gastronomic pleasure, and this packet certainly fulfilled the requirements.

Preparation

Wash rice till water is clear.

Add 2 cups water to coconut and blend, then strain to extract 3½ cups coconut milk. Add more water if necessary to make up required amount.

Shred screwpine leaves lengthwise and tie into a knot.

Peel and grate onion.

Microwave Cooking Method

In a deep bowl, place rice, coconut milk, onion and salt with knotted screwpine leaves.

Cover loosely with a sheet of kitchen paper and cook for 18-20 minutes on High (100%).

Fluff up with a fork when cycle is completed. Allow 5 minutes standing time covered with foil.

Remove screwpine leaves before serving.

Oboro (Mushroom Chicken Rice)

PREPARATION: 10 mins
COOKING: 700 watt – 23 mins
650 watt – 31 mins
500 watt – 41 mins
Times given here are for a
650 watt oven. Decrease time
by 15 seconds per minute for
a 700 watt oven. Increase time
by 20 seconds per minute for a
500 watt oven.
KCAL 2890
SERVES 6

2 cups short-grained rice
10 dried Chinese mushrooms
300 g (10 oz) chicken meat
½ cup *tamari shoyu*
4 tablespoons *mirin* or sherry
1 tablespoon palm sugar
2 eggs
salt
pepper
½ teaspoon five-spice powder
100 g (3½ oz) cooked peas
shredded lettuce

The reputation of Japanese food relies mainly on its delicacy of flavours and its impeccable presentation, whether it is in a formal tea ceremony, or in a rice dish steamed and served in a rice pot called domburi. *The Japanese use rice that is slightly sticky (what some may call 'new rice') so that it is picked up easily with pointed chopsticks.*

Preparation

Wash and drain rice.

Wash mushrooms, add water to cover mushrooms in a bowl, then cover bowl loosely with plastic wrap. Cook on Medium (70%) for 6 minutes. Remove mushrooms from water and slice into strips. Reserve mushroom stock.

Slice chicken thinly.

Microwave Cooking Method

In a shallow dish, place mushroom and chicken strips, *tamari shoyu, mirin,* palm sugar and ¼ cup of the reserved mushroom stock. Cover loosely with plastic wrap and cook on High (100%) for 4 minutes. Keep chicken and mushrooms warm under foil.

Beat eggs with salt, pepper and five-spice powder. Place in a greased dish in the microwave oven and cook on High (100%) for 50 seconds. As edges cook, move cooked parts to the centre of the dish. Shred cooked omelette into thin strips with a sharp knife.

In a deep Japanese pot called *domburi*, put rice and 3½ cups water (including remaining mushroom stock). Cook on High (100%) for 20 minutes, covered loosely with kitchen paper.

When rice is cooked, stir carefully, then spread chicken and mushroom strips over rice and stir well.

Serve garnished with green peas and lettuce shreds in the centre, surrounded by a ring of omelette strips.

Chicken Rice

PREPARATION: 15 mins
COOKING: 700 watt – 40 mins
          650 watt – 54 mins
          500 watt – 72 mins
Times given here are for a
650 watt oven. Decrease time
by 15 seconds per minute for
a 700 watt oven. Increase time
by 20 seconds per minute for a
500 watt oven.
KCAL 5530
SERVES 6

1 chicken, about 1½ kg (3⅓ lb)
2 star anise
2 × 2 cm (¾ × ¾ in) ginger
6 cloves garlic
2 cups rice
50 g (1⅔ oz) chicken fat
1 teaspoon sesame oil
3 stalks spring onion
1 extra teaspoon sesame oil
1 teaspoon dark soy sauce

Garnishes

1 cucumber, halved lengthwise
   and sliced
spring onion, shredded
   lengthwise and cut
   diagonally into 4 cm
   (1½ in) lengths
chilli garlic sauce or
   'Wee Nee Chilli'
1 tablespoon chopped pickled
   turnip (tungchye)

For first-timers in Singapore, lunch at Swee Kee's used to be a special treat. Here the steamy fragrance of chicken soup would assail your senses as you walked in, and amidst the chatter of humanity and the clink of china, bowls of hot rice were deftly upended on your plate while honey-pale chicken, shimmering on top of crisp, fresh cucumber, was served with a piquant chilli-garlic sauce.

Preparation

Clean chicken. Pound together star anise, ginger and garlic. Rub chicken with this mixture. Wash and drain rice and dry in the sun for a few minutes.

Dice chicken fat and cook on High (100%) for 10 minutes till oil is released. (Splatters can be cleaned off oven sides later.)

Drain chicken fat into rice. Add sesame oil and mix well. Dry roast rice in the microwave oven on High (100%) for 5 minutes, stirring twice during the cycle.

Microwave Cooking Method

Place spiced chicken in a casserole with 5 cups water, spring onions, salt and pepper to taste. Cover loosely with plastic wrap and cook for 19 minutes on High (100%), turning chicken so it is evenly cooked. Take chicken out and reserve stock.

Plunge chicken in icy water to stop cooking process. Wipe dry and rub all over with sesame oil and dark soy sauce. Cut into serving pieces and keep warm till needed.

Transfer rice to a casserole. Add 3 cups of the reserved stock. Liquid should be 2½ cm (1 in) above level of rice.

Cook, covered loosely with plastic wrap, for 20 minutes on High (100%). Stir rice after 14 minutes of the cycle and remove plastic wrap at this stage to continue cooking uncovered. Rice will be cooked when grains are separated.

Serving

Arrange pieces of chicken on a bed of cucumber slices and garnish with spring onion. Place rice in individual serving plates with saucers of chilli garlic sauce or 'Wee Nee Chilli'. Serve with bowls of chicken soup garnished with *tungchye*.

Note: When chicken stock boils, skim off the top and add this to chilli sauce for flavour.

Chicken Rice (202)

Clockwise from top: Rest House Nasi Goreng (205),
Brown Rice (199) and Nasi Lemak (200)

Rest House Nasi Goreng

PREPARATION: 12 mins
COOKING: 700 watt – 17 mins
           650 watt – 23 mins
           500 watt – 31 mins
Times given here are for a
650 watt oven. Decrease time
by 15 seconds per minute for
a 700 watt oven. Increase time
by 20 seconds per minute for a
500 watt oven.
KCAL 2900
SERVES 6

6 rashers bacon
2 small carrots
2 green capsicums
100 g (3½ oz) button mushrooms
2 large onions
2 cloves garlic
3-4 stalks spring onion
10-12 peanuts
1 tablespoon oil
2 cups cooked rice
2 tablespoons thick soy sauce
1 tablespoon sesame oil
salt
pepper
crispy onions

At the turn of the century, Malayan Government Rest Houses had the best Hainanese cooks who produced excellent fried rice. In an era when fashionable clubs and sophisticated restaurants were unknown, these were the main watering holes of many a weary government servant.

Preparation

Place rashers between 3 sheets of kitchen paper. Cover loosely with 2 more sheets of paper. Cook on High (100%) for 5 minutes or till bacon is crisp. Chop bacon.

Peel, wash and cut carrots and capsicums into tiny cubes. Drain button mushrooms and quarter them.

Peel and chop onions, garlic and spring onions separately.

Toast peanuts in a dish on High (100%) for 3 minutes. Stir once during the cycle to distribute heat evenly. Watch them or they could easily burn.

Microwave Cooking Method

Heat a browning dish on High (100%) for 6 minutes.

Add 1 tablespoon oil and brown garlic – it will sizzle at once in hot oil. Add onions and cook on High (100%) for 2 minutes.

Add carrots and capsicums. Cook on High (100%) for 3 minutes.

Add button mushrooms, bacon, rice, soy sauce and sesame oil. Stir well so ingredients are well mixed. You may need to transfer contents of dish to a larger casserole in order to mix well.

Cook, covered loosely with plastic wrap, for 4 minutes on High (100%), stirring once during the cycle. Correct for salt and pepper.

Remove plastic wrap and fluff up rice. Cover with foil to stand for 5 minutes.

Garnish with chopped spring onions, nuts and crispy onions.

Note: Bacon rashers may be omitted and fresh shrimps used instead.

Lo Mai Kai

PREPARATION: 20 mins
COOKING: 700 watt – 20 mins
           650 watt – 26 mins
           500 watt – 35 mins
Times given here are for a
650 watt oven. Decrease time
by 15 seconds per minute for
a 700 watt oven. Increase time
by 20 seconds per minute for a
500 watt oven.
KCAL 1900
SERVES 6

300 g (10 oz) glutinous rice
300 g (10 oz) chicken, preferably
   thighs and wings

Marinade
¼ cup thin soy sauce
2 tablespoons thick soy sauce
2 teaspoons sesame oil
2 teaspoons sugar
2 teaspoons oyster sauce

10 shallots
3 cloves garlic
2 tablespoons oil
1 × 1 cm (½ × ½ in) ginger
¼ cup light soy sauce
crispy shallots

This is another hawker food that used to arrive steaming hot in bowls late at night. You overturned the contents of the bowl onto a plate and there was this fragrant little mound of shining glutinous rice coloured brown with sauce and crowned with chicken. Best eaten with a little chilli sauce.

Preparation

Wash rice and soak in water for 2-3 hours.

Cut chicken into 4 × 4 cm (1½ × 1½ in) pieces and mix with marinade.

Peel and slice shallots thinly, chop garlic till fine and bruise ginger.

Microwave Cooking Method

Place soaked rice in an ovenproof dish with water about 3 cm (1¼ in) above rice level. Cover loosely with plastic wrap. Cook for 16 minutes, stirring once to soften rice grains.

Meanwhile, in a *wok* on a conventional stove, heat some oil and brown shallots and garlic, draining them on a piece of absorbent paper once browned.

Brown chicken pieces in remaining oil.

Add pan juices, remaining marinade, light soy sauce and bruised ginger to steamed rice, stirring to mix well.

In a casserole, place alternate layers of chicken and rice. Sprinkle with browned shallots and garlic and sprinkle with ½ cup water. Cover with plastic wrap and steam on Medium (70%) for 10 minutes.

Serve garnished with crispy shallots.

Aneka Nasi Kukus

PREPARATION: 15 mins
COOKING: 700 watt – 23 mins
          650 watt – 31 mins
          500 watt – 41 mins
Times given here are for a
650 watt oven. Decrease time
by 15 seconds per minute for
a 700 watt oven. Increase time
by 20 seconds per minute for a
500 watt oven.
KCAL 1100
SERVES 4

3 onions
3 cloves garlic
1 red chilli
2 tomatoes
2 tablespoons peanuts or
   almonds
2 tablespoons oil
½ cup raisins
½ tablespoon soy sauce
½ tablespoon sesame oil
salt
pepper
1½ cups long-grained rice

Garnishes
parsley
egg omelette strips
red chillies, cut into narrow strips
   lengthwise (attached at stalk
   end) and immersed in icy
   water to curl

This quick version of the Nasi Goreng, done entirely in the microwave oven, is simple and economical. Add any leftovers in place of shrimps for an even more economical meal.

Preparation

Peel and chop onions and garlic separately.

Seed and chop chilli. Dice tomatoes.

Roast nuts on High (100%) for 2 minutes, turning once during the cycle for even roasting.

Shell and devein shrimps.

Microwave Cooking Method

Heat a browning dish for 6 minutes on High (100%). Add oil and chopped garlic which will brown while oil sizzles.

Stir in chopped onions and cook for 1 minute on High (100%).

Add shrimps, and cook for 2 minutes on High (100%).

Add chopped tomatoes and chilli, raisins, nuts, soy sauce and sesame oil. Finally add salt and pepper and mix well.

Cook for 2 minutes on High (100%).

Transfer contents of browning dish to a deep ovenproof bowl, adding rice and water up to 2½ cm (1 in) above level of rice. Stir mixture well.

Cover the bowl with kitchen paper to prevent splatters and cook on High (100%) for 18 minutes. Fluff up with a fork and let it stand for 5 minutes, covered with foil.

Garnish with sprigs of parsley, strips of egg omelette and chilli flowers.

Note: A refreshing sauce to serve with Nasi Goreng and Aneka Nasi Kukus is a mixture of chilli and cucumber strips immersed in a marinade of vinegar and sugar. Refrigerate this till required.

Rajput Rice Pilaf

PREPARATION: 10 mins
COOKING: 700 watt – 20 mins
650 watt – 27 mins
500 watt – 35 mins
Times given here are for a
650 watt oven. Decrease time
by 15 seconds per minute for
a 700 watt oven. Increase time
by 20 seconds per minute for a
500 watt oven.
KCAL 2528
SERVES 6

2 cups rice
2 shallots
½ teaspoon saffron threads
**1 cup buttermilk or evaporated
milk curdled with juice of
2 limes**
100 g (3½ oz) almonds, blanched
**1 heaped tablespoon ghee or
butter**
salt
pepper
3-4 cardamoms
a few stalks coriander

*The Pilaf, Pilau or Pulao is a preparation of rice cooked with fruit and
vegetables, often confused with Beryani which is cooked with meat.
Pilafs have their origin in the northern part of India and Pakistan but can
today be found in all parts of the world where Indians have settled.*

Preparation

Wash and drain rice. Peel and slice shallots thinly. Soak saffron
threads in milk.

Slice almonds thinly, then toast on High (100%) for 2½ minutes,
turning once during the cycle.

Microwave Cooking Method

Heat ghee and shallots in a deep casserole on High (100%) for 3
minutes.

Stir in rice and cook for 3 minutes on High (100%), stirring once
during the cycle.

Add salt, pepper, cardamoms, and saffron with milk. Pour in
water till liquid comes up to 2½ cm (1 in) above rice level.

Cook rice on High (100%) for 18 minutes, covered with kitchen
paper to prevent splatters.

Stir rice well with a fork and let it stand to complete cooking
(cover with foil for best results).

Garnish with almonds flakes and coriander leaves.

Pineapple Rice

PREPARATION: 12 mins
COOKING: 700 watt – 21-22 mins
650 watt – 28-30 mins
500 watt – 37-39 mins
Times given here are for a
650 watt oven. Decrease time
by 15 seconds per minute for
a 700 watt oven. Increase time
by 20 seconds per minute for a
500 watt oven.
KCAL 2158
SERVES 6

2 cups rice
1 medium pineapple
1 large onion
2 stalks lemon grass
2 × 2 cm (¾ × ¾ in) ginger
1 tablespoon oil
salt
1 can sliced pineapple
1 cucumber, peeled and sliced

Since pineapple is found in most Southeast Asian countries, this rice dish may be found almost everywhere, although the spices and garnishes may vary with each country.

Preparation

Wash and drain rice. Place on a tray to dry.

Skin and cut pineapple into cubes, reserving juice.

Peel and chop onion and bruise lemon grass. Peel and grate ginger.

Microwave Cooking Method

Heat a browning dish on High (100%) for 6 minutes. Add oil and heat on High (100%) for 30 seconds. Cook onion, ginger and pineapple cubes on High (100%) for 3 minutes, turning to brown once or twice during the cycle.

Transfer contents of dish to a deep ovenproof bowl and add all other ingredients, including any pineapple juice. Add water till liquid is 2½ cm (1 in) above rice level.

Cover loosely with kitchen paper and cook on High (100%) for 18-20 minutes or until water is absorbed. Fluff up rice with a fork to separate rice grains.

Garnish with pineapple rings and cucumber slices and serve with a fish or egg curry.

Note: A folded dry towel in the microwave oven will absorb any moisture from the rice.

Parsee Fruit Pilaf

PREPARATION: 10 mins
COOKING: 700 watt – 15 mins
                650 watt – 20 mins
                500 watt – 27 mins
Times given here are for a
650 watt oven. Decrease time
by 15 seconds per minute for
a 700 watt oven. Increase time
by 20 seconds per minute for a
500 watt oven.
KCAL 1970
SERVES 6

¼ cup dried apricots
¼ cup raisins
¼ cup glace ginger
6-8 strands saffron
2 sticks cinnamon
4-6 cloves
salt
pepper
1 cup rice
a few drops rose water
2 teaspoons lime juice
1 tablespoon butter or margarine

The opulent feasts of the middle-easterners almost always contained a rice dish served with fruit, aromatic pomegranate seeds and spices. Some of this distinctive cuisine followed the Parsees to India and, today, equally opulent meals are served in the trading houses of northwest India. This rice complements a roast or mild curry.

Preparation

Place fruits with saffron, cinnamon, cloves, salt and pepper in a bowl and cover with plastic wrap. Microwave in 4 cups water on High (100%) for 8 minutes or till fruit is soft but not mushy. Drain liquid and use to cook rice.

Wash rice till water is clear.

Microwave Cooking Method

Pour 2½ cups fruit and reserved liquid into a deep bowl of rice. Liquid should be about 2½ cm (1 in) above rice level. Add rose water and lime juice. Cover with kitchen paper and cook on High (100%) for 12 minutes.

While still hot, pile into a buttered ring mould and let it stand, covered with foil, till ready to eat.

Serving

Unmould by immersing the base of the mould a few seconds in hot water. Overturn onto a plate, giving base a light tap.

Fill the centre with fruit and serve with a roast lamb.

Aburage Domburi

PREPARATION: 18 mins
COOKING: 700 watt – 29 mins
650 watt – 38 mins
500 watt – 51 mins
Times given here are for a
650 watt oven. Decrease time
by 15 seconds per minute for
a 700 watt oven. Increase time
by 20 seconds per minute for a
500 watt oven.
KCAL 936
SERVES 6

2 cups rice
3-4 sheets aburage
  (frozen soybean sheets)
2 cups chicken stock
4 tablespoons tamari shoyu
4 tablespoons mirin or dry sherry
2 teaspoons brown sugar
salt
pepper
a few stalks spring onions

A soup served with rice that makes a light and nutritious lunch in itself.

Preparation

Wash and place rice in a bowl with 3½ cups water. Cover with kitchen paper and cook on High (100%) for 18 minutes.

Cover *aburage* with hot water then drain. Cut each sheet into 8 pieces.

Microwave Cooking Method

Cover *aburage* pieces with chicken stock, *tamari shoyu*, *mirin*, brown sugar and cover the bowl loosely with plastic wrap.

Cook on Medium (70%) for 15 minutes then lower heat to low (30%) and cook for 5 minutes. Test for salt and pepper sufficiency.

Serve as a soup, ladled over rice and garnished with spring onions cut into strips and allowed to curl in icy water. Vegetables and radish pickle could also be served with Aburage Domburi.

Anand's Dilemma

PREPARATION: 2 mins
COOKING: 700 watt – 5 mins
650 watt – 7 mins
500 watt – 9 mins
Times given here are for a
650 watt oven. Decrease time
by 15 seconds per minute for
a 700 watt oven. Increase time
by 20 seconds per minute for a
500 watt oven.
KCAL 400
SERVES 1

1 packet instant noodles
1 egg
shredded vegetable, e.g. cabbage,
  leafy greens

Named after Anand, my 'batching' son, whose survival instincts taught him early to improvise with whatever was in the cupboard. This is one result which a nine-year-old could achieve.

Microwave Cooking Method

Place 1½ cups water and noodles in a bowl and cover with plastic wrap. Cook on High (100%) for 4½ minutes. Noodles will plump up as they boil.

Break an egg, shredded cabbage or any choice of vegetable onto noodles, mix and cook a further 2 minutes on High (100%).

Note: Cook noodles in serving bowl to save washing an additional bowl.

Norimaki Sushi

PREPARATION: 30 mins
COOKING: 700 watt – 21 mins
650 watt – 28 mins
500 watt – 37 mins
Times given here are for a
650 watt oven. Decrease time
by 15 seconds per minute for
a 700 watt oven. Increase time
by 20 seconds per minute for a
500 watt oven.
KCAL 1400
SERVES 6

2 cups short-grained rice
2 × 2 cm (¾ × ¾ in) dried kelp
   (kombu)
3 tablespoons sugar
1 tablespoon salt
3 tablespoons white vinegar
2 tablespoons mirin or dry sherry

Filling
6 dried Chinese mushrooms
2 tablespoons tamari shoyu
1 tablespoon sugar
2 large eggs
¼ teaspoon salt
oil
1 cucumber
pickled radish

nori sheets
wasabe

'Sushi, a delight to the eye, a revelation to the tongue, an engrossing culinary happening,' writes Donald Richie in Taste of Japan. *Properly made, Sushi should answer to all these counts and actually have all the rice grains facing the same direction.*

Preparation

Stir sugar, salt, vinegar and *mirin* in a bowl till sugar dissolves.

Place rice with *kombu* and 2¼ cups water in a casserole and cover loosely with kitchen paper. Cook for 18 minutes on High (100%). At the end of the cycle, stir rice, remove *kombu* and gradually stir sauces into rice. Allow to cool.

Wash mushrooms, cover with a little water and microwave on High (100%) for 3 minutes, covered with plastic wrap. Trim off stems and slice mushrooms thinly. Cook mushrooms in a mixture of *tamari shoyu* and sugar with 2 tablespoons water on Medium (70%) for 5 minutes till mushrooms are tender and soft.

Beat eggs with salt. Grease a flat pie dish and cook for 50 seconds to a minute on High (100%), moving cooked mixture to the centre of the plate as edges cook first. Cook eggs a few seconds extra if centre of omelette is still runny, but not too long as eggs will turn rubbery. Shred omelette into thin strips.

Peel cucumber, discard soft core and julienne.

Cut pickled radish into julienne strips.

Heat *nori* sheets by holding over a flame on a conventional cooker.

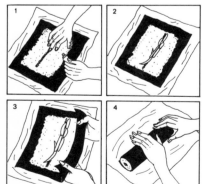

Assembly

Divide rice and fillings into 5 equal portions. Place a *nori* sheet flat on a work surface. Spread rice flat on the sheet, centering it so as to leave a small border of *nori* uncovered at the 4 edges.

In the middle of rice, run a strip of *wasabe* paste. On this place strips of omelette, vegetables and mushroom.

Roll up Sushi, keeping the roll firm as if you were rolling up coins in paper. Heat roll for 30 seconds on Medium (70%).

Refrigerate the rolls when cool. To serve, slice with a very sharp knife into 6 cylindrical pieces.

Serve on a plate with decorative garnishes of spring onion curls or radish pickles. Delicacy is the very soul in Sushi arrangement.

Norimaki Sushi (212)

Clockwise from top right: Omani Date Chutney (226), Wee Nee Chilli (222), Tamatar Chutney (224), Pooma's Puli Chutney (225)

Nonya's Birthday Rice

STRAITS CHINESE

PREPARATION: 10 mins
COOKING: 700 watt – 22-24 mins
               650 watt – 29-32 mins
               500 watt – 39-43 mins
Times given here are for a
650 watt oven. Decrease time
by 15 seconds per minute for
a 700 watt oven. Increase time
by 20 seconds per minute for a
500 watt oven.
KCAL 1988
SERVES 6

2 cups rice
1 large onion
1 tablespoon ghee
2-3 cloves
2-3 cardamoms
1 teaspoon turmeric powder
3½ cups water
1 chicken stock cube
salt

Served in Malaysia and Singapore on festive occasions such as weddings, birthdays or coming of age, this rice is rich in colour and flavour.

Preparation

Wash and drain rice.

Peel and dice onion.

Microwave Cooking Method

Heat a browning dish for 6 minutes on High (100%). Add ghee which will melt instantly. Brown onion for 2 minutes.

Add spices, rice and turmeric powder. Stir and cook for 3-4 minutes on High (100%). Stop cycle to stir a few times. Transfer contents of browning dish to a casserole.

Add water, stock cube and salt. Stir and cook on High (100%) for 18-20 minutes.

Stir to fluff up rice before serving.

Braised Prawn Noodles

PREPARATION: 15 mins
COOKING: 700 watt – 13½ mins
              650 watt – 18 mins
              500 watt – 24 mins
Times given here are for a
650 watt oven. Decrease time
by 15 seconds per minute for
a 700 watt oven. Increase time
by 20 seconds per minute for a
500 watt oven.
KCAL 1270
SERVES 4

10 dried Chinese mushrooms
300 g (10 oz) large prawns
1 teaspoon dark soy sauce
2 cloves garlic
2 × 2 cm (¾ × ¾ in) ginger
200 g (7 oz) fine egg noodles
200 g (7 oz) Chinese cabbage
   (*wong ah pak*)
1 tablespoon groundnut oil
1 cup prawn stock (or 1 anchovy
   bouillon cube with 1 cup water)
1 teaspoon salt
½ teaspoon pepper
½ teaspoon sesame oil
crispy fried onions

Our old grimy kitchen with the acrid smell of 'rubber' wood burning was in use all day, as each of our wartime friends cooked for their families who shared our home. Ma Ee's noodles, cooked in a great crater of a wok, created the most interest. The homemade noodles and the home-grown vegetables made a tasty meal, though scarce went into it.

Preparation

Wash mushrooms and soak in a cup of water. Cook, covered with plastic wrap, for 3 minutes on High (100%). Drain liquid, slice caps thinly.

Shell prawns, but keep the tail, and devein them. Pat dry with kitchen paper. Add soy sauce and stir in well.

Peel and pound garlic and ginger together.

Cover egg noodles in 1 cup water. Cook, covered with plastic wrap, for 5 minutes on High (100%). Separate noodles with chopsticks.

Wash and shred Chinese cabbage.

Microwave Cooking Method

In a 2 litre casserole dish, heat oil for 2 minutes on High (100%).

Add pounded garlic and ginger. Stir and cook, uncovered, for 2 minutes on High (100%).

Stir in stock and mushrooms. Cook, covered, for 3 minutes on High (100%).

Add cabbage, salt, pepper and sesame oil. Stir to mix and cook for 3 minutes on Medium (70%). Remove from heat.

To serve, place noodles in small bowls. Ladle hot prawns and some soup with cabbage over noodles. Garnish with crispy onions.

SAUCES & CHUTNEYS

Microtips on Storing Chutneys

Chutneys may be cooked in their own storage jars to save time and washing. However, as the boiling point of mixtures is raised when sugar or salt is added, you should use only ovenproof or heat-resistant utensils.

Sterilising Storage Jars.   Use only ovenproof or heat-resistant jars. Heat some water in each jar in the microwave oven on High (100%). When water boils, remove jar from the oven (with oven gloves), pour water out and shake excess drops clear of jar. Fill at once with blended chutney ingredients and cook as instructed. Allow jars to cool before covering and storing in the refrigerator.

Remember to remove metal lids of jars before microwaving.

Cooking in a Casserole.   Cook the chutney first, then sterilise the containers. Pour hot chutney immediately into hot jars or bottles and allow to cool before covering and storing.

Almondine Sauce

PREPARATION: 5 mins
COOKING: 700 watt – 8 mins
650 watt – 10 mins
500 watt – 13 mins
Times given here are for a 650 watt oven. Decrease time by 15 seconds per minute for a 700 watt oven. Increase time by 20 seconds per minute for a 500 watt oven.
KCAL 1522

4 tablespoons butter or margarine
½ cup almond slivers
1 tablespoon flour
½ cup milk
salt
pepper
chopped parsley

A classic sauce which enhances the most commonplace fish dish.

Microwave Cooking Method

Melt butter in a small casserole for 1 minute on High (100%).

Throw in almond slivers and cook for 3 minutes on High (100%).

Remove almonds and set aside. Stir in flour and cook on Medium (70%) for 2 minutes.

Add milk and seasoning and cook for 2 minutes on High (100%). Stir carefully with a whisk. Add almonds. Cook a further 2 minutes on Medium (70%).

When thickened, remove from heat, garnish with parsley and serve over grilled or poached fish.

Devilled Butter Sauce

PREPARATION: 5 mins
COOKING: 700 watt – 1½ mins
                  650 watt – 2 mins
                  500 watt – 3 mins
Times given here are for a
650 watt oven. Decrease time
by 15 seconds per minute for
a 700 watt oven. Increase time
by 20 seconds per minute for a
500 watt oven.
KCAL 1069

4 tablespoons butter
2 egg yolks
½ teaspoon mustard powder
½ teaspoon salt
½ teaspoon chilli powder
2 teaspoons Worcestershire
  sauce
2 teaspoons red wine or wine
  vinegar

Microwave Cooking Method

In a small casserole, melt butter for 1 minute on High (100%).

Whisk all other ingredients with melted butter. Cook for 30 seconds on Medium (70%).

Stir, then cook for another 30 seconds on Medium (70%).

Serve with poached or grilled fish.

Selva's Mayonnaise

PREPARATION: 1 min
COOKING: 700 watt – 3 mins
                  650 watt – 5 mins
                  500 watt – 6 mins
Times given here are for a
650 watt oven. Decrease time
by 15 seconds per minute for
a 700 watt oven. Increase time
by 20 seconds per minute for a
500 watt oven.
KCAL 2610

A
½ cup lemon juice
4 teaspoons flour
½ teaspoon salt
1 teaspoon sugar
½ teaspoon mustard powder

2 eggs
1 cup olive oil

In places where commercially prepared imported products are expensive, it is useful to know a straightforward mayonnaise recipe. This one has been perfected by my husband who considers himself a cook who needs no recipe book.

Preparation

Mix all ingredients 'A' together with ½ cup water. Stir well. Cook on High (100%) for 1 minute till mixture bubbles.

Boil on Medium (70%) for 3½ minutes, stirring two or three times during the cycle.

Cool thoroughly and beat 2 eggs and 1 cup olive oil into the product.

Cho Kan Jan (Sesame Seed Sauce)

PREPARATION: 2 mins
COOKING: 700 watt – 4 mins
650 watt – 5 mins
500 watt – 7 mins
Times given here are for a
650 watt oven. Decrease time
by 15 seconds per minute for
a 700 watt oven. Increase time
by 20 seconds per minute for a
500 watt oven.
KCAL 1342

1 red chilli
1½ tablespoons sugar
3 tablespoons vinegar
3 tablespoons light soy sauce
½ teaspoon sesame oil
½ cup sesame seeds

Preparation

Slit chilli and discard seeds.

In a bowl, mix sugar, vinegar, light soy sauce, sesame oil and the red chilli till sugar dissolves.

Microwave Cooking Method

Cook sesame seeds on a pie plate on High (100%) for 3 minutes, stirring once for even toasting.

Cook an extra 2 minutes on High (100%), stirring once more during the cycle so that seeds roast evenly. Watch the oven for seeds may burn!

Cool and crush sesame seeds roughly in a mortar.

Mix sauce ingredients and bottle. Serve as a dip for appetisers.

Note: Appetisers may be pickled radish strips, carrot and celery sticks, or egg and beef strips tied in bundles with chives.

Kajang Satay Sauce

PREPARATION: 10 mins
COOKING: 700 watt – 18 mins
             650 watt – 24 mins
             500 watt – 32 mins
Times given here are for a
650 watt oven. Decrease time
by 15 seconds per minute for
a 700 watt oven. Increase time
by 20 seconds per minute for a
500 watt oven.
KCAL 1370

10 shallots
2 cloves garlic
3 stalks lemon grass
1 × 2 cm (½ × ¾ in) dried
   shrimp paste (*belacan*)
6 blanched almonds
1 tablespoon mixed curry powder
   (coriander, cummin, fennel)
1 teaspoon chilli powder
½ coconut, grated
2 × 2 cm (¾ × ¾ in) tamarind
   paste
2 teaspoons oil
½ cup crunchy peanut butter
1 teaspoon sugar
salt
pepper

Childhood trips to friends in Seremban were always exciting, partly because of the devious bends in the road. We were never sure when we'd round a bend to find a makeshift durian or chempedak stall. Part of the excitement, however, was the inevitable stopover at Kajang for an incomparable satay feast. The satay sauce at Kajang was what really made the satay. In the microwave oven, it takes only a fraction of the conventional cooking time.

Preparation

Peel and chop shallots and garlic roughly.

Clean lemon grass and use only the thick fleshy stem, 2 cm (¾ in) from the root. Slice thinly.

Roast *belacan* for 3 minutes on High (100%), turning over after 1½ minutes so both sides are well roasted.

Roast almonds for 3 minutes on High (100%), also turning once during the cycle to brown them.

Blend together shallots, garlic, *belacan* and almonds till smooth. Stir in curry and chilli powder.

Blend grated coconut with ¼ cup water and strain for ½ cup thick coconut milk.

Work tamarind with ¼ cup water and strain for ¼ cup tamarind juice.

Microwave Cooking Method

In a deep casserole, heat oil on High (100%) for 2 minutes. Add blended ingredients and cook on High (100%) for 3 minutes or till oil separates from the mixture. Cook a little longer if the mixture appears uncooked.

Add peanut butter, tamarind juice, sugar, salt and pepper, and stir well. Cook on Medium (70%) for 4-5 minutes. Do not cover but stir during the cooking cycle.

Gradually pour in coconut milk and stir gently to mix well. Cook on Medium (70%) for 6-8 minutes. Remove from heat.

Note: Satay sauce keeps well frozen.

Chilli Tamarind Mix

PREPARATION: 3 mins
COOKING: 700 watt – 7 mins
650 watt – 9 mins
500 watt – 12 mins
Times given here are for a
650 watt oven. Decrease time
by 15 seconds per minute for
a 700 watt oven. Increase time
by 20 seconds per minute for a
500 watt oven.
KCAL 591

50 g (1⅔ oz) tamarind
½ cup vinegar
3 cloves garlic
2 × 2 cm (¾ × ¾ in) ginger
½ teaspoon mustard seeds
50 g (1⅔ oz) sugar
1 tablespoon chilli powder (or
less)
30 g (1 oz) sultanas
salt

'Old Grandpa', whose relationship to our family was never quite worked out, lived a colourful life as a young man, on the run from the British Raj in India. As a medical student, he was arrested for being too vociferous about independence and spent the rest of his life working his way down through Burma and eventually to Malaysia. This Chilli Tamarind Mix was his recipe, which he vowed kept him alive through his trek. He mixed it with rice and this apparently kept the rice fresh for days. The Indians have a similar dish called Puli Satham, and perhaps this is a variation.

Preparation

Work tamarind with ¼ cup vinegar into a thick juice and strain.

Grind mustard seeds till fine and blend with garlic and ginger, using the remaining vinegar to facilitate blending.

Microwave Cooking Method

Boil garlic-ginger mixture with sugar and chilli powder, covered with plastic wrap, for 2 minutes on High (100%).

Stir in sultanas, tamarind and salt and cook for 2 minutes more, covered, on High (100%).

Uncover and cook another 5 minutes, on Medium (70%), till chutney is thick and jelly-like. If chutney is too dry, add 2-3 tablespoons vinegar to reconstitute a liquid texture.

Cool before bottling.

Wee Nee Chilli

PREPARATION: 10-15 mins
COOKING: 700 watt – 8 mins
           650 watt – 10 mins
           500 watt – 13 mins
Times given here are for a
650 watt oven. Decrease time
by 15 seconds per minute for
a 700 watt oven. Increase time
by 20 seconds per minute for a
500 watt oven.
KCAL 610

500 g (1 lb) red chillies
100 g (3½ oz) garlic
100 g (3½ oz) ginger
¾ cup vinegar
1 cup sugar
1 teaspoon salt (or more)

The homemade chilli sauce my brother can't do without. This is served in the seafood restaurants of Port Kelang (formerly Port Swettenham).

Preparation

Wash and pick off stems of chillies. Drain and pat dry with paper towels.

Peel and slice garlic and ginger.

Blend chillies, garlic and ginger together, using vinegar to facilitate blending. Add sugar and salt and continue blending till a smooth paste is obtained.

Microwave Cooking Method

Half-fill two bottles with warm water. (Remove metal covers.) Bring to a boil in about 4 minutes on High (100%).

Take out bottle (use oven gloves) and pour out water quickly. Fill about three-quarters full with the chilli blend and cook on Medium (70%) for 4 minutes.

Stir and cook for 2 minutes on High (100%) or till mixture boils.

Remove from the oven. Cover instantly and allow to cool.

Note: The taste of the sauce can be varied by adding more or less of any ingredient, e.g., more garlic gives a stronger garlic flavour.

To sterilise bottles, never wipe with a towel. Pour boiling water out, shake to remove excess water and fill instantly with food.

Pinang Acar

PREPARATION: 30-45 mins
COOKING: 700 watt – 19½ mins
               650 watt – 26 mins
               500 watt – 35 mins
Times given here are for a
650 watt oven. Decrease time
by 15 seconds per minute for
a 700 watt oven. Increase time
by 20 seconds per minute for a
500 watt oven.
KCAL 1255
SERVES 6

400 g (14 oz) cucumber
salt
300 g (10 oz) cauliflower
200 g (7 oz) carrots
100 g (3⅔ oz) french beans
100 g (3⅔ oz) cabbage

Blend A
2 × 1 cm (¾ × ½ in) piece dried
**   shrimp paste (*belacan*)**
3 × 3 cm (1¼ × 1¼ in) galangal
**   (*lengkuas*)**
10 shallots
20 dried chillies

Mixture B
2 cups vinegar
2 teaspoons salt

½ cup oil
2 tablespoons sugar
1 teaspoon salt

Our old rambling home in Klang was refuge to four homeless families during the war. Though most were impoverished then, ties were strong and all food, work and especially festivals were shared. Whatever the festival or mood, New Year Acar invariably made its appearance.

Preparation

Peel and halve cucumbers lengthwise. Scoop out seeds. Cut boat-shaped halves into strips, about 5 × 1 cm (2 × ½ in). Work cucumber and a generous sprinkling of salt with fingers in a bowl and leave it for a while for liquid to drain out. Squeeze out liquid and pat cucumber dry.

Cut cauliflower into 3 × 5 cm (1¼ × 2 in) flowerets.

Cut carrots into strips of the same size as cucumber.

String french beans and slice into 5 cm (2 in) lengths.

Tear cabbage into small bite-size pieces.

Roast *belacan*, uncovered, for 2 minutes. Peel galangal and shallots, and seed dried chillies. Blend all four ingredients till fine.

Microwave Cooking Method

Organise yourself so that all vegetables are in individual bowls.

Scald each vegetable, covered with plastic wrap, for 1-2 minutes on High (100%), depending on quantity, in the vinegar-salt mixture. Drain off vinegar each time.

Preheat a browning dish for 7 minutes on High (100%). Heat oil in the dish for 1 minute on High (100%) – it should not be heated too long.

Add blended shallot-chilli-galangal-*belacan* ingredients and cook for 3 minutes, uncovered, on High (100%).

Stir in sugar and salt. Cook for 2 minutes, uncovered, on High (100%).

Add drained vegetables and stir well into blended mixture.

Cook for 4 minutes on High (100%), covered with plastic wrap. Stir, then continue cooking, covered, for another 2 minutes on High (100%). Stir and remove from heat.

Cool and bottle into sterilised jars. Pinang Acar will be well pickled and ready to eat after 2 days.

Keep Pinang Acar refrigerated.

Tamatar Chutney

PREPARATION: 12 mins
COOKING: 700 watt – 14 mins
650 watt – 19 mins
500 watt – 25 mins
Times given here are for a
650 watt oven. Decrease time
by 15 seconds per minute for
a 700 watt oven. Increase time
by 20 seconds per minute for a
500 watt oven.
KCAL 1800

**500 g (1 lb) ripe or over-ripe
tomatoes**
1 small ripe papaya
2-3 red chillies
1 green capsicum
2 large onions
6 cloves garlic
1 cup brown sugar
salt
½ cup white vinegar
4-5 cloves
1 tablespoon mustard seeds
1 stalk curry leaves
½ cup sultanas (optional)
1 tablespoon cornflour

*My parents' dinner parties I remember as a festive array of dishes on
gleaming white tablecloth. Invariably, the main meat dish would be
surrounded by colourful bowls of chutney, like the sun and its galaxy of
stars. Now, in these leaner, more health-conscious days, a simple
chutney still adds a note of luxury.*

Preparation

Dip tomatoes in boiling water for a few seconds so skins can be
peeled. You can also microwave them on High (100%), 30
seconds for each tomato.

Chop peeled tomatoes roughly, reserving both pulp and liquid.

Peel and seed papaya, then chop roughly.

Seed chillies and capsicum and chop roughly.

Peel and chop onions and garlic.

Microwave Cooking Method

Mix chopped onions, garlic, sugar, salt, vinegar, cloves, mustard
seeds and curry leaves (stripped from their stalk) in a large bowl.
Cook for 5 minutes on High (100%), or till onions are transparent
and cooked. Stir well.

Add tomatoes, papaya, chillies, capsicum and sultanas if you are
using them. Mix well. Shake cornflour over the mixture, whisking
or mixing with a fork.

Cook for 6 minutes on High (100%). Stir twice during the cycle to
make sure cornflour is well integrated. Test for salt and spice
sufficiency.

Cook for another 8 minutes on High (100%), stirring every 2
minutes until chutney has thickened.

Pour into sterilised bottles when cool and refrigerate.

Pooma's Puli Chutney

PREPARATION: 10 mins
COOKING: 700 watt – 5 mins
             650 watt – 6 mins
             500 watt – 8 mins
Times given here are for a
650 watt oven. Decrease time
by 15 seconds per minute for
a 700 watt oven. Increase time
by 20 seconds per minute for a
500 watt oven.
KCAL 665

150 g (5 oz) tamarind paste
1 teaspoon fennel
50 g (1⅔ oz) pitted dates
2 teaspoons chilli powder
2 tablespoons sugar
salt
6 green chillies
½ teaspoon mustard seeds

A South Indian favourite, this pickle goes equally well with Indian curry and western food. Surprisingly, it is best eaten with cold slices of chicken or ham.

Preparation

Work tamarind with 1 cup water into a paste and strain to obtain the thick pulp.

Roast fennel seeds for 1 minute on High (100%), then grind to a powder.

Blend dates, tamarind pulp, fennel, chilli powder, sugar and salt.

Slit chillies and remove seeds.

Microwave Cooking Method

Cook tamarind chutney with chillies and mustard seeds for 3 minutes on High (100%). Stir and blend well, then cook for another 2 minutes on Medium (70%) or until chutney starts bubbling.

Remove from heat, cool and store in sterilised bottle.

Note: Raisins may be added to this chutney. Cook together with chillies and tamarind paste.

Omani Date Chutney

PREPARATION: 10 mins
COOKING: 700 watt – 10-12 mins
          650 watt – 13-16 mins
          500 watt – 17-21 mins
Times given here are for a
650 watt oven. Decrease time
by 15 seconds per minute for
a 700 watt oven. Increase time
by 20 seconds per minute for a
500 watt oven.
KCAL 1841

500 g (1 lb) pitted dates
4 cloves garlic
2 × 2 cm (¾ × ¾ in) ginger
1 cup vinegar
100 g (3½ oz) sugar
1 teaspoon cloves
2 cm (¾ in) cinnamon stick
2 tablespoons chilli powder
salt to taste

As part of the Middle Eastern tradition, dates and coffee are served before any business is conducted. Fresh dates in Oman tasted wonderful until my husband discovered they were fruit-fly contaminated. Date Chutney is an infinitely safer way to eat dates if you have had a similar experience.

Preparation

Blend dates, garlic and ginger with ½ cup vinegar to obtain a thick mixture.

Microwave Cooking Method

Put sugar and remaining ½ cup vinegar in a deep casserole and cover with plastic wrap. Cook for 2 minutes on High (100%).

Add cloves and cinnamon and cook for 1 minute on High (100%), or till sugar melts.

Add date-garlic-ginger blend, chilli powder and salt. Stir well and cover with plastic wrap.

Cook for 10 minutes on Medium (70%), uncovered, stopping the cycle three times to stir.

If date chutney is too thick, add ¼ cup vinegar and cook for 3 minutes more.

Pour into sterilised bottles while. still hot and cool before refrigerating.

Anush's Apricot Chutney

PREPARATION: 5 mins
COOKING: 700 watt – 17 mins
650 watt – 23 mins
500 watt – 31 mins
Times given here are for a
650 watt oven. Decrease time
by 15 seconds per minute for
a 700 watt oven. Increase time
by 20 seconds per minute for a
500 watt oven.
KCAL 810

200 g (6⅔ oz) dried apricots
4 dried chillies
2 cloves garlic
2 × 2 cm (¾ × ¾ in) ginger
½ cup vinegar
200 g (6⅔ oz) sugar
salt
2 tablespoons sultanas (optional)

My daughter increased the chilli and spice in a traditional Australian chutney and came up with this Eurasian result.

Preparation

Wash apricots and soak in water while the other ingredients are being prepared.

Blend chillies, garlic and ginger with a little vinegar to facilitate blending.

Microwave Cooking Method

Cover apricots and water with plastic wrap. Cook for 10 minutes on High (100%) till soft and mushy.

Remove plastic wrap. Add vinegar, sugar, salt and blended ingredients to soft apricots. Stir well and cook uncovered for 10 minutes on Medium (70%). The liquid will gradually thicken as sugar melts. Stir once during the cycle, correcting for salt.

Cook for 3 minutes more on High (100%), to thicken the chutney.

Note: Add sultanas in the last few minutes of cooking time, if preferred.

Mangga Chutney

PREPARATION: 15 mins
COOKING: 700 watt – 20 mins
          650 watt – 26 mins
          500 watt – 35 mins
Times given here are for a
650 watt oven. Decrease time
by 15 seconds per minute for
a 700 watt oven. Increase time
by 20 seconds per minute for a
500 watt oven.
KCAL 3532

20 unripe medium-sized mangoes
3 × 3 cm (1¼ × 1¼ in) ginger
6 cloves garlic
½ cup blanched almond slivers
1 cup vinegar
2 cups sugar
2 teaspoons salt
2 teaspoons chilli powder
200 g (6⅔ oz) raisins

This versatile chutney has satisfied many a craving in my life.

Preparation

Peel and quarter mango, discarding tough skin and seeds. The flesh should weigh at least 400 g (14 oz).

Peel and slice ginger and garlic and pound or blend till fine.

Roast almonds for 3 minutes on High (100%), stirring once to prevent burning.

Microwave Cooking Method

Put vinegar, sugar and salt in a deep bowl and cover with plastic wrap. Cook on High (100%) for 3 minutes, stirring once. Sugar should be dissolved. If not, stir to mix thoroughly.

Add chilli powder and blended garlic and ginger and cook, covered, for 2 minutes on High (100%). Stir well.

Add mangoes and cook for 15 minutes on Medium (70%), stirring every 3 minutes or so. Add more vinegar if chutney is thickening too quickly. Add raisins for the last 5 minutes of cooking and remove plastic wrap.

Stir well and cook, uncovered, for 3 minutes on High (100%).

Bottle at once in sterilised bottles and cool before covering.

DESSERTS & SWEETS

Microtips on Baking

The main advantage of baking cakes in the microwave oven is the little time it takes — usually about 25 minutes. And cakes can be made in ovenproof dishes or heat-resistant plastic containers.

Choose round containers in preference to oblong or square ones. Round ring cake containers are ideal. Always use containers with straight sides so cooking is even.

Finally, always place the container on an inverted plastic or glass stand (or an inverted saucer), so the microwaves can penetrate and cook from many angles.

Microwaved cakes are best eaten fresh as they tend to dry out. To remedy microwave-dry cakes, moisten with a jam spread, a thick syrup of rum and water, or sugar and water, boiled in the microwave oven — one such mixture is ¼ cup water, 2 tablespoons rum and 2 teaspoons sugar cooked on High (100%) for 3 minutes. Icing on a microwaved cake also helps keep it moist.

Cake and Teabreads. Mix all ingredients together. It is better to undercook a cake than to overcook when baking. If the centre looks moist, return it to the oven for another minute, then remove it, cover with a plate and let it cook in its own heat. The moisture will disappear.

'5-minute' Packet Cake Mix. Follow directions on the packet, but instead of using a cake beater, beat cake mix with a fork. Microwave cooking needs little aeration; in fact, excessive aeration makes the cake hard and dry.

Grease and flour a non-metallic cake ring mould or use a round casserole with a paper cup filled with rice in the centre, to hold a ring shape. (Microwaves cook better on the outer edges.)

Cook for 5 minutes on High (100%). The centre may look moist, but a plate inverted over the cake for 30 seconds will dry it as the cake cooks in its own heat. Let it stand for 3 minutes before inverting onto a plate.

Pastry

PREPARATION: 15 mins
COOKING: 700 watt – 6 mins
               650 watt – 8 mins
               500 watt – 11 mins
Times given here are for a
650 watt oven. Decrease time
by 15 seconds per minute for
a 700 watt oven. Increase time
by 20 seconds per minute for a
500 watt oven.
KCAL 1506

200 g (6⅔ oz) flour
salt
2½ tablespoons (50 g/1⅔ oz)
margarine
2½ tablespoons (50 g/1⅔ oz)
butter
yellow food colouring or egg yolk

Pastry made in the microwave will not brown but is just as tasty, flaky and of good consistency. Top with a variety of fillings.

Preparation

Sift flour and salt to remove lumps.

Work flour and salt with margarine with the fingers till flour takes on a crumbly texture.

Add butter and, gradually, ¼ cup icy water, working quickly with the fingertips so as not to warm the pastry.

Form pastry into a ball. Do not knead.

Microwave Cooking Method

Roll pastry on a board and cut out to fit a 23 cm (9 in) non-metallic pie plate.

Colour pastry by brushing with food colouring (mixed with water) or with a beaten egg yolk.

Prick pastry all over with a fork. Cook for 8 minutes on High (100%), rotating plate after 4 minutes.

Take out and cool before filling with the desired filling.

Note: An egg-yellow colouring can be used if you feel pastry must be browned. The taste will remain the same with or without colouring.

*Clockwise from bottom: Drunken Bananas (256), Seri Muka (241),
Cory Coconut Custard (252)*

Nanas Down Under (233)

Nanas Down Under

PREPARATION: 12 mins
COOKING: 700 watt – 11 mins
         650 watt – 14 mins
         500 watt – 60 mins
Times given here are for a
650 watt oven. Decrease time
by 15 seconds per minute for
a 700 watt oven. Increase time
by 20 seconds per minute for a
500 watt oven.
KCAL 2521
SERVES 6

2 tablespoons butter
1 large can (500 g or 1 lb)
  pineapple rings
5-6 glace cherries, halved
150 g (5 oz) self-raising flour
1 tablespoon baking powder
150 g (5 oz) margarine
3 large eggs
150 g (5 oz) soft brown sugar
2 tablespoons golden syrup

When you need to impress someone without too much effort, try this Pineapple Upside Down Cake.

Preparation

Use a deep, curved non-metallic bowl and grease it liberally with 2 tablespoons butter.

Drain pineapple, reserving syrup and spreading ¼ cup of it over the butter. (It will sink to the bottom of the bowl but let it remain so.)

Arrange pineapple rings to cover the bottom and sides of the bowl, with cherry halves in the centre of the rings. Chop up the remaining rings to add to cake mix.

Sift flour with baking powder.

In another mixing bowl, cream margarine, eggs and sugar. Add chopped pineapple, and the flour sifted with baking powder. Beat with a fork while adding some of the remaining pineapple syrup to give a pouring texture.

Microwave Cooking Method

Pour cake mix carefully into the pineapple bowl, taking care not to disarrange the rings.

Cook, covered with plastic wrap, for 12 minutes on Low (30%).

Continue cooking for 2 minutes on High (100%) then remove from the oven. Let it stand for 5 minutes, remove the plastic wrap and unmould carefully.

Spoon golden syrup over the cake to keep it moist.

Vim Cheese Cake

PREPARATION: 10 mins
COOKING: 700 watt – 11-13 mins
                650 watt – 14-17 mins
                500 watt – 19-23 mins
Times given here are for a
650 watt oven. Decrease time
by 15 seconds per minute for
a 700 watt oven. Increase time
by 20 seconds per minute for a
500 watt oven.
KCAL 1975
SERVES 6

60 g (2 oz) butter
120 g (4 oz) whole wheat, or
crumbs from crushed graham
crackers/marie biscuits
1 teaspoon crushed palm sugar
1 teaspoon allspice

Filling
500 g (1 lb) Philadelphia cream
cheese
200 g (6⅔ oz) condensed milk
2 eggs
1½ tablespoons lemon or lime
juice
pinch of salt

1 tablespoon almonds

Although cheese cake is European in origin, it is today popular all over the world. For centuries, the Russians have made an Easter cake called Pascha, rich and heavy with eggs, almonds and cream cheese, which is probably the ancestor of the universal favourite.

Microwave Cooking Method

Use a 23 cm (9 in) round dish, preferably with straight sides, or a fluted flan dish. Grease it well.

Melt butter in the dish on High (100%) for 30-40 seconds. Do not let butter froth.

Sprinkle in wheat/crumbs, sugar and allspice and rub in with fingers to mix with butter. Press crumb mixture firmly and evenly onto the base of the dish and microwave on High (100%) for 1 minute or so. Rotate dish twice. Cook a further 30 seconds on High (100%).

Beat cream cheese, adding condensed milk slowly, then eggs, lemon juice and salt, until mixture is smooth and creamy.

Microwave in the mixing bowl on High (100%) for 3-4 minutes, until it thickens. Stir to evenly distribute heat.

Spread the base with the cream cheese filling and cover loosely with plastic wrap. Cook the whole cake on Medium (70%) for about 6-8 minutes until the filling is firm to the touch. Rotate dish 3 times during the cooking cycle. Let it stand to cool.

Note: Cut wedges while crust is soft and cooling. As the base will be covered with filling, mark the top of the pie dish where the wedges are so you can cut through the crust layer easily when serving.

Apple Spice Cake

PREPARATION: 8 mins
COOKING: 700 watt – 15 mins
650 watt – 20 mins
500 watt – 27 mins
Times given here are for a
650 watt oven. Decrease time
by 15 seconds per minute for
a 700 watt oven. Increase time
by 20 seconds per minute for a
500 watt oven.
KCAL 1906
SERVES 6

4 green apples
150 g (5 oz) plain flour
150 g (5 oz) castor sugar
2 tablespoons vegetable oil
2 eggs
1 teaspoon soda bicarbonate
1 teaspoon salt
1 teaspoon cinnamon powder
¼ teaspoon clove powder
¼ teaspoon grated nutmeg
2 tablespoons raisins
cinnamon powder
sugar

A nutritious cake using fruit which serves well with a scraping of butter on each slice, but one that can be eaten plain as well.

Preparation

Peel and core apples. Cut into cubes and cook with ¼ cup water on High (100%) for 8 minutes. Mash the apple.

Put all ingredients, except mashed apple and the raisins in a blender or food processor and blend till well mixed. Stir in the fruit.

Microwave Cooking Method

Grease and line the base of a small 15 cm (6 in) ovenproof bowl.

Pour cake mix into the bowl and microwave on Medium (70%) for 8 minutes. Turn the bowl twice during the cycle.

Cook on High (100%) for 4 minutes, turning the bowl 180° twice. When the wet patch on top disappears, the cake is cooked.

Let the cake stand for 6-8 minutes before turning onto a wire rack to cool. Sprinkle cinnamon and sugar on top for garnish.

Honey Cake

PREPARATION: 10 mins
COOKING: 700 watt – 10 mins
               650 watt – 13 mins
               500 watt – 17 mins
Times given here are for a
650 watt oven. Decrease time
by 15 seconds per minute for
a 700 watt oven. Increase time
by 20 seconds per minute for a
500 watt oven.
KCAL 2544
SERVES 6-8

200 g (6⅔ oz) butter
200 g (6⅔ oz) self-raising flour
4 tablespoons crushed soft brown
  sugar
4 tablespoons clear honey
200 g (6⅔ oz) eggs
4 tablespoons milk
1 teaspoon cinnamon powder
1 teaspoon cardamom powder
½ teaspoon nutmeg powder
½ teaspoon clove powder
50 g (1⅔ oz) almonds
pinch of salt

Icing
1 cup icing sugar
2 tablespoons butter
1 tablespoon ginger wine

A light and subtle cake. Tamara bakes us her version which often comes in foot-long loaf pans.

Preparation

You will need a small 23 × 11 cm (9 × 4½ in) loaf pan of ovenproof or toughened plastic. Grease and line the base of the pan with greaseproof paper.

Beat all ingredients except almonds together with an electric mixer till mixture is smooth and creamy.

Microwave Cooking Method

Pour cake mix into the prepared pan and place on a cake rack or on an upturned saucer. Microwave on High (100%) for 10 minutes, rotating cake twice during the cycle (after every 4 minutes).

Cover and let the cake stand to complete cooking, then turn onto a cooling rack.

Toast almonds on High (100%) for 3 minutes. Turn once during the cycle for even toasting.

Cream sugar and butter together then add ginger wine. Spread icing on the cake and press toasted almonds on top in a decorative layer.

Shanghai Sugared Walnuts

CHINESE

PREPARATION: 5 mins
COOKING: 700 watt – 7 mins
          650 watt – 9 mins
          500 watt – 12 mins
Times given here are for a
650 watt oven. Decrease time
by 15 seconds per minute for
a 700 watt oven. Increase time
by 20 seconds per minute for a
500 watt oven.
KCAL 2071
SERVES 4

300 g (10 oz) walnuts
200 g (6⅔ oz) honey
200 g (6⅔ oz) icing sugar
1 tablespoon lime juice

An unusual Chinese dessert as most dinners round off with fresh or canned fruits.

Preparation

Marinate walnuts in a mixture of honey, sugar and lime juice for 4 hours or less.

Microwave Cooking Method

Cook walnuts in syrup marinade for 6 minutes on High (100%). Stir once or twice during the cycle.

Sugar will caramelise and coat walnuts. Cook a further 3 minutes on High (100%). Remove and place on greaseproof paper to cool. Serve with after-dinner coffee.

Thagu Pyin

BURMESE

PREPARATION: 12 mins
COOKING: 700 watt – 20 mins
          650 watt – 26 mins
          500 watt – 35 mins
Times given here are for a
650 watt oven. Decrease time
by 15 seconds per minute for
a 700 watt oven. Increase time
by 20 seconds per minute for a
500 watt oven.
KCAL 3610
SERVES 6

1 cup sago
2 cups palm sugar, chopped
  roughly
pinch of salt
1 teaspoon butter
1 white coconut, grated

Most Asian sweets rely heavily on palm sugar and coconut, but this Burmese sweet made out of sago is refreshingly different.

Microwave Cooking Method

Wash sago and drain to remove dust. Add sago to 2 cups boiling water and cook on High (100%) for 12 minutes, stirring once during the cycle. Set aside till needed.

Dissolve palm sugar in 1 cup hot water and cook on High (100%) for 6 minutes, stirring twice during the cycle to break down the sugar.

Stir syrup and salt into sago and continue cooking the mixture on Medium (70%) for 8 minutes, stirring once during the cycle.

Pour the mixture into a greased tray to set.

When set, roll spoonfuls of sago in coconut flakes and serve.

Note: For more flavour, add screwpine leaves while cooking sago, removing before sugar is added.

Peanut Brittle

PREPARATION: 5 mins
COOKING: 700 watt – 11 mins
650 watt – 15 mins
500 watt – 20 mins
Times given here are for a
650 watt oven. Decrease time
by 15 seconds per minute for
a 700 watt oven. Increase time
by 20 seconds per minute for a
500 watt oven.
KCAL 4810
SERVES 6

100 g (3½ oz) sesame seeds
1 teaspoon butter
2 cups sugar
400 g (14 oz) roasted peanuts
½ teaspoon baking soda

Every Malaysian corner store or coffee shop has its gula or sweet section where large dusty plastic-lidded glass jars stand holding squares, cubes and circles of tasty peanut-based cookies – some crunchy and satisfying, others puffing up into flaky showers as you bite into them. They have to be eaten fresh otherwise they soften into limpid lumps with the humidity: an ideal excuse to stuff ourselves sick every shopping trip!

Microwave Cooking Method

Roast sesame seeds for 3 minutes on High (100%) or until brown.

In a buttered casserole, melt sugar in 1 cup water by cooking for 4 minutes on High (100%). Stir once during the cycle to dissolve sugar.

Add peanuts. Mix well and continue to cook for 5 minutes on High (100%), stirring twice during the cycle.

Stir in sesame seeds. Cook for 3 minutes on High (100%) until sugar crystallises, adding baking soda which will cause the mixture to foam slightly.

Pour quickly into a flat greased tray and cut into squares as peanut brittle begins to harden. Or let it cool and break bits off.

Store in an airtight container.

The Gladys Fluff

PREPARATION: 8 mins
COOKING: 700 watt – 13 mins
                650 watt – 18 mins
                500 watt – 23 mins
Times given here are for a
650 watt oven. Decrease time
by 15 seconds per minute for
a 700 watt oven. Increase time
by 20 seconds per minute for a
500 watt oven.
KCAL 555
SERVES 6

1 large (400 g/14 oz) can pineapple
1 teaspoon gelatin
2 tablespoons cornflour
2 egg yolks
3 egg whites
salt
2 teaspoons grated nutmeg
1 teaspoon cinnamon powder

This dessert may have its origins in the west, but it remains popular in Sri Lanka. Since curries are hot and spicy, fresh or canned fruit is usually served for dessert. In this case, the light pineapple fluff or soufflé complements the substantial curry meal perfectly.

Preparation

Drain syrup from canned pineapple into a bowl. Add sufficient water to make up 1 cup liquid.

Mix gelatin with 2 tablespoons of the diluted syrup and microwave on Medium (70%) for 1 minute or till gelatin dissolves.

Chop pineapple into bits.

Stir some diluted syrup with cornflour to make a smooth paste.

Place chopped pineapple with remaining liquid, cornflour paste and gelatin in a soufflé dish and stir well with a fork or whisk.

Beat egg yolks. Beat egg whites separately with a little salt till stiff.

Microwave Cooking Method

Cook the pineapple mixture on High (100%) for 5½ minutes till it thickens.

Add beaten egg yolks to a little of the thick custard, whisking well. Gradually add this to the rest of the custard. Stir carefully. Cook on High (100%) for 1 minute. Cool.

Fold beaten egg whites, half the grated nutmeg and all the cinnamon powder into the custard.

Garnish with the remaining nutmeg and cook on Low (30%) for 10 minutes or until pudding has set.

Serve hot or cold with cream.

Pistachio Ice Cream

PREPARATION: 10 mins
COOKING: 700 watt – 3 mins
          650 watt – 4 mins
          500 watt – 5 mins
Times given here are for a
650 watt oven. Decrease time
by 15 seconds per minute for
a 700 watt oven. Increase time
by 20 seconds per minute for a
500 watt oven.
KCAL 3200
SERVES 10

2 litres vanilla ice cream
200 g (6⅔ oz) pistachios
  or blanched almonds
green colouring
1 teaspoon cardamom powder
2 tablespoons sherry (optional)
1 can whipped cream

The first time I served this Kulfi to my Australian friends, they were intrigued by the cardamom spice in it and dubbed it 'curry ice cream'. Curry ice cream it remains to this day!

Microwave Cooking Method

Soften ice cream on Low or Defrost (30%) for 2-4 minutes or until ice cream is soft enough to mix with a spatula.

Mix nuts, colouring, cardamom powder and sherry, working quickly.

Fold in the whipped cream.

Return tub to the base of the freezer. The ice cream container should touch the freezer wall or base to set well. Leave for 4 hours at least.

Serve garnished with mint leaves and more cardamom powder.

Flambé Fruit

PREPARATION: 3 mins
COOKING: 700 watt – 7 mins
          650 watt – 9 mins
          500 watt – 12 mins
Times given here are for a
650 watt oven. Decrease time
by 15 seconds per minute for
a 700 watt oven. Increase time
by 20 seconds per minute for a
500 watt oven.
KCAL 1081
SERVES: 6

60 g (2 oz) butter
100 g (3½ oz) sugar
rind of 1 lime
2 tablespoons lime juice
5 tablespoons orange juice
fresh fruit (pineapple pieces,
  passion fruit, bananas,
  orange wedges or mango
  slices)
  or drained canned peaches/
  pears
3 tablespoons brandy

'Flambé' is a method of warming brandy, pouring it over fruit and then lighting it. The flavour is superb.

Microwave Cooking Method

Cook butter, sugar and rind in a shallow glass dish on High (100%) for 3 minutes.

Stir then add fruit juices. Stir to mix with syrup and cook on High (100%) for 4 minutes.

Add syrup to fruit and let it warm on Medium (70%) for 2 minutes.

In a cup or dish, warm brandy for 20 seconds on High (100%). Set brandy alight and wait for flame to die down. Stir brandy into fruit.

Serve topped with some whipped cream.

Seri Muka

PREPARATION: 15 mins
COOKING: 700 watt – 31 mins
         650 watt – 41 mins
         500 watt – 55 mins
Times given here are for a
650 watt oven. Decrease time
by 15 seconds per minute for
a 700 watt oven. Increase time
by 20 seconds per minute for a
500 watt oven.
KCAL 3110
SERVES 8-10

Rice Layer
250 g (8 oz) glutinous rice (*pulut*)
1 teaspoon salt
1¼ cups thick coconut milk
   from 1 grated coconut
1 tablespoon sugar

Custard Topping
6 eggs
200 g (6⅔ oz) sugar
½ teaspoon salt
6 screwpine leaves, pounded to
   extract green juice and
   essence
2 tablespoons rice flour
1¼ cups thick coconut milk

The creamy coconut custard on top of the compressed rice makes an unusual yet rich dessert with an apt name meaning 'beautiful faced'. The contrast of textures and tastes adds to the visual delight of this Malaysian dessert.

Rice Layer

Soak glutinous rice in salted water for 2 hours.

Drain rice at the end of that time, cover with coconut milk and add water to 2½ cm (1 in) above rice layer. Stir in 1 tablespoon sugar.

Steam rice for 18 minutes, covered with plastic wrap. Remove the wrap at the end of the cooking cycle.

Press rice onto a 20 cm (8 in) greased plate so that it forms a firm flat sheet. Use the back of a spoon to smoothen the layer which should be about 1½ cm (⅔ in) high.

Custard Layer

Beat eggs lightly, adding sugar and salt and beating till sugar dissolves.

Add screwpine juice and rice flour to coconut milk. Stir carefully into egg mixture and pour over the compressed rice layer.

Bake on Low (30%), covered with plastic wrap, for 15 minutes. Rotate the dish so that the centre will cook as well as the edges. At the end of the cycle, remove the wrap and continue cooking uncovered for 8 minutes on Low (30%).

Cool and cut into wedges.

Quezon Fancy

PREPARATION: 5 mins
COOKING: 700 watt – 13 mins
                650 watt – 18 mins
                500 watt – 23 mins
Times given here are for a
650 watt oven. Decrease time
by 15 seconds per minute for
a 700 watt oven. Increase time
by 20 seconds per minute for a
500 watt oven.
KCAL 3504
SERVES 6

3-4 medium-sized sweet potatoes
½ cup white sugar
½ cup brown sugar
½ cup butter
1 cup condensed milk
3 eggs, beaten
½ cup raisins
6 cloves
2 teaspoons cinnamon powder
1 teaspoon nutmeg powder

The Filipinos serve some of the best desserts in Asia and decorate them beautifully.

Preparation

Peel and grate sweet potatoes. You should have 4 cups.

Microwave Cooking Method

Add 3 tablespoons water to both kinds of sugar. Cook on High (100%) for 3 minutes, stirring to melt sugar.

Melt butter in a heatproof dish on Roast (70%) for 30 seconds.

Mix grated sweet potato with syrup, condensed milk, beaten eggs, raisins and spices. Add to heated butter, stir well and cover loosely with plastic wrap.

Cook on Medium (70%) for 12 minutes. Loosen with a spatula as edge cooks.

Uncover and cook on High (100%) for a further 2 minutes. Uncovering too long may dry and toughen the sweet potato.

Cool and serve with a cream lemon sauce.

Creamy Lemon Sauce

PREPARATION: 6 mins
COOKING: 700 watt – 2¼ mins
                650 watt – 3 mins
                500 watt – 4 mins
Times given here are for a
650 watt oven. Decrease time
by 15 seconds per minute for
a 700 watt oven. Increase time
by 20 seconds per minute for a
500 watt oven.
KCAL 795

50 g (1⅔ oz) butter
90 g (3 oz) castor sugar
1½ teaspoons cornflour
grated rind of 1 lemon
2½ tablespoons lemon juice
2½ tablespoons water
1 egg, beaten lightly

Preparation

Soften butter in the microwave oven on High (100%) for 20-30 seconds.

Microwave Cooking Method

Cream butter, sugar and cornflour together, blending with all other ingredients till mixture is smooth.

Microwave mixture on High (100%) for 2½ minutes or until mixture becomes clear and thick. Stir once or twice.

Pour while warm over Quezon Fancy.

Apple Crunch

PREPARATION: 15 mins
COOKING: 700 watt – 10 mins
            650 watt – 13 mins
            500 watt – 17 mins
Times given here are for a
650 watt oven. Decrease time
by 15 seconds per minute for
a 700 watt oven. Increase time
by 20 seconds per minute for a
500 watt oven.
KCAL 2740
SERVES 6

4 crisp green apples
1 teaspoon salt
3 tablespoons sugar
125 g (4 oz) frozen butter
1 teaspoon cinnamon powder
**1 packet commercial butter cake
  mix**
3 tablespoons brown sugar
½ cup desiccated coconut
⅓ cup chopped peanuts

A practical and simple way to prepare dessert, this is a reminder of my stay in Kingsburg, California with Granny E who introduced me to Yosemite and the giant Redwoods.

Preparation

Peel, core and slice apples. Sprinkle with salt to prevent discoloration. Place in a shallow dish with 3 tablespoons sugar and just enough water to wet them (1-2 tablespoonfuls).

Cook for 6 minutes on High (100%). Stir to mix evenly.

Slice hardened butter into thin slices or flakes.

Microwave Cooking Method

Spoon cooked apples into a square baking dish. Sprinkle with half the cinnamon powder.

Sprinkle with a layer of dry cake mix and cover this layer with butter flakes.

In a bowl, combine brown sugar, desiccated coconut, chopped peanut and the remaining cinnamon. Spoon this over the apple mix.

Cook for 7 minutes on High (100%). Place under a grill for 3-4 minutes to brown the crunch. (Use a conventional grill or microwave browner.)

Note: This Crunch can be served on its own or with an ice cream topping. Evaporated milk makes a delicious topping.

Cendol

PREPARATION: 10 mins
COOKING: 700 watt – 9 mins
                650 watt – 12 mins
                500 watt – 16 mins
Times given here are for a
650 watt oven. Decrease time
by 15 seconds per minute for
a 700 watt oven. Increase time
by 20 seconds per minute for a
500 watt oven.
KCAL 1570
SERVES 4-6

**6-8 screwpine leaves (*daun
    pandan*)**
1 teaspoon green food colouring
salt
**100 g (3½ oz) packet green bean
    flour (*hoenkwe*)**

1 coconut, grated
**6 tablespoons palm syrup (see
    recipe below)**

*School holidays meant visits to the museum in Kuala Lumpur or a cultural
evening at the British Council as my mother subscribed to the belief that
20 dollars bought either one dress or varied cultural experiences for the
entire family. These cultural visits were tempered with bribes, however,
so we used to race enthusiastically through the museum just to get to the
Cendol (pronounced chen-dol) man in Lake Gardens. The Cendol men
are a dying breed today, and we must solace ourselves with the watered
down versions in the posher watering holes of sophisticated Kuala
Lumpur.*

Preparation

Chop screwpine leaves and blend with ¼ cup water to pulp
them. Strain the green liquid and add green food colouring. Add
water to make up 3 cups of liquid.

Stir 1 cup of the green liquid with the green bean flour till lumps
are smoothened out. Set aside.

Microwave Cooking Method

Boil the remaining green liquid (about 2 cups) in the microwave
oven on High (100%) for 4 minutes, uncovered. Stir once or twice
during the cycle.

Stir and add green bean flour paste and cook on High (100%) for
3 minutes or until it boils. Stir two or three times during the cycle –
it is not necessary to stir continuously as lumps do not form easily
in the microwave oven.

Place a large-hole grater or strainer over a basin of icy water to
which a few cubes of ice have been added. Press the warm
green bean mixture through to form tear-drop shapes which
should set in the icy water. Drain when done.

Extract ¾ cup thick coconut milk from grated coconut. Add 5
cups water to the residue and blend in a blender. Strain to extract
5 cups thinner coconut milk. Add a little salt to coconut milk to
enhance its taste. (The salt also helps preserve it.)

Serving

Spoon green Cendol into tall glasses. Add crushed ice, coconut
milk and top with a tablespoon each of thick coconut milk and
palm syrup.

Palm Syrup

COOKING: 700 watt — 8 mins
650 watt — 10 mins
500 watt — 13 mins
Times given here are for a
650 watt oven. Decrease time
by 15 seconds per minute for
a 700 watt oven. Increase time
by 20 seconds per minute for a
500 watt oven.
KCAL 2005

500 g (1 lb) palm sugar (*gula melaka*)
1 cup water
3 tablespoons golden syrup
4-5 screwpine leaves, shredded and tied into a knot

Microwave Cooking Method

Chop palm sugar roughly so it will melt quickly.

Put all the ingredients together in a large mixing bowl and cook for 10 minutes on High (100%), stirring once or twice to melt down palm sugar.

Strain, then bottle and refrigerate till required.

Kluay Lae Kaopot Buat

PREPARATION: 5 mins
COOKING: 700 watt — 8 mins
650 watt — 11 mins
500 watt — 15 mins
Times given here are for a
650 watt oven. Decrease time
by 15 seconds per minute for
a 700 watt oven. Increase time
by 20 seconds per minute for a
500 watt oven.
KCAL 1110
SERVES 6

5 large green bananas (*pisang hijau*), about 500 g (1 lb)
1 medium can sweetcorn
3 tablespoons sesame seeds
3 tablespoons palm sugar
1 cup thick coconut milk
½ teaspoon jasmine essence (*yod nam malee*)

Thai desserts are always exquisitely presented. Use fresh flowers and a lot of imagination to present this unusual dessert. Served with vanilla ice cream, or on its own, this dessert goes well with all Southeast Asian dishes.

Preparation

Peel and cut bananas diagonally into 2½ cm (1 in) pieces and place in a bowl. Drain sweetcorn and add to bananas.

Toast sesame seeds for 3 minutes on High (100%), stirring once to brown evenly.

Microwave Cooking Method

Break or grate palm sugar. Add 3 tablespoons water and cook for 3 minutes on High (100%) or till sugar melts. Stir well, cool and add to thick coconut milk.

Pour coconut milk and palm sugar mixture over bananas and sweetcorn. Stir and cook for 5 minutes on Low (30%). Stir, then add jasmine essence and sprinkle with toasted sesame seeds.

Refrigerate before serving.

Payasam (Sago Pudding)

PREPARATION: 2 mins
COOKING: 700 watt – 17 mins
          650 watt – 23 mins
          500 watt – 30 mins
Times given here are for a
650 watt oven. Decrease time
by 15 seconds per minute for
a 700 watt oven. Increase time
by 20 seconds per minute for a
500 watt oven.
KCAL 1830
SERVES 6

½ cup sago
2 tablespoons butter or ghee
50 g (1⅔ oz) vermicelli
2 tablespoons raisins
1 tablespoon cashew nuts or
    almonds
4-5 cardamoms
½ cup sugar or golden syrup
1½ cups evaporated milk,
    diluted to make 2 cups liquid
salt
1 teaspoon rose water
2 egg whites

Payasam or 'Christmas Eve Magic' as we called it at home was always produced in bulk for carollers who visited late on Christmas Eve. We had the Chinese church singers and the Wesley choir, but the noisiest and most festive were the Tamil singers who sang to the accompaniment of drums, cymbals and tambourines. Their music, quick and happy, truly heralded Christmas.

Preparation

Soak sago in water for 10 minutes.

Melt butter or ghee for 30 seconds on High (100%) in a deep casserole. Turn vermicelli in the hot oil and roast for 3 minutes on High (100%), stirring once during the cycle. Remove vermicelli with a slotted spoon.

Plump raisins in remaining butter or ghee for 1 minute on High (100%). Drain raisins and set aside.

Cook cashew nuts or almonds in the same bowl for 2 minutes on High (100%). The nuts may be broken up roughly in a mortar.

Peel cardamom pods to extract seeds and crush seeds slightly so that flavours will penetrate the Payasam.

Microwave Cooking Method

Drain water from sago. Pour sago, cardamom seeds, sugar and milk into the casserole used to brown other ingredients. Stir well.

Cook for 8 minutes on High (100%), whisking well after 4 minutes and taking care not to let the pudding mix boil over. Keep stirring as mixture cooks.

Check to see if sago has turned transparent, an indication that it is cooked. Whisk well to loosen any lumps. Cook a further 3 minutes on High (100%).

Add browned nuts, vermicelli and raisins. Test for sugar and salt sufficiency. Cook on Low (30%) for 5 minutes to soften nuts and vermicelli.

Whisk rose water and stiffened egg whites into the mixture and serve hot or cold.

Mt Lavinia Special

PREPARATION: 10 mins
COOKING: 700 watt – 8 mins
          650 watt – 10 mins
          500 watt – 13 mins
Times given here are for a
650 watt oven. Decrease time
by 15 seconds per minute for
a 700 watt oven. Increase time
by 20 seconds per minute for a
500 watt oven.
KCAL 810
SERVES 4

4 green tart apples
8 cloves
3 tablespoons soft brown sugar
1 teaspoon nutmeg
½ teaspoon allspice
½ teaspoon cinnamon powder
1 tablespoon sultanas
1 tablespoon butter

This was a favourite dessert of the British colonials wherever the Empire extended. An optimistic historian might claim that these baked apples reminded them of home. A cynic would more likely point out that apples which have travelled half the world by ship are only good for baking. Luckily, whoever is right, the result is still delicious.

Preparation

Core apples by cutting a V-shaped plug out, leaving bottoms intact.

Poke 2 cloves into each apple.

Mix sugar, spices and sultanas and fill the cored apples with this mix.

Microwave Cooking Method

Arrange apples in a greased dish and spread some butter on the tops. Cover with plastic wrap.

Cook for 8 minutes on High (100%). Check if apples are soft by pricking with a fork. Cook a further 2 minutes to soften the tough skins.

Serve with a custard or cream, or chilled whipped evaporated milk.

Hung Tau Sui (Red Bean Sweet)

PREPARATION: 5 mins
COOKING: 700 watt – 26 mins
           650 watt – 35 mins
           500 watt – 47 mins
Times given here are for a
650 watt oven. Decrease time
by 15 seconds per minute for
a 700 watt oven. Increase time
by 20 seconds per minute for a
500 watt oven.
KCAL 1260
SERVES 4

250 g (8 oz) red beans
2 × 2 cm (¾ × ¾ in) ginger
½ cup sugar

A tasty, filling 'stomach liner', this bubur *used to be popular in the school canteen where ten cents bought one a large bowlful, eaten with a chipped enamel Chinese soup spoon.*

Preparation

Pick out stones/grit from beans and wash thoroughly. Soak for at least 30 minutes in water if time permits.

Wash, peel and shred ginger.

Microwave Cooking Method

Place beans with 2 cups water in a deep casserole (do not use a wide-mouthed casserole).

Cook beans for 25-30 minutes on High (100%), covered with plastic wrap. Stir once during the cycle.

Stir in sugar and ginger. Add another ½ cup water if beans have thickened too quickly or a thinner consistency is desired. (Beans should be slightly mushy to taste right.)

Cook for another 5 minutes on High (100%). Stir well and remove from heat.

Serve as a sweet after a main meal or as a tea-time snack.

Option: For a different flavour, add dried orange peel during the cooking process, and serve with coconut cream.

Red Bean Sweet (248)

Devils on Horseback, Savoury Roasted Nuts (261)

Chocaholic Slice

PREPARATION: 2 mins
COOKING: 700 watt – 4 mins
                  650 watt – 5 mins
                  500 watt – 7 mins
Times given here are for a
650 watt oven. Decrease time
by 15 seconds per minute for
a 700 watt oven. Increase time
by 20 seconds per minute for a
500 watt oven.
KCAL 3540
SERVES 6

1¼ cups self-raising flour
pinch of salt
120 g (4 oz) butter or margarine
1 tablespoon desiccated coconut
4 tablespoons castor sugar

Topping
1 tablespoon butter
1½ tablespoons cocoa, sifted
1 cup icing sugar, sifted
2 tablespoons milk

The Spanish kept their discovery of chocolate to themselves for nearly a hundred years. The Italian Benzoni in 1541 wrote that the drink 'was more suited to pigs than to man' (though he later changed his mind). We can't blame him for having thought so, for chocolate was at the time believed to have been 'ground on flat stones, mixed with red pepper, cinnamon and achiotte, a red colouring seed'!

Microwave Cooking Method

Sift flour and salt into a bowl.

Melt butter on High (100%) in 30 seconds. Add melted butter, desiccated coconut and castor sugar to sifted flour and mix well.

Place mixture in a tray and press down firmly.

Cook for 4½ minutes on Medium (70%).

In a separate bowl, melt 1 tablespoon butter in 20 seconds on High (100%). Add sifted cocoa, milk and icing sugar, mixing in with a fork until the icing is smooth.

Wait till the base is cool before spreading with icing.

Cut into slices to serve.

Cory Coconut Custard

PREPARATION: 15 mins
COOKING: 700 watt – 24 mins
650 watt – 32 mins
500 watt – 43 mins
Times given here are for a
650 watt oven. Decrease time
by 15 seconds per minute for
a 700 watt oven. Increase time
by 20 seconds per minute for a
500 watt oven.
KCAL 1840
SERVES 4-6

4 eggs
½ cup sugar
¼ teaspoon salt
3 tablespoons grated coconut

Caramel
200 g (6⅔ oz) sugar
200 ml (⅘ cup) water

2 cups milk
1 teaspoon vanilla essence
1 teaspoon grated nutmeg

A Filipino custard dedicated to a brave and admirable Filipina. In the Philippines coconut is often used with Spanish and American ingredients.

Preparation

Beat eggs, sugar and salt till sugar has melted.

Grease individual custard cups.

Toast coconut on High (100%) for 3 minutes, stirring once during the cycle.

Make the caramel by cooking sugar with water on High (100%) for 17-18 minutes in a heatproof dish. Do not stir but watch caramel towards the end of cooking time as it turns brown very fast and could burn. Pour a little caramel into each custard cup.

Microwave Cooking Method

Cook milk in a clear heat-resistant bowl for 4½ minutes on High (100%), or until tiny bubbles appear on the edges of the bowl. Add vanilla essence.

Beat egg mixture a little and stir into warm milk. Pour milk into the custard cups. Sprinkle the top with toasted coconut flakes and grated nutmeg.

Arrange heat-resistant cups in a circle on the outer edges of the circular microwave tray. Cook, uncovered, for 7 minutes on High (100%), or till custard looks thickened.

Chill before serving, turned into serving cups, or serve in cups custard was cooked in.

Banana Filipina

PREPARATION: 5 mins
COOKING: 700 watt – 4 mins
650 watt – 5 mins
500 watt – 7 mins
Times given here are for a
650 watt oven. Decrease time
by 15 seconds per minute for
a 700 watt oven. Increase time
by 20 seconds per minute for a
500 watt oven.
KCAL 1790
SERVES 6

6 large green bananas (*pisang hijau*)
2 tablespoons lime juice
1 tablespoon butter or margarine
4-6 cloves
¼ teaspoon cardamom powder
2 tablespoons honey
1 cup orange juice
½ cup white grated coconut
2 tablespoons Grand Marnier
  or ¼ cup brandy
  or 1 teaspoon vanilla essence
  if alcohol is not preferred
ice cream

A banana dessert from the Philippines. This one includes a light orange liqueur to perk the tastebuds.

Preparation

Peel and halve bananas lengthwise. Sprinkle with lime juice.

Microwave Cooking Method

Place banana halves in a shallow dish and dab on butter or margarine. Add cloves and cardamom powder and drizzle in honey and orange juice.

Cover loosely with plastic wrap and cook on High (100%) for 4 minutes.

Add coconut and Grand Marnier and cook on High (100%) for 1 minute. If brandy is used, warm brandy on High (100%) for 30 seconds and pour over bananas.

Pour liquor over bananas and ignite before serving. Each banana half may be topped with a scoop of ice cream. (Drizzle some sauce over the ice cream.)

Foenander Marshmallow

PREPARATION: 5 mins
COOKING: 700 watt – 6 mins
                650 watt – 8 mins
                500 watt – 10 mins
Times given here are for a
650 watt oven. Decrease time
by 15 seconds per minute for
a 700 watt oven. Increase time
by 20 seconds per minute for a
500 watt oven.
KCAL 2845
SERVES 6-8

30 g (1 oz) gelatin
500 g (1 lb) castor sugar
½ teaspoon vanilla essence
any pastel food colouring
¼ cup cornflour
½ cup icing sugar

A wonderful lady single-handedly turned cake-making into an art form in Malaysia. Her pupils not only learned all about cakes but picked up hints from Kathleen on home management and basic nutrition. I have used her marshmallow recipe to produce several hundred packets for countless fêtes and fairs. Here is the recipe adapted for use in the microwave oven.

Preparation

Put 1 cup cold water in a bowl and sprinkle gelatin over water. Cook for 2 minutes on High (100%) or till gelatin dissolves.

Stir well. Cook for another 30 seconds on High (100%).

Stir in castor sugar. Cook for 5 minutes on High (100%), stirring twice during the cycle.

When sugar has dissolved, remove from the oven. Do not overboil the mixture as this will harden it.

Beat the mixture with an electric cake mixer till it is stiff and thickening and has the texture of ice cream.

Add flavouring and any light colour. Beat a little longer to mix flavouring and colour evenly and pour into a greased 12 cm (5 in) square cake pan to cool.

Sift cornflour with icing sugar. Sprinkle some of this mixture over the marshmallow block to prevent stickiness when handled.

When cold, cut into squares on a board sprinkled with cornflour and icing sugar mixture.

Toss marshmallows in icing sugar.

Note: Pastel colours are traditionally used for sweets.

Natasha's Offering

PREPARATION: 2 mins
COOKING: 700 watt – 6-8 mins
              650 watt – 8-10 mins
              500 watt – 11-13 mins
Times given here are for a
650 watt oven. Decrease time
by·15 seconds per minute for
a 700 watt oven. Increase time
by 20 seconds per minute for a
500 watt oven.
KCAL 1715
SERVES 10

a small can of lychees
1 packet crystallised ginger
  or ginger in syrup
1 × 1 cm (½ × ½ in) paraffin wax
300 g (10 oz) cooking chocolate
1 tablespoon rum
waxed paper

In the Aztec empire, chocolate was served to the warriors and withheld from the cowardly. Even today, it takes a strong will not to polish off the entire plate when Natasha, our Russian friend, brings home these tempting chocolate-coated treats.

Preparation

Drain lychees from syrup and wipe dry with paper towels.

Stuff lychees with bits of ginger.

Microwave Cooking Method

Melt wax and chocolate in a rounded bowl for 2 minutes on High (100%). Stir well.

Dip lychees quickly in chocolate and place on waxed paper. (You will need to keep reheating the chocolate mixture till all lychees are coated otherwise chocolate will set.)

Refrigerate to harden, then place in cases or on a pretty plate to serve after dinner.

Drunken Bananas

PREPARATION: 5 mins
COOKING: 700 watt – 5 mins
            650 watt – 6 mins
            500 watt – 8 mins
Times given here are for a
650 watt oven. Decrease time
by 15 seconds per minute for
a 700 watt oven. Increase time
by 20 seconds per minute for a
500 watt oven.
KCAL 1500
SERVES 8

4 large green bananas (*pisang hijau*)
1 lime or lemon
50 g (1⅔ oz) pitted prunes
½ cup orange juice
3 tablespoons dark rum
60 g (2 oz) butter
4 tablespoons soft brown sugar
1 teaspoon whole cloves
8 cherries

This is a lovely dessert, served on its own or as a topping for vanilla ice cream. Use the tiny golden bananas (pisang mas) for variety and flavour.

Preparation

Peel and halve bananas diagonally. Squeeze lemon or lime juice over them to prevent discoloration.

Dice prunes and soak in a mixture of orange juice and rum for 3-4 hours or overnight.

Microwave Cooking Method

Cook butter and sugar in a shallow non-metallic dish for 2 minutes on High (100%). Stir once during the cycle.

Add prunes and their marinating liquid, and cloves. Stir well. Cook for 2 minutes on Medium (70%).

Add bananas, spooning sauce over them and arranging them on the outer edges of the dish to cook better. Add cherries to the dish. Cook for 2 minutes on High (100%), covered with plastic wrap.

Cool and serve as a sweet, placing a piece of banana on a dish and spooning some sauce over it with a cherry on each serving.

Burfi Bhawani

PREPARATION: 5 mins
COOKING: 700 watt – 19 mins
             650 watt – 25 mins
             500 watt – 33 mins
Times given here are for a
650 watt oven. Decrease time
by 15 seconds per minute for
a 700 watt oven. Increase time
by 20 seconds per minute for a
500 watt oven.
KCAL 2183
SERVES 6-8

2 cups milk powder
2 cups ground almonds
½ cup castor sugar
1 teaspoon cardamom powder
1¼ cups cream

A traditional Indian almond and milk candy, made simple the microwave way by my talented friend Bhawani.

Preparation

Mix all ingredients in a bowl, using cream to blend sugar and milk powder.

Pour into a greased 20 cm (8 in) pie plate.

Microwave Cooking Method

Cook on Medium (70%) for 25 minutes or till set. The centre may appear wet. Let it stand, covered, for 5 minutes to cook on its own heat.

Cut into diamond shaped slices and refrigerate when cool.

Note: For a variation, use desiccated or fresh grated coconut instead of almonds.

Sankhagnua Mak Phao Laos

PREPARATION: 5 mins
COOKING: 700 watt – 9 mins
650 watt – 12 mins
500 watt – 16 mins
Times given here are for a
650 watt oven. Decrease time
by 15 seconds per minute for
a 700 watt oven. Increase time
by 20 seconds per minute for a
500 watt oven.
KCAL 1900
SERVES 4

4 (small) young coconuts
8 eggs
1 cup sugar
1 cup thick coconut milk
(from 1 old coconut, grated)
4 screwpine leaves

This coconut custard served in coconut shells is a traditional Laotian sweet which is easier to prepare in the microwave oven than when using the conventional steaming method. Laotian food is like a blend of Thai and Vietnamese food and coconut forms the basis.

Preparation

Remove husks from the 4 coconuts. Curve into shape and cut off a slice from the top to leave a sizeable hole. Cut off a smaller slice off the bottom so coconuts can sit upright. Reserve the top slices to use as lids.

Pour out coconut water in the shell. Leave the young meat lining the inside.

In a bowl, beat eggs with sugar and thick coconut milk till sugar has dissolved and mixture is thick. Shred each screwpine leaf lengthwise by running down its length with a fork. Tie the shreds of each leaf into a knot and add to the mixture.

Microwave Cooking Method

Divide the mixture equally into the coconut shells. Set reserved caps on top.

Steam for 6 minutes on High (100%), two at a time (total time 12 minutes).

Serve custard in the shells, with long serving spoons.

Bubur Kacang Hijau

PREPARATION: 8 mins
COOKING: 700 watt – 27 mins
650 watt – 36 mins
500 watt – 47 mins
Times given here are for a
650 watt oven. Decrease time
by 15 seconds per minute for
a 700 watt oven. Increase time
by 20 seconds per minute for a
500 watt oven.
KCAL 4196
SERVES 6

500 g (1 lb) green beans
4 screwpine leaves
2 coconuts, grated
300 g (10 oz) sago
pinch of salt
300 g (10 oz) brown sugar

This is a tea-time or after-dinner sweet, often cooked during the Muslim fasting month of Ramadan when the sun-up to sun-down fast is broken with something a little special. This particular recipe employs both conventional and microwave methods for quick results.

Preparation

Roast green beans for 6 minutes on High (100%), stirring two or three times during the cycle.

Shred screwpine leaves by running a fork down their length and tie into a knot.

Add ¾ cup cool boiled water to grated coconut and blend, then strain to extract 1½ cups thick coconut milk.

Microwave Cooking Method

Cook green beans in 3 cups water for 25 minutes on High (100%), covered loosely with plastic wrap. Leave a vent in the wrap so that a spoon can be inserted to stir the green beans as they cook. Stir 4-5 times to cook evenly. (Do not leave the spoon in the oven during the cooking cycle.)

Meanwhile, on a conventional stove top, boil 2 cups water. Add sago and salt to boiling water and cook till sago turns translucent. (About 10-15 minutes.)

Drain and wash sago in water till excess starch has washed off.

When green beans are cooked, stir and drain off liquid.

Cook sugar and ½ cup water with shredded screwpine leaves for 3½ minutes on High (100%) till syrup boils. Remove screwpine leaves before using syrup.

To serve, scoop green beans into individual bowls, and add some sago, syrup and thick coconut milk.

SAVOURIES

Kaju Badam Masala

PREPARATION: 10 mins
COOKING: 700 watt – 11 mins
              650 watt – 15 mins
              500 watt – 20 mins
Times given here are for a
650 watt oven. Decrease time
by 15 seconds per minute for
a 700 watt oven. Increase time
by 20 seconds per minute for a
500 watt oven.
KCAL 2158
SERVES 6-8

100 g (3½ oz) cashew nuts
100 g (3½ oz) almonds
200 g (6⅔ oz) peanuts
2 tablespoons ghee
2 teaspoons chilli powder
   (less if preferred)
1 teaspoon *garam masala*
6-8 curry leaves
100 g (3½ oz) rice crispies
salt

My aunt believed that to pass exams one had first to eat one's fill. So my memory of exams is of keeping awake all hours, jogging around quadrangles to stay awake, and consuming mountains of 'Mixture'. This recipe, quick and simple, comes highly recommended for the scholars in your home.

Preparation

Clean and rub off skins of peanuts and cashew nuts.

Microwave Cooking Method

Cook cashew nuts on High (100%) for 3 minutes, turning nuts over after 1 minute or so to prevent burning.

Cook almonds in the same way. Peanuts will need at least 5 minutes. Keep turning nuts so that they roast evenly.

In a larger mixing bowl, melt ghee by cooking on High (100%) for 1 minute.

Add spices and torn curry leaves. Heat for 1 minute on High (100%).

Mix in rice crispies and nuts and stir well. Cook on High (100%) for 2 minutes. Stir and take out of the oven.

Sprinkle in salt to taste. Cool and bottle in an airtight container.

Note: If nuts and crispies soften, recrisp by heating for 1-2 minutes on High (100%).

Devils on Horseback

PREPARATION: 15 mins
COOKING: 700 watt – 6 mins
            650 watt – 8 mins
            500 watt – 11 mins
Times given here are for a
650 watt oven. Decrease time
by 15 seconds per minute for
a 700 watt oven. Increase time
by 20 seconds per minute for a
500 watt oven.
KCAL 635
SERVES 6 or more

6 bacon rashers
12 pitted prunes
100 g (3½ oz) cream cheese
  or 12 pitted dates
toothpicks
½ tablespoon butter

All Asians love parties, and seize any opportunity to have a makan kecil or 'small meal'. This recipe and the two that follow will take care of the unexpected party or get-together of friends.

Preparation

Cut rind carefully off bacon and cut into two lengthwise. They should be long enough to wrap around a prune twice.

Make a slit in each prune and stuff with cream cheese or a pitted date. Wrap a length of bacon like a belt around each prune, making sure it is enclosed.

Secure with a toothpick.

Microwave Cooking Method

Heat a browning dish for 6 minutes on High (100%). Coat the dish with butter and arrange Devils on Horseback on the dish. Cover with a paper towel to prevent splatters.

Cook for 1 minute on High (100%), then turn over and cook for another minute on High (100%). Bacon will sizzle as it cooks.

Serve hot as an entrée.

Savoury Roasted Nuts

COOKING: 700 watt – 2½ mins
            650 watt – 3½ mins
            500 watt – 4½ mins
Times given here are for a
650 watt oven. Decrease time
by 15 seconds per minute for
a 700 watt oven. Increase time
by 20 seconds per minute for a
500 watt oven.
KCAL 813
SERVES 4-6

100 g (3½ oz) nuts (any kind)
garlic salt
chilli powder (optional)
½ teaspoon butter

This comes under the category of 'arm's length food', for once you start on it, you're never satisfied till it's all gone.

Microwave Cooking Method

Cook nuts for 3 minutes on High (100%), turning once during the cycle.

Sprinkle with garlic salt and chilli powder and roll in ½ teaspoon butter.

Cook for 30 seconds on High (100%).

Cool and serve at once or store in an airtight bottle.

Bacon Appetiser

PREPARATION: 10 mins
COOKING: 700 watt – 13 mins
              650 watt – 18 mins
              500 watt – 23 mins
Times given here are for a
650 watt oven. Decrease time
by 15 seconds per minute for
a 700 watt oven. Increase time
by 20 seconds per minute for a
500 watt oven.
KCAL 2135
SERVES 10 (3 per person)

10 blanched almonds
10 rashers bacon
5 prunes
6 medium-sized prawns
6 black olives
60 g (2 oz) pineapple cubes
60 g (2 oz) cocktail sausages

This makes a pretty variety of appetisers.

Preparation

Toast almonds on High (100%) for 4 minutes, turning once during the cycle.

Stuff prunes with toasted almonds.

Cut each strip of bacon into three lengthwise.

Shell and devein prawns. Stone olives.

Wrap thin bacon strips around olives, drained pineapple cubes,, prawns and cocktail sausages. Fasten with wooden toothpicks.

Place several layers of kitchen paper on a plate. Arrange 10 appetisers slightly apart and cover with a layer of paper.

Microwave Cooking Method

Cook each dish of 10 appetisers for 4½ minutes on High (100%). You may need to vary the time, depending on the size of bacon and stuffing.

Drain well and place on a serving tray. The appetisers may be reheated if necessary for a few seconds before serving.

Note: This is good cocktail fare. Use thin Polish salami strips instead of bacon, or strips of corned beef, sliced thinly.

Anytime Open-face Snacks

PREPARATION: 10 mins
COOKING: 700 watt – 15-29 mins
                  650 watt – 20-38 mins
                  500 watt – 27-51 mins
Times given here are for a
650 watt oven. Decrease time
by 15 seconds per minute for
a 700 watt oven. Increase time
by 20 seconds per minute for a
500 watt oven.
KCAL 1550
SERVES 6-8

1 teaspoon sesame seeds
200 g (6⅔ oz) spiced ham
100 g (3½ oz) shelled prawns
200 g (6⅔ oz) minced pork
2 medium-sized potatoes
6 stalks spring onion, chopped
pepper
1 teaspoon garlic/celery salt
1 teaspoon chilli powder
2 tablespoons grated cheese
butter
a few slices bread
1 egg, beaten

These can be added to Bacon Appetisers and Devils on Horseback (opposite and on page 251) for greater variety.

Preparation

Toast sesame seeds for 3 minutes on High (100%), stirring once during the cycle.

Chop spiced ham and prawns and mix with minced pork.

Wash and cook potatoes for 8 minutes on High (100%). Peel and mash.

Add mashed potatoes, chopped spring onions, pepper, chilli powder, garlic/celery salt and cheese to the meat and mix thoroughly.

Butter a few slices of bread and cut out fancy shapes with cookie cutters.

Pat a little of the mixture onto pieces of bread and smooth into a rounded dome. Brush with beaten egg.

Microwave Cooking Method

Place about a dozen pieces on a flat dish. Cover loosely with plastic wrap and cook on High (100%) for 5 minutes or till meat is cooked.

Garnish with toasted sesame seeds.

If a crisp golden colour is preferred, place under a conventional grill for 2-3 minutes.

Repeat till all pieces are cooked. Serve hot, reheating for a few seconds if necessary in the microwave oven.

Gang Yui

PREPARATION: 5 mins
COOKING: 700 watt – 4 mins
           650 watt – 5 mins
           500 watt – 7 mins
Times given here are for a
650 watt oven. Decrease time
by 15 seconds per minute for
a 700 watt oven. Increase time
by 20 seconds per minute for a
500 watt oven.
KCAL 360
SERVES 4-6

2 eggs
1 teaspoon light soy sauce
6 stalks young spring onion
6 chives
100 g (3½ oz) beef fillet

Marinade
1 tablespoon ginger juice
1 teaspoon sesame oil
1 teaspoon soy sauce
½ teaspoon pepper

In Japan, even snacks must be a visual feast.

Preparation

Beat eggs with soy sauce.

Soften spring onions and chives by wetting slightly and heating on Medium (70%) for 2 minutes on kitchen paper.

Slice beef into thin strips, but not so thin that they tear apart. Season beef in marinade.

Microwave Cooking Method

Cook eggs on High (100%) for just over a minute. Stop after 30 seconds of the cycle to move cooked egg at the edges to the centre of the plate. Cool and cut into strips.

Stir-fry beef in an oiled plate for 2 minutes on High (100%).

Tie a bundle of some beef and egg strips with chive and spring onion 'ties'.

Serve with a sesame seed sauce.

DRINKS

Microtips on Heating Liquids

If you have a 650 watt microwave oven, it takes about 2½ minutes to boil a cup of water or beverage if the liquid is at room temperature.

When microwaving more than 1 cup, arrange the containers in a circle with a space in the centre. Leave spaces between the containers as well so that microwaves can circulate easily.

When a cup of water is boiled in a microwave oven, and a spoon or a teabag is inserted, it comes to a boil once more, so be wary of hot liquids.

Marshmallow Cocoa Mocha

PREPARATION: 2 mins
COOKING: 700 watt – 4 mins
          650 watt – 5 mins
          500 watt – 7 mins
Times given here are for a 650 watt oven. Decrease time by 15 seconds per minute for a 700 watt oven. Increase time by 20 seconds per minute for a 500 watt oven.
KCAL 1010
SERVES 4-6

3 teaspoons cocoa
2 cups milk
6 marshmallows
3 teaspoons sugar
1 teaspoon instant coffee powder
½ teaspoon nutmeg powder
½ teaspoon cinnamon powder

Another one for the chocaholics.

Preparation

Mix cocoa with 3 tablespoons cold milk till smooth.

Cut marshmallows in half.

Microwave Cooking Method

Heat remaining milk for 4 minutes on High (100%). Do not let it boil over.

Add cocoa mixture and mix with a whisk, adding sugar, instant coffee powder, nutmeg and cinnamon. Stir well.

Pour into 2 cups. Top with halved marshmallows and microwave on High (100%) for 1 minute. Marshmallows will puff up when heated. Serve hot.

Papa's Hot Jaffna Cure

PREPARATION: 2 mins
COOKING: 700 watt – 3 mins
          650 watt – 4 mins
          500 watt – 5 mins
Times given here are for a
650 watt oven. Decrease time
by 15 seconds per minute for
a 700 watt oven. Increase time
by 20 seconds per minute for a
500 watt oven.
KCAL 395
SERVES 1

1 cup milk
2 tablespoons sugar
1 teaspoon instant coffee powder
1 egg
1 tablespoon brandy or rum
nutmeg or cinnamon powder

Although my father insisted that his cough came from 'the home country', I have found many recipes similar to this purporting to be cures for upset stomachs and the common cold. When ill, however, we were quite happy to tuck into bed with this potion containing a heady dose of brandy that came out of hiding on such decisive occasions.

Microwave Cooking Method

Heat a cup of milk on High (100%) for 3 minutes.

Add sugar and coffee, stirring to dissolve. Cook for another 1 minute on High (100%), taking care not to let it boil over.

Meanwhile, beat egg till frothy and add gradually to boiling coffee, stirring all the while so that egg mixes without coagulating.

Add brandy or rum and top with spice. Serve hot.

Lake Club Special (Irish Coffee)

PREPARATION: 2 mins
COOKING: 700 watt – 3 mins
          650 watt – 4 mins
          500 watt – 5 mins
Times given here are for a
650 watt oven. Decrease time
by 15 seconds per minute for
a 700 watt oven. Increase time
by 20 seconds per minute for a
500 watt oven.
KCAL 700
SERVES 2

2 cups strong black coffee
4 teaspoons sugar (or to taste)
4 tablespoons Irish whiskey
2 tablespoons whipped cream

The Lake Club in Kuala Lumpur used to be the bastion and symbol of white domination. I am convinced it was worth breaking those barriers if only to taste this lovely concoction in the orchid festooned lounge.

Microwave Cooking Method

Microwave coffee with sugar in two tall heatproof Irish coffee glasses on High (100%) till boiling (about 3-4 minutes). Stir to melt sugar.

Add whiskey and stir. Carefully spoon cream on top and serve hot. Cream will gradually seep into coffee.

Note: A coffee liqueur may be used instead of Irish whiskey.

Do not use crystal in the microwave oven as there is lead content in crystal.

Top to bottom: Marshmallow Cocoa Mocha (265),
Lake Club Special (266), Aunty Lily's Gingertea (269)

Left to right: The Flores Meatloaf (123),
Fred's Favourite Hamburger Casserole (115)

Aunty Lily's Gingertea

PREPARATION: 5 mins
COOKING: 700 watt – 8 mins
           650 watt – 10 mins
           500 watt – 13 mins
Times given here are for a
650 watt oven. Decrease time
by 15 seconds per minute for
a 700 watt oven. Increase time
by 20 seconds per minute for a
500 watt oven.
KCAL 150
SERVES 3-4

2 thick slices young ginger
4 cardamoms
2 cm (¾ in) cinnamon stick
4 teabags or 4 teaspoons tea
   leaves
1 teaspoon sugar
milk

The cure for all ailments, this Jaffna gingertea made an appearance when we had chicken pox, measles, or even when someone had an upset stomach. Although strangely spicy in flavour, one easily acquires a taste for Aunty Lily's hot gingertea. Many have grown addicted to it.

Incidentally, ginger is a cure-all throughout Asia, as it is believed to drive away 'wind'. It is imbibed therefore in many forms.

Preparation

Bruise or pound ginger till soft but not pulpy.

Peel cardamom pods to extract the tiny seeds. Bruise the seeds in a mortar.

Microwave Cooking Method

Put the following in an ovenproof jug: 4 cups hot water, ginger, cardamom seeds and cinnamon. Cook on High (100%) for 10 minutes or till mixture boils.

Meanwhile, place tea in a teapot. Pour boiling ginger-water into the pot and leave it to steep for 4 minutes.

Strain into cups and add milk and sugar to taste.

Spicy Lime Tea

PREPARATION: 2 mins
COOKING: 700 watt – 8 mins
          650 watt – 10 mins
          500 watt – 13 mins
Times given here are for a
650 watt oven. Decrease time
by 15 seconds per minute for
a 700 watt oven. Increase time
by 20 seconds per minute for a
500 watt oven.
KCAL 50
SERVES 4

1 tablespoon orange peel
1 tablespoon lime peel
2 stalks lemon grass
2 cinnamon sticks
4 teaspoons tea leaves
1 lime, sliced

A touch of Eastern mystique and elegance to the mundane cuppa char.

Preparation

When you peel orange and lime skins make sure the white pith is not lifted with the rind.

Wash and cut off leafy part of the lemon grass, using only the fleshy stem about 1 cm (½ in) from the root.

Microwave Cooking Method

Boil 4 cups water with the fruit peel, cinnamon and lemon grass on High (100%) for 10 minutes.

Stop the cycle once or twice to stir water to release citrus oils. Continue cooking till water boils.

Pour boiling water over tea leaves in a teapot. Cover and let it steep for a few minutes.

Strain and serve hot with lime slices for garnish. Add sugar to taste. Do not add milk.

Note: Spicy Lime Tea can also be served chilled.

For a lovely cuppa, fill a cup a quarter full with milk, add a teabag and stew on High (100%) for 45-50 seconds. Squeeze out the teabag, top with hot water and add sugar if desired.

Puncha Crème

PREPARATION: 6 mins
COOKING: 700 watt – ¾ min
           650 watt – 1 min
           500 watt – 1⅓ mins
Times given here are for a
650 watt oven. Decrease time
by 15 seconds per minute for
a 700 watt oven. Increase time
by 20 seconds per minute for a
500 watt oven.
KCAL 2281
SERVES 8

peel of 1 lemon
3 eggs
1½ cups evaporated milk
1 cup dark rum (less if preferred)
1⅘ cups condensed milk
dash of angostura bitters
1 teaspoon grated nutmeg

Preparation

Peel only the rind of the lemon, taking care not to cut too deep. Leave the peel in thin curly lengths.

Beat eggs with lemon peel till thickened.

Microwave Cooking Method

Heat evaporated milk for 1 minute on High (100%).

Add rum and slowly dribble in beaten eggs while whisking continuously.

Add condensed milk and continue beating to thicken mixture.

Add a dash of bitters and cool in the refrigerator.

Serve in tall narrow glasses of crushed ice, garnished with grated nutmeg and a curl of lemon peel.

Planter's Rum

COOKING: 700 watt – 1 min
           650 watt – 1½ mins
           500 watt – 2 mins
Times given here are for a
650 watt oven. Decrease time
by 15 seconds per minute for
a 700 watt oven. Increase time
by 20 seconds per minute for a
500 watt oven.
KCAL 220
SERVES 2

2 tablespoons rum
1 tablespoon sugar
½ lime
dash of bitters
lime peel (zest with no white pith)

The early planters in British Malaya had a hard time of it. It took some effort to keep from 'going troppo' on lonely mosquito infested estates. Planters would drown stengahs (whiskey-water) in the early part of the evening to dull the sting of mosquito bites and in the later part of the evening, the mosquitoes would be too drunk to bite anyway! Planter's Rum is to help planters brave the mosquitoes and retain their sanity under these conditions.

Microwave Cooking Method

Cook rum, sugar and ¼ cup water in toughened glass for 1½ minutes on High (100%).

Stir well to mix and squeeze in lime juice. Cool then add bitters.

Serve with lime curls and crushed ice.

Menu Plans

Rasa-lah Nonya Weekend Dinner (for 8)

Although the pre-cooked, pre-packaged, frozen and hawker variety of food is always available, to be able to eat simple, wholesome home-cooked food is often a treat. This menu, designed for a family and a guest or two at the weekend, will not take you long to prepare if the countdown is followed accurately.

Shopping

Cater for normal recipe quantities. If you are feeding less people, buy two-thirds the quantity. If your spice shelf is well stocked, you won't have to buy the dry ingredients. Coconut can be bought grated and frozen till required.

On your return from shopping, clean, shell and devein prawns and freeze till needed. Chicken for Ayam Sioh should be bought in pieces and, if shopping is done on the eve of the dinner, marinated straight away in spices and refrigerated.

Morning of the Dinner

1 Roast, then microwave green beans for Bubur Kacang Hijau. Cook green beans up to the point liquid is drained off.

2 Blend fish for Nonya Otak Otak.

Afternoon of the Dinner

(Allow 2 hours.)

1 Set the table.

2 Cook Ayam Sioh, then fry conventionally, leaving sauce till later.

MENU

Ayam Sioh
Amah's Sambal Udang
Nonya's Otak Otak with Cucumber
Nara Dofu
Nasi Lemak
Bubur Kacang Hijau

3 Blend grated coconut and extract coconut milk for Nasi Lemak and Amah's Sambal Udang. Refrigerate till ready to use.

4 Cook Amah's Sambal Udang. Rice may be cooked conventionally if the microwave oven is used for Amah's Prawn Sambal.

5 Steam the Otak Otak.

6 Prepare vegetables for the Nara Dofu. Cook the dofu dish.

7 Heat tamarind sauce (adding cornflour) and pour over Ayam Sioh, heating both for 5 minutes.

When Your Guests Arrive

While dinner is being served, heat Bubur Kacang Hijau, adding coconut milk just before serving.

Balinese Night to Remember (for 10)

Asians are always ready for a night of festivity. Arrange a Balinese evening which promises colour, spirit and novelty. Send your invitations a fortnight early with the injunction that your guests dress in keeping with the theme – *sarungs*, leis or floral headpieces. Make little temple offerings – hibiscus, bougainvillea or jasmine floating in little bowls of water. Shred pandan leaves into slivers and sprinkle over the flowers. For music, a tape of Balinese *angklong* music would complete the setting.

Shopping

Make up the shopping list. Cater for quantities specified in the recipes except for rice (double quantity) and ginger tea (boil water conventionally).

A Week Ahead

1   Make Kaju Badam Masala and Rendang Indonesia according to recipe. Cool and store nut 'mixture' in bottles. Freeze the Rendang.
2   Clean prawns, devein and freeze. Clean and gut fish.
3   Order flowers and drinks (Bali Brem).

Eve of the Party

(Allow 2 hours' preparation.)

1   Make peanut sauce for Sumatran Gado-Gado.
2   Marinate Trade Winds Pork Chops.
3   Peel all onions and garlic for cooking the next day. Chop, blend or purée as required and refrigerate blended mixtures (remember to label them).
4   Make and refrigerate garnishes.

Afternoon of the Dinner

(Allow 2 hours.)

1   Defrost all frozen ingredients and cooked meats.
2   Set the table and assemble dessert plates, cups, sugar and milk on a separate tray.

> ### MENU
>
> Kaju Badam Masala
> Satay Prawns
> with Kajang Satay Sauce
> Ikan Merah Belanda
> Rendang Indonesia
> Trade Winds Pork Chops
> Sumatran Gado-Gado
> Pineapple Rice
> Nanas Down Under
> Aunty Lily's Gingertea

---

3   Marinate prawns and skewer onto Satay sticks. Refrigerate.
4   Cook stuffing for fish, stuff the fish and tie or skewer then refrigerate.
5   Start Pineapple Rice and bring it to the point where ingredients are assembled but water has not been added to cook rice.
6   Cook ingredients for Gado-Gado. Arrange them on a platter and refrigerate.

Ninety Minutes Before Dinner

1   Complete cooking of fish.
2   Heat Rendang on Low (30%).
3   Cook Trade Winds Pork Chops.
4   Bake Nanas Down Under but hold the syrup till ready to serve.

Countdown

1   While serving drinks and the nut 'mixture', cook Satay Prawns and rice.
2   Serve Satay Prawns, Rendang, Gado-Gado and Pineapple Rice.
3   While the main course is being served, complete the Nanas Down Under and make Aunty Lily's Gingertea (boiling water conventionally). Serve both on the prepared tray.

Festive Sunday Curry Lunch (for 12)

An authentic curry lunch in the tradition of the early colonials should have a balance of mild and spicy dishes, hot flavours tempered by mild chutneys, cold yogurt and of course fresh fruit to finish the meal. A curry seldom loses flavour if cooked ahead and reheated (quite the reverse in fact), and most of this menu has been designed so that last-minute touches can be added just prior to serving the meal.

Shopping

Cater for quantities recommended in the recipes but cook two servings of meat to make food sufficient for 12. Shop for double the quantity of Rajput Rice Pilaf and Drunken Bananas. Buy minced meat from the butcher and clean and blend prawns with spices upon your return from shopping.

Eve of Lunch

(Allow 3 hours' preparation.)

1   Prepare Pooma's Puli Chutney. Cool and refrigerate.
2   Prepare Ceylonese Prawn Patties. Cook, cool and refrigerate, wrapped in foil.
3   Cook Sambar Dhal to the point lentils are cooked, and just before tempering with spices.
4   Cook Lamb Peretal but do not add coconut milk or onion rings.
5   Soak prunes in marinade for Drunken Bananas and refrigerate.

Morning of Lunch

(Allow about 2 hours.)

1   Complete Lamb Peretal by adding coconut milk and onion rings. Cover with foil to stand.
2   Cook Papadams and store in an airtight container.
3   Assemble ingredients and utensils for Drunken Bananas. Do not peel bananas till needed.
4   Lay the table, assemble serving dishes and cutlery. Prepare drinks (chill wine, beer, etc.)

MENU

Entrée

Ceylonese Prawn Patties

Main Course

Lamb Peretal
Sambar Dhal
Rajput Rice Pilaf
Papadam
Pooma's Puli Chutney

Dessert

Drunken Bananas

Two Hours Before Lunch

1   Take Ceylonese Prawn Patties out of the refrigerator to bring to room temperature.
2   Finish Sambar Dhal: temper spices then heat Dhal and add tempered spices.
3   Cook Pilaf and stand in foil to keep warm.

One Hour Before Lunch

1   Heat Ceylonese Prawn Patties if you wish to serve them hot.

Countdown

1   Heat Lamb Peretal while entrée is being served (Low cycle, 6-7 minutes, stir to heat evenly and use plastic wrap to prevent drying out).
2   Serve the main course. Meanwhile, cook Drunken Bananas. The dessert may be left to cool till the main course is cleared. Boil water for coffee.
3   Clear the table and serve dessert and coffee.

Evening for Two

Celebrate an anniversary or a special event with candlelight, white linen and sparkling crystal. When you have only one guest, you will want to spend as much time as possible with that person. Preparation for this meal can be made ahead of time and any last-minute reheating or cooking done while your guest is having a drink.

Shopping

Make up your list. Do not forget drinks, coffee liqueur, garnishes and fresh, crisp lettuce for the Ma Uon. Debone chicken before freezing and freeze ice cream till needed.

Eve of the Party

(Allow 2 hours' preparation.)

1   Prepare chicken breasts for Surprise Wraps and refrigerate. Prepare filling for Surprise Wraps and freeze in plastic wrap.

2   Follow recipe for Ma Uon to completion, cooking in plastic patty moulds or small ovenproof bowls. Cool after cooking and refrigerate in plastic wrap till needed.

3   Assemble Surprise Wraps and freeze overnight. (Remember to take them out of the freezer early in the morning of the party to defrost.)

4   Roast and blend nuts for Green Tomato Salad. Wash and prepare salad ingredients. Keep refrigerated in an airtight container.

5   Make the Carol Kulfi and freeze so that container touches the base or side of the freezer.

Afternoon of the Dinner

(Allow an hour.)

1   Cut and prepare Green Tomato Salad, but keep ingredients separate till dinner is about to be served.

2   Wash lettuce for Ma Uon cups and place in serving bowls.

3   Prepare garnishes for Surprise Wraps, Green Tomato Salad and Carol Kulfi.

4   Lay the table and chill wine.

M E N U

Entrée
Ma Uon served in Lettuce Cups

Main Course
Green Tomato Salad
Surprise Wraps
White Rice

Dessert
Carol Kulfi (Pistachio Ice Cream)
Lake Club Special

Countdown

1   While giving your guest a drink, steam Ma Uon in plastic wrap for 4 minutes. Stand in foil till ready to serve.

2   Take Carol Kulfi out of the freezer and place on Defrost cycle for 50 seconds, then let it stand to come to room temperature slowly.

3   Cook 1 cup rice for 12 minutes. When rice is cooked, fluff up with a fork and let it stand, covered.

4   Lower Ma Uon into lettuce cups and serve your entrée. As your guest is finishing the entrée, toss the Green Tomato Salad and cook Surprise Wraps for 3 minutes on each side. You will have to leave the table to turn the Wraps over.

5   Remove entrée and serve the main course with rice and Green Tomato Salad. During the main course, boil water for the Lake Club Special. It can sit in the microwave oven till you finish eating.

6   Remove the main course. While scooping Carol Kulfi into bowls, reheat coffee. Serve dessert with coffee.

When Mum's Away

The microwave oven is the ideal cooker to use when Mum is away. The internal walls are not hot (though the food container will be heated by the food being cooked) and there is no fire hazard. If you have your basic shopping list up to date, the family will be able to cook up a storm in a jiffy.

Shopping

Your basic shopping list should include tomato soup in packets for just such eventualities. Don't forget the packets of instant noodles, apples, sugar, cinnamon, butter and chicken pieces, washed and frozen in family size packets.

One Hour Before Dinner

1   Defrost chicken slowly on Defrost cycle. Allow it to stand to come to room temperature slowly.
2   Core and fill apples with filling.
3   Season chicken. Slice vegetables for the noodle dish.

> **MENU**
> Tomato Soup in a Packet
> Krispy Korean
> Anand's Dilemma
> Mt Lavinia Special

4   Cook soup according to instructions on the packet, using the microwave oven (refer to notes on soups on page 37).
5   While soup is served, cook chicken and let it stand in foil.
6   Cook noodles. Add vegetables and complete cooking cycle.
7   Dish out and serve noodles and chicken.
8   While main meal is being eaten, bake apples which should be ready by the time the main part of the meal is over.

Mid-week Blues (for 4-6)

Too often we find ourselves returning depressed during the week with the thought of having to prepare a meal for the family. With the microwave oven, this drudgery can be avoided with some quick meals.

Shopping

Shop for basic ingredients each week so that you are sure to have these in your store. Have a standard shopping list made out and carry this with you always. Keep chicken pieces, rice and a variety of the root vegetables handy. These keep well.

Defrosting

This menu is designed on the premise that you haven't prepared for dinner beforehand, so give yourself time to defrost your chicken pieces.

> **MENU**
> Baked Chicken Mindanao
> Basic Stir-fried Vegetable
> White Rice

One and a Quarter Hours Before Dinner

1   Season chicken and let it sit in marinade.
2   Prepare your vegetables, onions, garlic, etc.
3   Cook chicken while washing rice. Let chicken stand in foil when done.
4   Cook rice. Fluff it up with a fork and let stand in foil.
5   Cook Stir-fried Vegetables.
6   Serve your dinner hot, by removing foil just before serving.

Q & A

Are microwaves safe?

The same question may be asked of a conventional cooker. We have all received minor burns and cuts from kerosene, gas, wood-fire or electric cookers. Remember the scares and rumours when gas cylinders were introduced? People have learnt to live with these devices quite happily. The unknown entity always causes anxiety.

Microwave ovens stay cool during cooking and have had to meet stringent mechanical and electrical safety requirements. It is merely a more direct method of cooking food using electrical power where waves are attracted to food rather than to the area around the food.

How does the food cook?

Directly. Instead of energy being used to heat up the inside of an oven or cooking utensil, electricity is transformed into microwave energy which generates heat directly within the food itself.

This energy is used only when the cooker is in action. The moment the door is opened, the oven is automatically turned off and a fan turned on.

What about escaping microwaves?

Most microwave ovens have 6 different safety factors. During manufacture the door is opened and closed on test machines 30,000 times. In any case, the waves are only as strong as those from your colour television.

Nevertheless, is there any way to check if the microwave oven is leaking radiation?

Microwave leakage detectors may be bought. They come with instructions on their use and should give you peace of mind.

What happens to the microwaves? Are they still in the food after cooking?

Microwaves are little pulses of energy which are used up in the heating process and disappear completely.

For a novel way to prove this, try this experiment (once only, or it damages the magnetron).

Place a light bulb in half a cup of milk. Place it in your microwave oven. Set it on High for 1½ minutes. The bulb will light up. Switch off the oven, and the bulb will go off, proof that no microwaves are left in the milk.

Won't microwaves travel and so escape through the door?

> Microwaves travel in straight lines and bounce off the walls of the oven. Waves that hit the door are deflected by the wire mesh in the door.

Is it dangerous to use metal in a microwave oven?

> It is not dangerous to the operator but the magnetron in the microwave oven will be damaged if metal is used.

What is likely to go wrong?

> The magnetron will need to be replaced. It is normally guaranteed for 3 years, rather like a television tube. A microwave oven needs to be serviced and tested for leaks once a year.

Does the microwave oven switch off automatically?

> Yes, immediately after the door release operation is touched.

Why don't plastic dishes melt?

> Microwaves pass through paper, glass, plastic or wood. They do not pass through metals and will be deflected back to the magnetron, damaging it.

Is it safe for children to use a microwave oven?

> Yes, probably far safer than using a conventional electric or gas cooker.

If steam escapes, can't harmful waves escape?

> Steam escapes by edging around the door but microwaves travel in straight lines and cannot escape.

Do I need gloves, rubber shoes or aprons to protect myself?

> There is no need for such protection. The waves are only attracted to food in the oven. Microwave ovens have been tested and in use in America, Japan and the United Kingdom for many years and safety rules are quite rigid in those countries.

Does microwave cooking save on fuel bills?

> The speed and efficiency in microwave cooking keeps down energy costs. It is possible to halve the energy used. For example:

		kWhr Used
4 chicken pieces	microwave	0.40
	conventional	1.14
2 fish	microwave	0.10
	conventional	0.25
2 eggs scrambled	microwave	0.30
	conventional	0.90
250 g (8 oz)	microwave	0.32
meat curry	conventional	1.10

What are the differences in microwave ovens?

They have some or all of the following features. Choose the model most suited to your needs.

- Turntable. This rotates the food and cooks it evenly.
- Temperature gauges or probes that automatically turn off when the desired temperature is reached.
- Browners that brown meat after cooking as microwaves do not brown.

What wattage do I need?

Wattage determines the time taken to cook each dish. A 700 watt oven would cook quicker than a 650 watt oven or a 500 watt oven. If your purpose in buying the oven is to save time, then certainly you should invest in a 700 watt oven.

How economical is it to cook for only two people?

In terms of cooking time and fuel economy, microwave ovens are a saving as there is no need to warm up a large oven, and the smaller the portion, the less time it takes to cook.

What interiors and doors are best?

Stainless steel interiors are easy to clean and metal edged doors set into a deep recess are best.

Does the capacity of the microwave oven make a difference?

Microwaves cook only the food. They do not heat the oven. Hence the quantity of food, not the capacity of the oven, determines cooking time. In a 650 watt oven, one potato takes 4 minutes, 4 potatoes take 16 minutes – and the times are the same whatever the size of oven.

It is wattage that counts, not capacity. It should be large enough, however, to take a baking or browning dish.

Is a browner necessary?

Not if you also have a conventional oven with grill.

How healthy is microwaved food?

Food is so quickly cooked in the microwave oven that nutrients are all retained. Salt is retained too, so food needs less salting in the microwave oven.

What happens if you reheat microwaved food?

There will be little or no change in its quality. It will be warmed, edible and not mushy. Reheating on a conventional stove, on the other hand, dries food and changes its texture.

What information can I obtain about my microwave oven?

Consult the marketing manager of the sole agency distributing your brand of oven in your country. The company should have a home economist to help with queries and problems.

How should I clean my microwave oven?

With damp cloth and kitchen paper only. Do not use scouring pads or strong detergents. Steam a cup of water in the oven to soften spilled food. Cleaning is easier after this.

Can I sterilise bottles, for example, a baby bottle?

Yes. Wash the bottle out thoroughly, rinse and shake out moisture and microwave on High (100%) until it is warm and liquid has evaporated.

How can I check if my microwave oven is losing power?

Bring a cup of water to boil in the oven. It should take no more than 3 minutes. If it takes longer, then there could be two reasons. You may be lacking power through a leak or the magnetron in your oven is due for a change. The life of a normal magnetron is about 2,000 cooking hours.

Is there any danger in using plastic wrap to cover food while cooking?

Plastic wrap or plastic seals made of polyethylene are safe. When polyethylene is heated to a stage where breakdown occurs, it gives off water and carbon dioxide which are harmless. Some other plastic wraps, however, emit noxious gases when heated at high temperatures. Look for the sign which says 'Microwave-safe Plastic Wrap'.

Glossary

Notes on Serves

Most Asian food does not lend itself easily to portion-counting. An Asian meal can extend itself to accommodate 5 or 10 people for the same meal, comprising one meat dish and rice, depending on the quantity of side dishes, pickles or vegetables and soups available, as long as extra rice is cooked to provide for the extra guests.

In this book I have indicated the number of serves for each recipe. This is a general estimate as in Asian homes the requirements of meat are low. In general I have allowed for 100 g (3½ oz) of meat per person as there is always an abundance of pickles, curries and the ever present, always available rice with which to eat the other dishes.

Coconut

Coconut is used as dried desiccated flakes and as coconut milk which is the milky liquid extracted from the kernel of the ripe coconut — not the colourless coconut 'water' found inside the nut.

Coconut Milk. To express coconut milk from a scraped coconut, break it in half and scrape it, using a metal scraper, or blend small chunks of kernel in a blender. Once steeped in some water and squeezed, the thick liquid extracted, the 'milk', is used in cooking. This 'milk' should be strained to remove the pieces of grated coconut. The thicker milk is merely the thicker cream which rises to the top when milk is refrigerated. 'Thick coconut milk' also refers to milk extracted with very little water, for example, adding ½ cup water to 1 coconut would give you thick milk. To obtain a thinner milk, add water to the once-squeezed flakes and blend once more, straining the liquid for use.

Today coconut milk is available in cans, in UHT packets, in powdered form or in solid coconut cream blocks. The Thai variety of canned coconut milk may be slightly sweetened and often alters the taste of the curry. However it can be successfully used in sweet dishes calling for coconut milk or cream.

Rice

Rice is the staple in most Asian cooking. There are two main varieties — long-grained, needing more water, and short-grained, needing less. Long-grained rice is used in Thailand, Malaysia, Indonesia, the Philippines, China and Japan while the short-grained variety is used in Laos, Cambodia, Burma and North Thailand.

Glutinous Rice is used in Asian desserts and cakes. There is also the 'black' rice grown in some parts of Asia, especially in Malaysia.

Basmati or Pakistani Rice is an aromatic long-grained variety of rice, usually the most expensive rice on the market. It is used for Pilafs and Beryani dishes.

Cooking Rice. For successful rice cooking, wash the rice several times in several rinses of water until the water is clear. The microwave cooks trouble-free rice if the intructions are followed accurately. See page 190 for tips on cooking rice. .

Tamarind

This paste provides the sour flavour in most Asian dishes. It is the fleshy fruit of the Tamarind tree. Tamarind liquid, rather than the whole fruit, is used in cooking. To obtain this liquid, the pulp should be soaked in a little water and stirred or worked with the fingers until it dissolves. The liquid thus obtained can then be strained for use and the pulp discarded.

   Today it is possible to obtain small jars of homogeneous tamarind concentrate which is easily stirred into water or mixed directly into curries. As these are concentrates, one should use them sparingly.

Aburage (JAP)	Thin flat sheets of fried soybean curd — sold frozen.
Achuete	Annatto seeds, called 'achiotte' in South America. Red seeds used for colouring Filipino food. May be substituted with paprika.
Agar-agar JAP : kanten	Seaweed jelly used as sweet in Asia. Tengusa seaweed (Gelidium Amansi Lam Ourous) is the chief ingredient in Japanese confections.
Aka-miso	Bean paste — see Miso.
Allspice	A flavouring powder obtained from the berry of a West Indian tree.
Almond slivers	Almonds sliced thinly.
Amchur (INDIAN)	Dried green mango used as a sour ingredient.

Anise pepper
BOT   : *Xanthoxylum*
       pipesetum
CHIN   : faah jiu,
       Sichuan chiao
JAP   : sansho
	One of the five spices used in five-spice powder. It leaves an acidic taste on the tongue.

Aromatic ginger	See Galangal.

Achuete

Asafoetida
BOT : *Ferula asafoetida*
BURM : shingho
HINDI : hing
TAMIL : perunkaya

Resinous gum of an African tree used in Indian cooking to prevent 'wind' or flatulence. Used only in minute quantities.

Asam jawa (MALAY)

See Tamarind.

Asam gelugur (MALAY)

Dried skin of tamarind fruit used in cooking Malay and Straits Chinese food.

Azuki (JAP)

Red bean paste made into a sweet.

Bagoong

See Shrimp paste.

Bamboo shoot
BOT : *Gigantochlea nigruciliata*
BURM : honyit
CHIN : sun
INDON,
MALAY : rebung
JAP : takenoko
LAO : no mai lai

Sold in cans, braised in water. The fresh variety can be obtained at wet markets but takes a long time to boil. The canned variety is simpler to use. The tender stems are used in Chinese cookery. Once a can has been opened, the shoots keep for about 3 weeks, stored in brine or water.

Banana stem
BURM : ngapiyan oo

Tender banana stem, at the top of the tree, is used in Burmese cooking.

Banh pho (VIET)

Rice noodles. es.

Barbeque sauce

Red, tangy sauce, mixture of tomato and Worcestershire sauces.

Basil (sweet basil)
BOT : *Ocicum basilicum*
CHIN : luo lei cai
HINDI : babuitulsi
INDON,
MALAY : selasih/kemangi
LAO : phak itu lao
THAI : horapa

Herb used for seasoning red meats.

Baste

To pour liquid over meat as it cooks.

Beansprouts
BURM : pepinpauk
CHIN : dou ya
MALAY : tauge
TAMIL : tavkai moolai

Green mung beans, soaked and allowed to sprout.

Belacan

See Shrimp paste.

Besan (INDIAN)

Chickpea flour, used in Indian cooking. Coats well as a batter.

Bitters, Angostura

Herb used to flavour drinks.

Blanched

To whiten, by removing skin.

Brine

Salted water, saltwater

Brinjal
INDON,
MALAY : terung
LAO : mak kheva
TAMIL : katerikai

Aubergine, eggplant. Available large or small, round or long, deep to light purple, or light green to white.

Browning dish		Heatproof dish coated with tin oxide, prevents microwaves from penetrating dish and therefore heats up as a frying pan.
Buah keras		See Candlenut.
Burghul wheat		Cracked wheat grain in Middle Eastern cooking, e.g. Couscous.
Candlenut		A hard nut not unlike the almond, used to thicken curries in Malaysia and Indonesia. These nuts contain oil and were used as a primitive fuel, hence the name.
BOT	: *Alelunites moluccana*	
INDON	: kemiri	
MALAY	: buah keras	
Capsicum		Sweet peppers, large and green or red, not to be confused with chilli peppers.
BOT	: *Capsicum annuum*	
Cardamom		There are several varieties of cardamom, each with a slightly different flavour, the most common being the one grown in South India. Always store whole in the cupboard and extract seeds just before use. Cardamoms are used in Indian and Sri Lankan cooking. The Normans brought cardamoms to Britain in the 11th century.
BOT	: *Elettaria cardamonum*	
BURM	: palasi	
HINDI	: illiachi	
INDON	: kapulaga	
MALAY	: buah pelaga	
TAMIL	: yela kaii	
Cashew nuts		Small sweet kidney-shaped nuts. Raw or roasted cashews can be purchased from nut shops, health food stores or any grocer.
HINDI	: kaju	
INDON,		
MALAY	: biji gajus	
Cellophane noodles		Bean thread noodles – fine transparent noodles made from starchy mung beans. May be boiled or cooked in soups.
BURM	: kyazan	
CHIN	: dong fen	
INDON,		
PHIL	: sotanghoon	
JAP	: humusame	
MALAY	: suun	
THAI	: woon sen	
Champignons		See Mushrooms, button.
Char siew		Chinese barbecued spiced pork.
Cherries, glace		Sugared cherry preserves.
Chilli pepper		Hot green peppers which redden when ripe. There are many varieties – thin, long ones, small 'bird's eye' chillies and the large sweet capsicums.
BOT	: *Capsicum frutescens*	
INDON	: cabai, cili	
LAO	: mak phet	
MALAY	: lada, cili	
PHIL	: sili labuyo	
THAI	: prik	
Chillies, dried		These shrivelled looking dusky dark red chillies may need soaking in hot water or plumping with water in the microwave oven on High (100%) for 1½ minutes before blending or grinding. Dried chillies may be kept for a long time but after a year they may lose some flavour and 'hotness'.

Chinese coriander

These look like coriander leaves, hence the name. The leaves and stalks are larger however and have a distinctly different flavour. Malays call this *daun sup* or 'soup leaves', as they are usually chopped and used as a soup garnish.

Chinese wine

CHIN : bee chiu

Clear and potent white wine used in cooking. A little like gin in flavour.

Chocolate, semi-sweet

Cooking chocolate available in supermarkets. Melted easily in the microwave oven and used in sweets and cakes.

Cinnamon

BOT   : *Cinnamomum zeylanicum*
BURM   : Thitk-ya boh gauk
CHIN   : rou gui pi
HINDI : darcini
INDON.
MALAY : kayu manis
TAMIL : karuva pattai
THAI   : ob cheuy

The spiral bits of bark collected from the cinnamon tree. Adds flavour and tang to curries, drinks and desserts. Older trees have more mature stems.

Citrus leaf

Kaffir or double lime leaf, from the small local lime called *limau purut*. See Kaffir lime.

Cling or plastic wrap

The clear plastic material used to wrap food or cover containers of food before cooking in a microwave oven. To avoid drying out, food should always be loosely wrapped to allow steam to escape.

Cloves

BOT   : *Eugenia caryophyllata*
BURM   : ley-nyin-pwin
CHIN   : ding xiang
INDON.
MALAY : bunga cengkih
HINDI : laung
TAMIL : keramboo
THAI   : gram poo

Tropical tree native to the Moluccas. The part used in cooking are the dried flower buds used in the treatment of drastic toothaches in the Middle Ages. The clove is an essential sweet spice. A good clove will ooze a glistening oil when the stalk is pressed. It has warming, stimulating and digestive properties and has been known to be used both as an antiseptic and an anaesthetic. Cloves are named for the Latin nail, *clavus*.

Coconut

BOT   : *Cocos nucifera*
CHIN   : ye
INDON.
MALAY : kelapa
TAMIL : thenga

A large nut in a thick layer of husk. The white kernel is grated for the extraction of white coconut milk while the clear liquid within the cavity makes a cool and delicious drink. See notes on coconut milk at the beginning of the Glossary.

Coconut, desiccated

Dried coconut flakes, easily reconstituted by soaking in water.

Kaffir lime leaf

Coriander

BOT	:	*Coriandrum sativum*
BURM	:	nannambin (leaf) nannamsi (seed)
CHIN	:	yuan qian (leaf)
HINDI	:	dhania sabz (leaf) dhania (seed)
MALAY	:	daun ketumbar (leaf) ketumbar (seed)
PHIL	:	kinchay
TAMIL	:	malli kolunthu (leaf) kotthu malli (seed)
THAI	:	pak chee

The leaves of the coriander plant used in Asian cooking. The seed is the main ingredient in curry powder. All parts of the plant are used in cooking. Ripe seeds are strongly aromatic, sweet and pleasant, but the leaves on their own can also be rather strong in flavour. The name 'coriander' originates from the Greek *koriannon* meaning bug, a reference to the smell of the leaf and unripe seed. When coriander leaves are combined with chillies and other hot foods, they provide a cool, pungent and unique foil to the hot spices.

Cummin

BOT	:	*Cuminum cyminum*
BURM	:	samonnet
INDON, MALAY	:	jintan putih
TAMIL	:	nachiragam
THAI	:	mellet jira

The aromatic seed from a small annual, an essential ingredient in curry powder. The seed is similar to caraway in appearance but quite different in flavour. The seed is used also as an anti-flatulent and an aid to digestion.

Cummin, black

BOT	:	*Nigella sativa*
INDON, MALAY	:	jintan hitam
TAMIL	:	kala jeera
THAI	:	mellet jira

Aromatic and peppery – used as one of five spices called *panch phora*.

Cummin, sweet

See Fennel.

Curry powder

The word originated from the Tamil *karri* meaning sauce. Curry powder is a blend of many spices. Recipes vary as each home may have its own traditional recipe. Hence there is no single 'curry powder' as such in Asia. The Indian curry powder usually consists of various proportions of coriander, cummin, fennel, turmeric, cardamom, cinnamon and cloves. See Garam masala.

Curry leaves

BOT	:	*Murraya koenigui*
BURM	:	pyi ndaw thein
HINDI	:	kitha neem
INDON, MALAY	:	daun kari
TAMIL	:	karuva pillay, karipattai
THAI	:	bai karee

Used more frequently in India, Malaysia and Sri Lanka, the leaves resembling bay leaves are added to Indian curries. The tree is a native of Asia and its leaves keep their flavour when dried or frozen. However, they are generally added fresh with onions being sautéed at the start of curry-making. Cassia leaves (*Cinnamomum cassia*) are also used for the same purpose but are smaller and narrower.

Cus cus		Poppy seeds. Minute white seeds used in kurmah cooking.
BOT	: *Paparer somniferus*	
Daikon (JAP)		Giant white radish, about 25-38 cm (10-15 in) long. Mild in flavour. Pickled for use with Japanese food.
HKG	: lobak	
Dashi (JAP)		Clear soup stock made from seaweeds and dried bonito. An essential soup starter or part of a dripping sauce. Instant *dashi* is now available in food stores specialising in Japanese foods.

To make *dashi*, cook 4 cm (1½ in) *kombu* (or dried kelp) and 3 tablespoons bonito in 3 cups of water, covered with plastic wrap, for 15 minutes on High (100%). Strain for use.

Daun (INDON/MALAY)	Leaf or herb.
Daun pandan	Pandanus or screwpine leaf.
Daun salam	Mint-like herb used in Indonesian cooking. Substitute curry leaves.
Deveining	To make a cut down the back length of the prawn and remove the black 'vein' or intestine before cooking.

Dhal		A general term for lentils or split peas of which there are various colours and sizes. The staple food of Indians, particularly vegetarians. A few varieties are
HINDI	: tavoor arisi	
TAMIL	: parapoo	

mysore dhal	(yellow)
toor dhal	(red)
mung dhal	(green)
urad/ulunthu (split peas)	(black)
channa dhal (horsegram, chickpeas)	(brown)

Dhania (HINDI)	See Coriander.
Dried fish	Many varieties are available in Southeast Asia. Two popular ones are dried anchovy (*ikan bilis kering*) and dried threadfin (*ikan kurau kering*).

To clean the long-jawed variety of dried anchovy, remove the head and black stomach, wash quickly and dry well before frying. There is a smaller specimen called whitebait. In Southeast Asia, dried anchovy is cooked in hot dry curries called *sambals*, and marketed as Macassar red fish.

Fennel		Known as sweet cummin, it is used a great deal in Indian and Sri Lankan cooking. Ground and refrigerated, it keeps for a long time. Preroasting the seed heightens flavour. It is used in its powdered form, rather than as a paste.
BOT	: *Foeniculum vulgare*	
BURM	: samon saba	
HINDI	: sonf	
INDON, MALAY	: jintan manis adas	
TAMIL	: perinseeragam	

Fenugreek		Small, angular toffee-coloured seeds. Usually bitter but important in imparting flavour, in small quantities, especially in Indian fish curries. Fenugreek is also used to 'sour' the Indian black gram pancake, *dosai*.
BOT	: *Trigonella foenum-graecum*	
BURM	: penatha si	
HINDI	: methi	
INDON, MALAY	: halba	
TAMIL	: vendyam	

Fish sauce

BURM : ngan pya ye
CAMB : tuk trey
CHIN : yu lu
LAO : nam pa
PHIL : patis
THAI : nam pla
VIET : nuoc mam

Every Southeast Asian country has its own fish sauce which plays the same role in this region as soy or oyster sauce in China and Japan. It is prepared by steeping fish in brine for a long time. The thick browning liquid is bottled and used in cooking to bring out the flavour of food. Fish sauce is rich in Vitamin B.

Five-spice powder

CHIN : wu xiang fen

A Chinese spice used in Chinese cooking. It is reddish-brown and consists of star anise, fennel, cinnamon, cloves and Sichuan pepper.

Flambé

To set alight. The practice of setting a cake, fruit, pancake or roast alight with spirits so as to impart a distinctive flavour to the food.

Gabi leaves

Used in Burmese and Thai cooking. Closest to spinach.

Galangal, greater

BOT : *Alpinia galanga*
CHIN : lan jiang
INDON : laos
LAO : kah
MALAY : langkuas
THAI : ka

A delicate flavoured rhizome, also known as Siamese ginger. It has a yellow root with pink fibrous looking knobs. Galangal was regarded an aphrodisiac in medieval times. Today it is grown and used in Southeast Asia and in Iran. The Thai and Laotians use it as a digestive stimulant.

Galangal, lesser

BOT : *Alpinia officinarum*
BURM : zeodary
CHIN : sa leong kung
INDON,
MALAY : kencur
THAI : krachai

Also known as aromatic ginger. Native to China, the root is dried and should be pulverised before use. The Chinese use it as a medicinal herb, while the Malays use it as a spice.

Garam masala

Mixture of spices used in Indian cooking. Each family has its own blend. It should be made fresh and stored in small quantities in an airtight bottle. A good mixture would have
    2 tablespoons coriander seeds
    1 tablespoon cummin
    1 teaspoon cardamoms
    1 teaspoon black pepper
    ½ teaspoon cloves
    ½ teaspoon nutmeg
Cardamoms should be peeled to extract the small black seeds within. Roast ingredients in a shallow dish on High (100%) for about 4 minutes, stirring once during the cycle. Grind or mill finely then store in an airtight jar when cool.

Garlic

BOT : *Allium sativum*
CHIN : suan tou
INDON,
MALAY : bawang putih
PHIL : bawang
TAMIL : poondu

Probably originating in Central Asia, garlic is one of the oldest cultivated plants. It is perennial and the bulb is divided into many cloves. A small quantity of garlic heightens existing flavours. It is believed to be a powerful disinfectant and an antiseptic, preventing infection and the formation of bacteria in the stomach.

Ghee

Clarified butter used in Indian and Sri Lankan cooking. It does not burn as readily as butter and adds a distinctive flavour to food.

Giblets

'Innards' of animals, often cleaned and cooked successfully.

Ginger
BOT : *Zingiber officiale*
CHIN : jiang
INDON,
MALAY : halia
LAO : khing
PHIL : luya
TAMIL : inji
THAI : khing

A rhizome that grows wild in the damp tropical forests of Southeast Asia. Ginger is a tangy, pungent root used in most Southeast Asian cooking. Fresh ginger should be pounded and the juice or pulp used. It may also be chopped, sliced or bruised with a mortar or the flat side of a heavy cleaver before cooking. Ginger keeps indefinitely when frozen and can be reused with no loss of flavour. In the currency of the spirit world, the Lao believe ginger is gold.

Ginger powder

Used largely in cakes and in Western cooking.
Do not substitute the fresh for the dry variety as the flavours are quite different.

Glace

To coat with syrup – as in glace ginger or cherries.

Golden syrup

Thick syrup residue from sugar manufacture, used for sweetening food.

Grass jelly
CHIN : leung fun
MALAY : cincau

Black seaweed jelly bought fresh or in cans. Served with ice and syrup, it is popular in Malaysia and Singapore.

Green mung beans

Used as a vegetable and also as a sweet. Mung beans soaked and germinated are the beansprouts used often in Asian cooking.

Haeko (MALAY)

Black shrimp paste.

Ham

Chorizo del Bilbao, used in the Philippines for terrine.

Hoenkwe

Green mung bean flour used in making Malaysian and Indonesian cakes. It is obtained from Indonesia in small cylindrical packets and is sometimes called 'cendol' flour.

Hoisin sauce

A sweet, spicy, red-brown sauce. A mixture of garlic, sugar and soy beans. Used mainly to season pork or barbequed pork.

Ikan bilis (MALAY)

Anchovy.

Jasmine essence
THAI : yod num malee

An essence used in Thai cooking.

Julienne

To cut into thin strips.

Kaffir lime
BOT : *Citrus hystrix*
INDON,
MALAY : limau purut
THAI : makrut

This little known member of the citrus family has a bumpy dark green rind with a concentration of aromatic oils. Historically used in Malaysia and Sri Lanka as a medicinal oil, today used in Thai cuisine, where only the leaves and zest are used. Fresh citrus leaves and the grated rind of fresh limes can be substituted. The powdered kaffir lime obtained in Thai shops is also a good substitute.

Kangkung (MALAY)

Water convolvulus, a green leafy vegetable rich in iron and vitamins. Grows in wet or damp areas.

Kapee (THAI, VIET)

See Dried shrimp paste.

Kemiri (INDON)

See Candlenut.

Kimchee (KOREAN)

A pungent cabbage pickle.

Kombu (JAP)

Japanese kelp or seaweed. It is obtained in grey or black flat ribbons and is used to flavour dashi and sushi rice.

Krachai

See Galangal, lesser.

Kuali (MALAY)

CHIN   : wok
INDIAN : dekshi
TAMIL   : irumbu chatti

The round bottomed 'wok' used in Asian cooking. This is the ideal cooking vessel for stir-frying vegetables as the heat is distributed instantly.

Kuih (MALAY)

Cakes, usually made from rice flour.

Kurmah

A 'white' curry from North India, which uses the milder spices rather than the fiery chilli peppers from the South.

Kulfi

A creamy Indian ice cream made with pistachio nuts and cardamoms.

Kushi yaki

Skewers of beef cooked Japanese style.

Langkuas (MALAY)

Galangal, greater.

Laos (INDON)

See Galangal, greater. Laos is usually the dried powder of the root.

Leek

Vegetable closely related to the onion.

Lemon grass

BOT   : *Cymbopogon citratus*
BURM : zebalin
CHIN   : cong mao
HINDI : sera
INDON,
MALAY : serai
LAO   : bai mak nao
TAMIL : lampichepul
THAI   : takrai

One of the most used herbs in Southeast Asia, especially in Lao, Thai and Malaysian food. The plant has long grass-like leaves, the stem and leaves are fibrous and fill out near the root into a bulb-like base. It has a lemony scent and imparts a delicious flavour to food cooked in chilli or curry. The root can be dried and reconstituted with a little water. Use only the stem close to the root up to about 1¼ cm (½ in), after discarding the outer leaves. Mature stalks give a stronger aroma.

Lentils

See Dhal.

Lime

BOT   : *Citrus microcapa*
BURM : thambuya
CHIN   : qing ning meng (large lime) suan gan (small lime)
HINDI : niniboo
INDON,
MALAY : limau nipis (large lime), limau kasturi (small lime)
PHIL   : calamansi
TAMIL : elumchi palam

Small and round with a dark green skin. Aromatic and juicy, used to make refreshing drinks as well as in cooking. Do not confuse with the kaffir lime (limau purut), the lime with the bumpy rind and fragrant leaves shaped like the number 8.

Mackerel, Spanish, (*Scomberomorus commersoni*)

BURM : nga kyi kan
CHIN   : ma jun yu
HKG   : kau ye
INDON,
MALAY : tenggiri batang
PHIL   : tangigi
THAI   : pla ai bang
VIET   : ca thu ao

Aclaimed one of the finest food fishes of Southeast Asia, the flesh is firm and has a good flavour. As a curry fish, this is a favourite among Malaysian cooks.

Madeira wine	Sweet wine used as a liqueur. Originally from Madeira, Spain.
Maldive fish MALAY : ikan kayu SING : umbalakada TAMIL : maasi	Dried rock-hard tuna buried in the sand to dry. Broken into bits, it resembles wood chipping. Soaked in water to soften, it adds flavour to any vegetable or curry. Used in Sri Lankan cooking.
Malt sugar	Thick brown and like molasses, this is used in Chinese cooking. Usually bottled in an earthenware or a squat plastic jar.
Marinate	To steep meat or vegetables in a marinade (which could be spices, sauces, or a mixture of ingredients) so that its combined flavour is absorbed.
Mee	Yellow noodles made from wheat flour.
Meehoon	Thin, white rice flour noodles.
Mint	Several varieties are used in Asian cooking. The most common is polygonum or *daun kesum*, which is used in fish dishes.
Mirin	A golden cooking wine with low alcohol content. Essential ingredient in Japanese cooking, giving a sweet mildness to liquids, glazes and sauces. Sweet sherry is a suitable substitute.
Miso	Mixture of malt, salt and mashed fermented soy beans with its liquor. Rich savoury paste used only in traditional Japanese cooking, especially miso soup.
Mushroom	
Button	Also called champignons, these may be fresh or canned.
Dried Chinese	These dark brown mushrooms should be soaked in hot water or microwaved with a little water on High for 1½ minutes before slicing for use.
Straw	These mushrooms with a different texture and flavour can be substituted for the first two.
Mustard greens CHIN : cai xin HKG : choy sum MALAY : sawi hijau	Green leafy vegetable used a great deal in Chinese and Malay cooking. It has small yellow flowers.
Mustard seeds BOT : *Brassica nigra* HINDI : rai INDON, MALAY : biji sawi TAMIL : kadugu	Ground, this gives a yellow paste, which is used to remove infection or as a poultice. Used as a spice in cooking and pickling.
Nam pla (THAI)	See Fish sauce.
Nam prik pao	Green Thai curry paste.
Nori	Crisp seaweed sheets – sweet and seaweedy in flavour. It is rolled around sushi or vinegared rice. Slivered with scissors, it can be used as a garnish. Lightly toast to render it pliant for rolling around sushi.
Nuoc mam (VIET)	Fish sauce.
Offal	Intestines and stomach, gills, etc. of any animal that need to be discarded when cleaning the carcass. Also refers to parts of the animal (heart, kidneys) considered less valuable than the flesh.

Oil

    Blended vegetable   Blend of oil, mainly from nuts.

    Gingelly   Strong-flavoured, used in Indian and Sri Lankan cooking.

    Groundnut   Extracted from groundnuts and used often in Chinese cooking.

    Olive   Strong-tasting, used in Middle Eastern and Mediterranean cooking.

    Sesame   Strong and nutty flavour. Use sparingly in Burmese and Chinese cooking.

Olek sambal (INDON)   Indonesian chilli-garlic sauce.

Onion
BOT   : *Allium species*   One of the oldest herbs, with high content of Vitamin C, minerals, sulphur and trace elements. It has been used as an antiseptic and is believed to have a cleansing effect on the body. The large onion is the most common. As it holds a great deal of moisture, salt slices before frying to drain moisture to allow onions to crisp in the oil.

    'crispy onions'   Mentioned as a garnish in many recipes, this is particularly easy to make in the microwave oven. Peel and slice (crosswise) a large quantity (500 g or 1 lb) of shallots, place in a casserole with just enough oil to cover and cook on High (100%) for 20 minutes. Stir shallots, then return to the oven to cook for another 10 minutes. Watch carefully during these last minutes as they crisp and brown in a few seconds, after which they may burn. You now have a reserve of garnish to last a long while, minus the bother of stirring continuously at a conventional *kuali* or *wok*.

    shallot   The most commonly used onion in Asia, this is small, red or purple, and when slices are fried, they crisp very fast in hot oil.

    spring   In this book, this refers to the bulb and leaves resembling chives, used for garnish. The bulb and a short part of the stem from the base would be used, as these are stronger flavoured.

Oregano
BOT   : *Origanum vulgare*   Used more in Italian and Greek cooking, the word, derived from Greek, means 'joy of the mountains'. Its strong, distinctive flavour is good used with fish or meat.

Oyster sauce
CHIN   : hao you
HKG   : ho yau
MALAY   : kicap tiram

A thick brownish sauce which smells slightly fishy. Adds a delicate flavour to meat, fish or vegetable. It is a blend of oysters, soy sauce and brine and keeps best refrigerated once the bottle is opened.

Pak ban
(THAI, BURM)   Green spinach.

Palm sugar
BURM   : chandagar
CHIN   : ye tang
HINDI   : jaggery
INDON   : gula jawa
MALAY   : gula melaka
PHIL   : panutsia
TAMIL   : chakkarai
THAI   : nam tan peep

Dark caramelised sugar obtained from the sap of the coconut and palmyra palms. Sold in round, flat cakes, it keeps indefinitely if dry. Easily reconstituted into syrup in the microwave if chopped up and boiled in a little water.

Pandanus   See Screwpine.

Paprika   Red peppers, sweet and mild in flavour. Used more as colouring.

Parmesan cheese   Cheese used as a garnish for spaghetti. Obtainable in its grated form. Rather strong in flavour.

Peanut butter   Thick oily paste of ground peanuts. Used as a base for satay sauce.

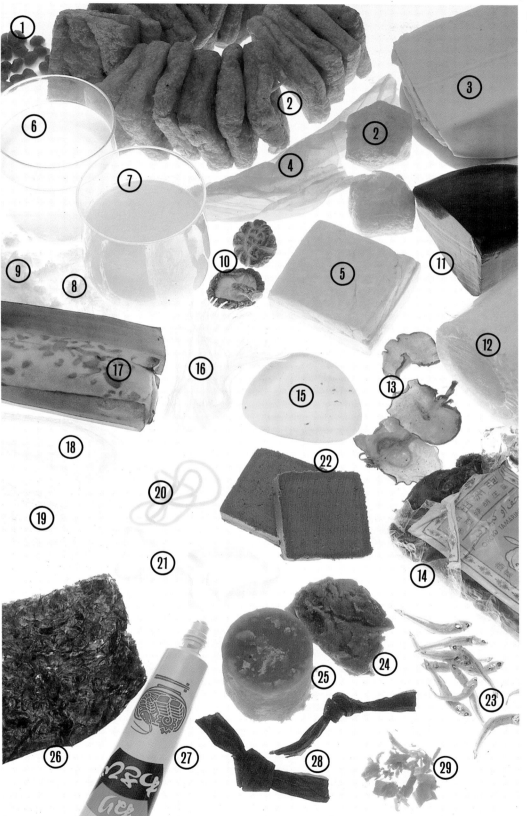

1 *preserved soy beans*
2 *dofu-pok*
3 *soft soybean square*
4 *dried soybean skin*
5 *firm soybean square*
6 *coconut water*
7 *coconut milk*
8 *grated coconut*
9 *coconut powder*
10 *dried Chinese mushrooms*
11 *grass jelly*
12 *banana stem*
13 *dried tamarind skin*
14 *tamarind paste*
15 *'papadam' (Indian crisp)*
16 *rice vermicelli*
17 *'tempe'*
18 *agar strips*
19 *cellophane noodles*
20 *egg noodles*
21 *flat rice noodles*
22 *dried shrimp paste*
23 *anchovy*
24 *palm sugar*
25 *palm sugar*
26 *nori sheet*
27 *'wàsabe'*
28 *'kombu'*
29 *'tungchye'*

Above and opposite: some Asian herbs

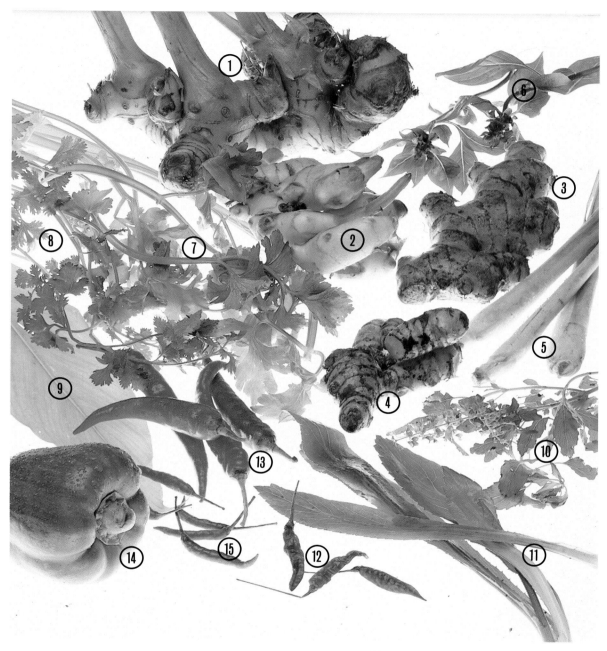

**Seeds and spices
from the Asian
kitchen**

turmeric powder	1
chilli powder	2
coriander powder	3
asafoetida	4
tolam dhal	5
mysore dhal	6
sambar dhal	7
black gram	8
fennel/sweet cummin	9
cummin	10
candlenuts	11
cardamoms	12
fenugreek	13
mustard seeds	14
red beans	15
cloves	16
sesame seeds	17
coriander	18
black peppercorns	19
star anise	20
saffron	21
cinnamon	22

Peel (lemon, orange)	Rind or outer skin, dried.
Pisang hijau (MALAY)	Large green bananas.
Plastic wrap	See Cling wrap.
Plum sauce	Sweet sauce made from Chinese plums, used in Chinese cooking.

Pomfret, black

BURM	: sin ngamoke	Grey flat fish, similar in appearance to the white pomfret, though not as esteemed and consequently less expensive. Often used in Southeast Asian cooking.
CHIN	: hei chang	
HKG	: hak chong	
INDON,		
MALAY	: bawal hitam	
PHIL	: duhay	
THAI	: pla jara met dum	
VIET	: ca' chim den	

Pomfret, white

BURM	: nga mote phyu	A flat and broad silvery white fish with a delicate flavour and texture. Similar to the black pomfret but much more expensive.
CAMB	: trey chap sen	
CHIN	: bai chang	
HKG	: pa chong	
INDON,		
MALAY	: bawal putih	
THAI	: pla jara met khao	
VIET	: ca chim trang	

Poppy seeds	See Cus cus.
Pulot (MALAY/INDON)	Glutinous rice.
Rice	See notes at the beginning of this section.
Ring mould	Mould with a depression in the centre. Ideal for microwave cooking as food cooks from the sides and the centre cooks last. See 'Microwave Ovensafe Utensils'.
Rose water	The diluted essence of rose petals used in Middle Eastern and Indian foods and foods reflecting an Arabic influence. It is strong-flavoured and should be used sparingly.

Saffron

BOT	: *Crocus sativus*	Threadlike bright orange stigma of the crocus. Saffron from Valencia is the most expensive spice on the market today. It has a strongly sweet, pungent smell. It is usually added to warm water or milk and the coloured liquid is added to food to give it the characteristic saffron colour and flavour. Not to be confused with turmeric or artificial saffron which has the colour but no fragrance.
HINDI	: kesar	
INDON,		
MALAY	: koma-koma	
TAMIL	: kunkum	

Sago	Starchy granules from the sago palm. Tapioca pearls may be substituted for sago.
Sake	Japanese rice wine used as a liqueur and also as a marinade for Japanese food. Sherry is a good substitute.

Sambal (INDON/MALAY)

TAMIL	: chumbal	Combination of chilli, onions and spices, cooked or blended together. A concentrated mix is traditionally eaten with rice. Often forms the base for seafood.

Santan (MALAY)	Coconut milk.
Satay (MALAY)	Meat on skewers, though the word sometimes describes the peanut and chilli-based sauce that goes with the meat on skewers.

Scallops

A seafood, soft, white and fleshy circles of meat not unlike crab in texture.

Screwpine

BOT : *Pandanus lati folia*

CHIN : xiang cai

INDON,

MALAY : daun pandan

PHIL : pandan

THAI : bai toey

Used as a flavouring in rice, and as both flavouring and colouring agent in some Southeast Asian sweets. When crushed or boiled, the flavour and green colour is released.

Sea bass
(Plectropomus)

BURM : kyauk nga

INDON,

MALAY : kerapu bara

PHIL : lapu lapu

THAI : pla kaang daeng jutfa

VIET : ca' mun cham

An excellent fish, suitable for Southeast Asian cooking. Light orange with dark blue spots, this is an expensive fish.

Semolina

MALAY : sugee

TAMIL : rulang

A coarse-grained wheat product used in Indian cooking and also in cakes. Commonly known as sugee, wheatola or 'breakfast delight'.

Senangin
(Eleutheromena tetraductylon)

BURM : nga ka tha

HKG : ma yau

INDON,

MALAY : kurau senangin

PHIL : mamal

See Threadfin.

Sesame

BOT : *Sesamum indicum*

CHIN : ma

INDON,

MALAY : bijan

JAP : goma

TAMIL : ellu

Tiny tear-shaped seeds used in Chinese, Japanese and Southeast Asian cooking, especially in sauces, sweets and cakes.

Sesame oil

CHIN : ma you

MALAY : minyak bijan

Oil extracted from toasted sesame seeds. It is golden brown with a nutty flavour. Not to be confused with Indian gingelly oil which has a slightly bitter taste.

Shad
(Hilsa toli)

BURM : nga thalaut yautpha

HKG : cho paak

INDON,

MALAY : terubuk

THAI : pla talum phuk

About 50 cm (20 in) long, this fish has a silver and rather oily body. The roe is used in *sambals* in Malaysia and it keeps its shape when cooked. A very popular fish in Burmese cooking.

Shallot

See Onion.

Shrimp paste, black		A thick dark paste used in Southeast Asian cooking. Essential in recipes (such as Rojak) calling for its use as it has a distinctive flavour. *Belacan* is a reasonable substitute.
INDON, MALAY, PHIL	: patis	

Shrimp paste, dried		A pungent prawn or shrimp paste used in Southeast Asian cooking. Light grey or dark brown, it is sold in the form of cakes or balls.
BURM	: ngapi	
CHIN	: ma la jian	
INDON	: terasi	Cut into 2 cm (¾ in) cubes and microwave 3 cubes for 2 minutes on High (100%). Cool and freeze in airtight jars. This keeps indefinitely if frozen.
LAO	: padek	
MALAY	: belacan	
PHIL	: bagoong	
THAI	: kapee	
VIET	: mam tom	

Snapper		Grey to pink fish, sometimes turning a darker pink after death. Excellent for steaming or baking whole. It is sometimes called Mangrove red snapper because it can be found in mangrove areas.
(Lutjanus argentimaculatus)		
BURM	: nga pahni	
CAM	: trey aukeuy prak	
CHIN	: hong yu	
HKG	: hung yau	
INDON, MALAY	: siakap merah	
THAI	: pla kaphong si thao	
VIET	: ca' huong van	

Soy beans, preserved		This is available in varying quality, ranging from a thick mixture of semi-mashed fermented soy beans to the whole fermented soybeans. There is also the Korean ground bean sauce (*mor sze jeung*).
CHIN	: dow see	
MALAY	: tauco	

Soybean squares		Made from soybeans, the most protean of vegetables, it is white and can be firm or soft with a delicate flavour.
CHIN	: dou gan (firm) dou fu (soft)	
JAP	: dofu	

Soy sauce		Dark sauce made from fermented soy beans, kept in vats until the right consistency is achieved. Many varieties available:
CHIN	: hei jiang you (dark) jiang qing (light)	• thick, dark and sweet sauce • dark soy sauce • light (saltier) soy sauce • mushroom sauce (soy sauce fermented with mushrooms) • Indonesian sweet sauce (*kicap manis*) • Japanese soy sauce (*tamari shoyu* or *shoyu*)
INDON, MALAY	: kicap	
JAP	: tamari shoyu	
VIET	: tuong	

Spam		Commercial preparation of spiced ham.

Star anise		The eight pointed star anise is one of the main ingredients of five-spice powder. Native to China.
BOT	: *Illicium verum*	
CHIN	: hui xiang	
INDON, MALAY	: bunga lawang	
THAI	: poy kak bua	

Sushi (JAP)		Rice flavoured with vinegar, salt and sugar and served as tiny rice savouries or wrapped into seaweed rolls as in Norimaki Sushi.

Tabasco		Hot, pungent chilli sauce, rather vinegary in taste, used for European food. Substitute *sambal olek* or chilli sauce.

Tamari shoyu Japanese soy sauce.

Tamarind Sour, pulpy fruit of a large tree, shaped like a bean. The leathery pod has dark seeds covered with the flesh. See the notes on Tamarind at the beginning of this section.

BOT	: *Tamaarindus indica*
BURM	: magyi thi
CHIN	: ya cau
HINDI	: imli
INDON, MALAY	: asam jawa
LAO	: mak kam
PHIL	: sampalok
TAMIL	: puli
THAI	: sam ma kham

Tandoori Clay oven used to bake food in India. Also refers to a special curry mix to coat meat for tandoori cooking.

Taucheo (CHIN) Fermented soy beans. See Soy beans.

Tempe (MALAY) Fermented soybean cake, rich in vitamins, used in Indonesian and Malay cooking.

Terasi (INDON) Dried shrimp paste.

Terrine Mixture of liver, brandy and spices, made like a cake – served on toast or with potatoes.

Threadfin The Threadfin Indian Tassel fish has a golden body up to a metre in length. The fish is found in the coastal waters of the west coast of Malaysia. An excellent fish and very good eating.
(Polynemus indicus)

BURM	: nga let khwa
CHIN	: wu yu
HKG	: ma yau
INDON, MALAY	: kurau, senangin
THAI	: pla kurau
VIET	: trey caro

Tomato purée Thick paste of tomato used in Indian and some Malay cooking.

Tuk trey (CAMB) See Fish sauce.

Tungchye Salted turnip bits, a garnish for soups and rice.

Tuong (VIET) Soy sauce.

Turmeric Rhizome of the ginger family. This yellow root is one of the main ingredients in curry cooking. Do not confuse this with saffron. It is antiseptic and a preservative used in cooking fish and meat.

BOT	: *Curcuma longa*
BURM	: fa nwin
HINDI	: haldi
INDON, MALAY	: kunyit
TAMIL	: manjal
THAI	: kamin

Vermicelli Thin wheat pasta strands, Italian in origin, used in Indian sweets.

Wasabe	Also known as horseradish, but this is a misnomer, as *wasabe* is the grated root of a riverside plant native to Japan. In sushi bars, *wasabe* is called 'tears' as it stings when eaten. Obtainable in powder form to be mixed with water into a paste. Also available as a paste, sold in tubes. Accompanies raw fish dishes.
Water chestnuts	Small vegetable with thin papery skin, crisp in texture. (See chestnuts.)
Wax paraffin	Clear edible wax used in the making of homemade chocolate.
Whisk	To beat with a many-pronged fork, to aerate.
Worcestershire sauce	Commercial sauce, rather spicy, with a distinctive flavour.
Yogurt	Fermented milk used to tenderise meat and chicken and flavour fish. For recipes in this book, unflavoured or plain white yogurt is used.
Zest	Outer skin of citrus fruit such as orange and lemon, used in cooking to impart a certain tangy flavour.

Shopping Guide

Listed below are some shops where one may buy oriental foods and/or utensils.

United Kingdom

Bombay Emporium Ltd
Radiant House
Pegamoid Road
London, N18

Harrods Ltd
Knightsbridge
London, SW1

*Hiruma Overseas Corporation
(U.K. Limited)*
4 Charlotte Place
London, W1

Indian Emporium Ltd
8 Great Russell Street
London, W1

Kwong Shang Lung Co. Ltd
Park Avenue
London, NW10

Lal Jolly Ltd (mail order)
70 Warwick Road
London, SW5

*Loon Fung Supermarket
Warehouse*
261 Water Road
Wembley, Middlesex

Oriental Store
Macclesfield Street
London, W1

Patak Spices Ltd
134 Drummond Street
London, W1

United States of America

EAST

House of Spices
76-17 Broadway
Jackson Heights
NY 11372
Tel: 476 1577

India Food & Condiments
811 Lexington Avenue
New York, NY 10016
Tel: 593 0295

India Food and Gourmet
110 Lexington Avenue
New York, NY 10021
Tel: 686 8955

Toko Garuda
336 East 50th Street, Room A
New York, NY 10022

Trinacria Importing Co.
415 Third Avenue
New York, NY 10016

Wing Wing Imported Groceries
79 Harrisson Avenue
Boston, Mass. 02111

Wing Woh Lung Co.
50 Mott Street
New York, NY 10013

MIDWEST

Asia Food Products
1509 Delmar Boulevard
St Louis, MO 63103

Manna International Market
1162 Broadway
Ann Arbor, MI 48105

WEST

B.C. Market
711 North Broadway
Los Angeles, CA 90012

Bezjian's
4725 Santa Monica Boulevard
Los Angeles, Calif.
Tel: 663 1503

Haig's Delicacies
642 Clement Street
San Francisco, Calif.
Tel: 752 6283

Kowloon Market
750 North Hill Street
Los Angeles, CA 90012

Nak's Oriental
1151 Chestnut Street
Menlo Park, CA 94025

Shing Chong & Co.
800 Grant Avenue
San Francisco, CA 90012

Wong On Lung Co.
686 North Spring Street
Los Angeles, CA 90012

Australia

CANBERRA ACT

Dickson Health Food Centre
14 Dickson Place
Dickson, ACT 2602

Holt Foodlands
Holt Place
Holt, ACT 2615

Kingston Health Foods
Kennedy Street
Kingston, ACT 2604

Mawson Health Foods
Shop 7, Mawson Place
Mawson, ACT 2607

Woden Health Foods
Shop L55, Woden Plaza
Phillip, ACT 2606

NEW SOUTH WALES

Newcastle

Kanda Aust. Pty Ltd
42 Northbridge Plaza
Sailor's Bay Road
Northbridge, NSW 2063

Mekong Asian Food Shop
394 Anzac Parade
Kingsford, NSW 2032

77 Spring Street
Bondi Junction
NSW 2022

Park Health Foods
108A Burwood Road
Burwood, NSW 2134

Yuen War Trading Co.
Hunter Street
Newcastle, NSW 2300

Sydney

Asian Provisions Pty Ltd
166 Victoria Avenue
Chatswood, NSW 2067

Burra Bazaar
Shop 16, Cremorne Centre
Military Road
Cremorne, NSW 2090

Castle Trading Pty Ltd
93 Belmore Road
Randwick, NSW 2031

David Jones Sydney Pty Ltd
The Food Hall
Market and Elizabeth Sts
Sydney, NSW 2000

Diamond Crest
94 Gould Street
Bondi Beach, NSW 2026

Eastern Foods Pty Ltd
18 Cambell Street
Sydney, NSW 2000

Eze and Sons
108 Brighton Boulevard
North Bondi, NSW 2026

Korean, Japanese and Chinese Food Store
14B Oxford Street
Sydney, NSW 2000

Pendle Hill Health Foods
135 Pendle Way
Pendle Hill, NSW 2145

Wing Yuen Tai
25 Little Hay Street
Haymarket, NSW 2000

QUEENSLAND

Brisbane

Far East Trading Co.
261 Wickham Street
Valley, Qld. 4000

G.F.R. Vysma
18 Hill Street
Kingston, Qld 4205

SOUTH AUSTRALIA

Adelaide

David Jones (Adel.) Ltd
44 Rundle Mall
Adelaide, SA 5000

Brighton

Orient Import
406A Brighton Road
Brighton, SA 5048

VICTORIA

Melbourne

Foon Kee
214 Little Bourke Street
Melbourne, Vic. 3000

Hong Oriental Pty Ltd
206 Little Bourke Street
Melbourne, Vic. 3000

Menorah Gourmet Pty Ltd
125-127 McKinnon Road
McKinnon, Vic. 3204
Tel: 586 304

Myer's Limited
Bourke Street
Melbourne, Vic. 3000

WESTERN AUSTRALIA

Perth

Hop Hing Pty Ltd
901 Canning Highway
Mt Pleasant, WA 6153

Acknowledgements

The ideas, hearts and stomachs of many friends have gone into the making of this book. They shared their recipes so that I could present a varied collection adapted for the microwave oven. These friends are fondly acknowledged in the recipes they contributed.

I would also like to thank Shirley Grafton-Williams, Natasha Daniloff, Michael and Robyn Spence, Mary Whitehead and my son Rajah who spent many hours proofreading, laughing at and offering advice on countless details, Lina Flores for her efficient and organised word processing, Geoff Croft for the initial artwork, Dr Gomathy Arumugam, my sister-in-law, who put aside a week of surgery to help me with photographic sessions, and Michelle and Gi Sandhu, my niece and her husband, who opened their lovely home so generously for those sessions.

It has been an inspiration to work with talented people. Lee Jen's photography is proof of his unusual talent. I thank him for his patience and Shirley Hew and the team at Times Books International for their advice and the expert professionalism with which they handled my book through all its stages of production.

Finally, I wish to thank my family for their supportive reassurance and tolerance during the months when they had to endure tested meals or no meals at all!

The Author

Carol Selvarajah has successfully combined two careers — raising a family and being a full-time teacher. Brought up in Malaysia and resident for long periods in North America and Australia, Carol knows at first hand the difficulties of combining these two roles in Asian and non-Asian environments.

She first realised the advantages of microwave cooking when running a fast-food restaurant in Sydney and quickly adapted the microwave oven to home use. *The Asian Microwave Cookbook* is the fruit of ten years' experience and experimentation with recipes for both simple and appetising family meals and more sophisticated and elaborate full-scale entertaining.

Carol lives in Sydney with her husband, Dr Selvarajah, sons Rajah and Anand, and daughter Anusha, an excellent cook herself.